EDIBLE FOREST FOODS OF TRIBALS IN SOUTH INDIA

EDIBLE FOREST FOODS OF TRIBALS IN SOUTH INDIA

(Carotene Content, Medicinal and Culinary Aspects)

Dr. P. Rajyalakshmi

Kalpaz Publications
NEW DELHI-110 052

EDIBLE FOREST FOODS OF TRIBALS IN SOUTH INDIA
(Carotene Content, Medicinal and Culinary Aspects)
Rs. 690/-

ISBN: 81-7835-028-9

Published in 2002 in India by
Kalpaz Publications
C-30 Satyawati Nagar
New Delhi-110 052

Laser Typesetting at: Power Photocomposers, New Delhi-110 002
Printed at: Mehra Offset Printers, Delhi-110 002.

CONTENTS

FOREWORD

Forests form one of the largest ecosystems of the world, bountifully bearing nutrient rich as well as plants of medicinal value of immense significance to the mankind. Tribals living in the forests exploit nature to meet their food and health needs through these plants. Information available on the wild edible and medicinal flora is scanty and scattered.

Vitamin A deficiency is the major public health problem in India and other developing countries. Although Vitamin A prophylaxis programme has been in operation in India for the last two decades yet it has not had the desired impact, particularly in the backward rural and tribal areas. Plant foods form the main source of vitamin A in Indian dietaries. ICMR and FAO steadfastly supported programme dealing with production, availability and consumption of vitamin A foods to combat the deficiency problem.

The work reported in this book is the outcome of a ICAR adhoc research scheme entitled *"Screening of forest foods consumed by tribals of South India for β-carotene content"*, carried out during 1997-2000. It provides information on total Carotenoids and β-carotene content of more than hundred forest species and foods (green leafy vegetables, other types of vegetables, fruits, roots and tubers) consumed by tribals. In addition, it also contains first hand information on attitudes and beliefs of tribals, pertaining to foods in general but also native treatment adopted by them for eye related diseases.

The book also provides brief description along with photographs of wild edible plants with an account of salient characters, phenology, distribution and medicinal value which would help in easy identification of the flora in the field. It also gives details of the culinary practices followed by the tribals for the foods they collect and consume and also dwells on the effect of processing by the tribal method, on beta carotene content. A chapter on overview of carotenoids provides current information on its biological role, as well as important food sources of vitamin A.

The book focuses on a number of important conceptual and substantive issues: It is also of great relevance as the information provided in it serves as a useful guide to all National and International scientists in the field of Food Science & Technology, Health and Nutrition, Agriculture, Botany and Biotechnology.

I congratulate the authors of the book and, all the staff and students associated with the work reported here and, wish more contributors from them in future for the benefit of the society. It is my fond hope that the information contained here will be used widely for the benefit of not only the tribal populations but also for the benefit of the society at large.

M.V. Rao

PREFACE

Vitamin A deficiency remains a serious public health problem in India and other developing countries. It is reported that 25 per cent of the world's total number of 15 million blind live in India of whom about 5th can trace the origin to VAD. Studies carried out in India and elsewhere showed that even mild vitamin A deficiency is associated with increased risk of morbidity and mortality in young children. Vitamin A prophylaxsis programme has been in operation for the last 20 years has not had the desired impact. It is very well known that VAD is primarily due to dietary inadequacy. Though vitamin A can be derived from both animal and plant foods, the former is prohibitory because of economic and ethnic reasons. Fruits and vegetables especially green leafy vegetables are cheaper and provide more than 80 per cent of vitamin A as provitamin carotenoids in developing countries. Among various carotenoids in nature, β-carotene is the most abundant in Indian foods and has the maximum vitamin A activity. Therefore, increasing the production and consumption of plant foods is most logical approach to combat VAD. However, in view of the increase in the population demands and insufficiency of the traditional foods rich in β-carotene, expanding newer source of beta carotene can form a truly sustainable solution to the problem.

Forests as the repository of various foods rich in nutrients is not yet fully realised. Tribals who inhabit forest clad mountains exploited nature to meet their food demands which may be unconventional to us and exceptionally rich in β carotene content.

The tribals possess abundant traditional knowledge about various plant species which ensures their regeneration. The exploration of wild edible plant resources in a developing country like India is of paramount importance.

This humble work of "Screening of forest foods consumed by tribals for β-carotene content" provide a brief description of wild edible plants with a significant characters, phenology, distribution, medicinal value and carotene content. Also culinary practices of tribals, effect of processing on carotene content in foods, perception of diseases and native treatment adopted by tribals are discussed. The information provided serves as a useful guide to the common man, National and International scientists in the field of health, nutrition, food science and technology, biochemistry, medicine, botany, horticulture, agriculture and forest organisers as well, besides all other interested in wild plants at the district level.

This work is not at all the final word as there is a good scope for those interested in the subject to add further data on the distribution and the range of edible plant species growing wild in the tribal habitat all over India. Planning workable strategies for production and promotion of the wild plant species in non-tribal areas need special attention in all our developmental plans. New methods, recipes and value added products that have potential for market and to be accepted into practice by non-tribal members need to be worked out.

Inspite of the care which had been exercised in every way, there are bound to be some errors and omissions, especially for a work of this kind. I shall appreciate suggestions for improvement by the users of this book.

I place on record my deep sense of gratitude to Indian Council of Agricultural Research (ICAR) for providing funds to the ad hoc research scheme "Screening of forest foods consumed by the tribals for beta carotene content" for the period from Aug. 1997 to Jan. 2000, which made possible in bringing out this valuable piece of work; and to all those who were directly, indirectly involved in the execution of the work.

Dr. P. Rajyalakshmi
Principal Investigator
ICAR Ad hoc Research Project on "Screening of forest foods consumed by tribals for β-carotene content"

Dept. of Foods and Nutrition
Post Graduate & Research Centre
Acharya N.G. Ranga Agricultural University, Rajendranagar,
Hyderabad-500 030.

Date: 4.08.2001

PROJECT STAFF

Principal Investigator : **Dr. P. Rajyalakshmi,** M.Sc., Ph. D.
Associate Professor

Co-investigator : Dr. R. Manorama, M.Sc., Ph.D.
Assistant Professor

Research Associates :
1. Mrs. K. Venkata Lakshmi, M.Sc. (Horticulture)
2. Mrs. K. Venkata Lakshmamma, M.Sc. (Foods and Nutrition)
3. Ms. T.V.N. Padmavathi, M.Sc. (Foods and Nutrition)

DEPARTMENT OF FOODS AND NUTRITION
COLLEGE OF HOME SCIENCE
POST GRADUATE & RESEARCH CENTRE
ACHARYA N.G. RANGA AGRICULTURAL UNIVERSITY
RAJENDRANAGAR, HYDERABAD-500 030.

ACKNOWLEDGEMENTS

The project staff expresses their immense gratitude to Indian Council of Agricultural Research (ICAR) Krishi Anusandhan Bhavan, New Delhi for providing funds to carry on the study.

They are immensely thankful to Dr. Tej Verma, Assistant Director General, (Home Science), ICAR, for her cooperation and timely action for smooth running of the project work.

The staff place on record with great reverence the following individuals who helped in identification of botanical nomenclature of the forest GLV's.

Dr. Thammanna	Horticultural Advisor Government of Andhra Pradesh Secretariat, Hyderabad
Dr. M. Venkaiah	Assistant Professor Department of Botany Andhra University Visakhapatnam
Dr. Y.N.R. Verma	Associate Professor Department of Botany P.G. College of Science Saifabad, Hyderabad

The staff wish to acknowledge the contributions made by the following individuals who extended their cooperation and assistance at various stages of the project work.

Dr. Bhaskara Chary	Technical Assistant, National Institute of Nutrition, Jamia Osmania, Tarnaka, Hyderabad.
Mr. Chandra Raju	Technical Assistant, Tribal Cultural Research and Training Institute, Masab Tank, Hyderabad.

Mr. Rajasekhar	Programme Officer, Integrated Tribal Development Agency, Parvathipuram, Vizianagaram Dist.
Mrs. Damayanthi	Programme Officer, Integrated Tribal Development Agency, Parvathipuram, Vizianagaram Dist.
Mr. K. Ramakrishna Rao IAS	Programme Officer, Integrated Tribal Development Agency (ITDA), Paderu, Visakhapatnam Dist.
Mr. Jayesh Rajan, IAS	Project Officer, Integrated Tribal Development Agency, Rampachodavaram, East Godavari Dist.
Mr. K. Tulasi Rao	Bio-diversity cell, Srisailam Project, NSRT
Mr. Veerabhadrudu	Project Officer, ITDA Srisailam, Kurnool Dist.
Mr. Venkataiah and the Staff	Asst. Project Officer, ITDA, Srisailam, Kurnool Dist.
Mr. Srinivas	Deputy Executive Engineer, ITDA, P. Konavalasa.
Mrs. Y. Ratnakumari	Child Development Project Officer, Maredumilli, E. Godavari Dist.
Mrs. Ramannamma	Child Development Project Officer, Gummalaxmipuram, Vizianagaram District.
Mrs. Jayalakshmi	Mandal Development Officer, Gummalaxmipuram, Vizianagaram District.
Mrs. Kameswari	Child Development Supervisor, Gummalaxmipuram, Vizianagarain Dist.
Mrs. Manikeswari	Child Development Supervisor, Munching Putt, Paderu, Vizag Dist.

Dr. Arun Sathe	Director, Research Centre for Medical and Aromatic Plants Acharya N.G. Ranga Agricultural University, Rajendranagar, Hyderabad.
Dr. Srimannarayana	Silviculturist, Department of Forestry, Acharya N.G. Ranga Agricultural University, Rajendranagar, Hyderabad.
Dr. B.S. Kulkarni	Associate Professor, Department of Mathematics and Statistics, Acharya N.G. Ranga Agricultural University, Rajendranagar, Hyderabad.
Mr. S. Triloknath	Artist-cum-Photographer, Agricultural Information Centre Acharya N.G. Ranga Agricultural University, Rajendranagar, Hyderabad.
Mr. Sagar	Computer Operator, M/s. Sagar Computers and Xerox Rajendranagar, Hyderabad.

The staff would like to record their sincere gratitude and indebtedness to the people of the respective tribal communities without whose cooperation the work could not be accomplished.

We are thankful to the Directors of the following institutions for permitting us to use their Library.

- Tribal Cultural Research and Training Institute, Telugu Sankshema Bhavan, Masab Tank, Hyderabad.
- National Institute of Nutrition, Indian Council of Medical Research (ICMR), Jamai Osmania, Tarnaka, Hyderabad.
- Andhra Pradesh Forest Department, Saifabad, Hyderabad.
- National Academy of Agricultural Research Management, (NAARM) Rajendranagar, Hyderabad.
- Post-graduate College of Science, Osmania University, Saifabad, Hyderabad.

Special thanks are due to Ms. Y. Jyothsna, Ms. K. Balachandramani Devi, Ms. Suneetha, T. Nandana, students of Post-Graduate and Research Centre for their valuable contributions to the research work.

The staff owe a special word of gratitude to Prof. Dr. P. Geervani, who was the source of inspiration behind the work.

The staff wish to place on record the cooperation and encouragement provided by the concerned university Administrative staff, teaching and non-teaching staff of Post Graduate and Research Centre, Acharya N.G. Ranga Agricultural University, Hyderabad during the study period.

LIST OF FIGURES AND ILLUSTRATIONS

LIST OF TABLES

CHAPTER 1

IMPORTANCE AND RELEVANCE OF THE PROBLEM

The World Health Organisation (WHO) Micronutrient Deficiency Information System (MDIS) indicates that over 90 countries have a public health problem with regard to clinical and/or sub-clinical vitamin A deficiency (VAD) as it contributes to a considerable proportion of the blindness in children. It is reported that 25 per cent of the 15 million blind in the world are from India; about a fifth can trace the origin to VAD. Supplementation of vitamin A may be envisaged as a short term measure to tackle the problem immediately. It is very well known that VAD is primarily due to dietary inadequacy.

The National Nutrition Policy (1993) and National plan of action on nutrition (1995) adopted by Government of India has set virtual elimination of VAD as one of the goals. As it's corner stone, Food and Agricultural Organisation (FAO) has steadfastly supported the increased production and consumption of vitamin A rich foods as the only sustainable solution to the problem. Since in India, a large number of people depend on vegetarian diets, inexpensive foods of vegetable origin that are rich in Beta-carotene need to be explored. The long term solution to the problem lies in identifying newer sources of Beta-carotene and expanding the production, availability and consumption of the wild flora.

Forests are one of the largest ecosystems of the world bountifully bearing omnivorous resources for sustenance of humans. The vast potential of forest and forest land has a repository of variety of nutritious foods is not yet fully realised. It offers a potential for providing many more yet unknown benefits to future generation. Forest clad mountains are the original habitat of many tribal groups of our country. More than 300 main tribal communities are distributed from Himalayas down to Indian ocean and from the Arabian sea to Bay of Bengal and Eastern frontiers. The total recorded area of forests in the country is 75.06 m. ha.

which is 22.8 per cent of the total land area of the country (BISR, 1984). The total population of scheduled tribes in the country is 683.81 lakhs and they constitute an important segment of the population of India representing 8.08 per cent of the total population of the country (Census of India, 1991) Fig. 1.

Tribals who live close to nature collect and consume variety of foods from forests which may be unconventional to us and exceptionally good in Beta-carotene content. The cultural pattern of each community determines the nature and extent of food behaviour found in the area. Some of the traditions followed by the tribals may be good and should be preserved. Moreover, as most of the foods need to be processed before consumption, the effect of processing on carotene content need to be studied.

Knowledge of the attitudes and beliefs towards foods in health and common ailments and in eye related problems is essential in planning appropriate nutrition and health education programmes. Information of this nature in the tribal population is very limited. The present study is an effort in this direction.

The objectives of the study are as follows:

Specific objective

- To screen forest foods consumed by tribals for Beta-carotene content.

General objectives

- To explore Beta-carotene rich forest foods available in different seasons.
- To collect information on consumption pattern, storage, processing practices, attitudes, beliefs, attached to forest foods from the tribals.
- To analyse fresh forest foods and processed by tribal method for Beta-carotene content.
- To find the plant material used and native treatment adopted by tribals for diseases related to eye.

CHAPTER 2

PROFILE OF THE STUDY

The tribal habitat of Andhra Pradesh, India exists in the central southern tribal region has 7th largest tribal population (4.2 million) in the entire country accounting for 6.3 per cent of the state population.

The state of Andhra Pradesh is situated on the eastern coast of India bounded on the north by the states of Maharashtra, Madhya Pradesh and Orissa, on the west by Karnataka and Maharashtra and on the south by Tamil Nadu and Karnataka. It lies between latitudes 12° 37' and 19° 54' north and longitude 76° 46' and 84° 46' East, with a total geographical area of 275068 sq. km. Andhra Pradesh is the fifth largest state in India, constituting 8.75 per cent of the total area of the country. It is also the fifth most populous state in India with a total population of 66.5 million in 1991. Forest area in Andhra Pradesh form 6397.1 thousand hectares which accounts for 23.2 per cent of total land area in the state (BISR, 1984).

The scheduled area constitute 11 per cent of total geographical area of the state. The main concentration of tribals extending over 30030 km. is distributed in 8 districts namely Srikakulam, Vizianagaram, Visakhapatnam, East Godavari, West Godavari, Khammam, Warangal and Adilabad. There are 33 tribal groups in the state. Chenchu, the primitive tribal group (PTG) inhabit the contagious forest tracts of the Nallamalai hills which extend over six bordering districts: Mahaboobnagar, Kurnool, Prakasam, Guntur, Nalgoda and Ranga Reddy.

The tribal areas in Andhra Pradesh has been divided into 5 geographical regions based on common geoethnic characteristics (TCR & TI, 1993) Table 1.

Location, particulars of the study area

The study area comprised of five districts from eastern ghats of Andhra Pradesh namely Vizianagaram, Visakhapatnam, East Godavari. Kurnool and Prakasam districts under Integrated Tribal Development Agency Fig. 2. The general area profile of the selected five districts from

Andhra Pradesh, India are given in Table 2. Two mandals from each district were selected on the basis that they are relatively isolated and unaffected by the outside contacts. The geographical particulars of each of the districts and the mandals selected are described herewith.

TABLE 1

Geographical Regions of Tribal Habitat in Andhra Pradesh

	Region	*District covered*	*Major tribal groups*
1.	Gond-Kolem region	Adilabad	Gond, Kolam, Pardhan, Thoti
2.	Koya-konda Reddy region	Warangal Khammam W. Godavari E. Godavari	Koya, Konda Reddi, Konda Kammara, Valmiki
3.	Khond-Savara region	Visakhapatnam Srikakulam Vizianagaram	Khond-savera, Bagata, Valmiki, Konda dora Kotia, Gadaba, Porja, Konda Kammara, Mali
4.	Chenchu region	Mahaboobnagar Nalgonda Kurnool Prakasam and Guntur	Mannemdora Chenchu
5.	Plain areas (non scheduled areas)	All other areas	Yanadi, Yerukula Lambada

TABLE 2

General area profile of the selected districts from Andhra Pradesh, India

S. No.	*District*	*ST population (in lakhs)*	*% ST population in total population*	*Total Geographical area (Hect. lakhs)*	*% Forest area to total geographical area*
1.	Vizianagaram	1.90	9.0	2.84	62.32
2.	Visakhapatnam	4.69	14.3	15.30	74.50
3.	East Godavari	1.76	3.9	10.36	49.42
4.	Kurnool	0.56	1.9	17,658 sq. km	3,535 sq. km
5.	Prakasam	0.99	3.6	17,629 sq. km	4,42,499.00 hec.

Source: Census of India, 1991

Fig. 1. Map of India
Showing Predominantly Tribal Areas.

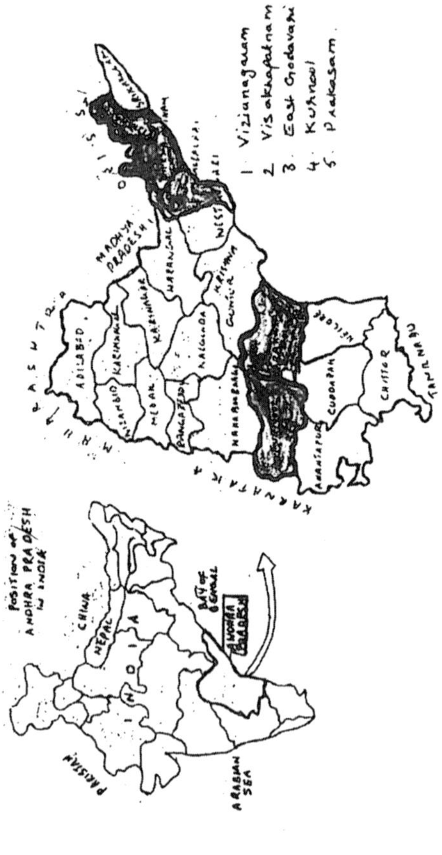

Fig.2: Location of the study area in Andhra Pradesh, South India

AREA PARTICULARS OF THE SELECTED DISTRICTS

Vizianagaram district

The total geographical area of the district is 2.84 lakhs hectares. Agency area covers 1.19 sq. kms. constituting 18.3 per cent of the total geographical area of the district. The major tribal groups of the district are savara, gadaba and mannemdora.

In Vizianagaram district, two agency blocks namely bhadragiri and pachipenta where the tribal population of the district is concentrated were selected. Bhadragiri is bordered by Orissa state on the north. Seethampet on the east, Kurupam on south and Parvathipuram on the west. There is no urban area in the block. Pachipenta is bounded by salur towards north, Gajapathipuram towards south, salur samithi on east and Orissa state in the west Fig. 3(a).

Visakhapatnam district

Visakhapatnam district has a geographical area of 11,167 sq. kms. of which the agency area covers 6239 sq. kms. constituting 56.1 per cent of the total geographical area of the district. Visakhapatnam district occupies third place as far as percentage of tribal population to total is concerned. Visakhapatnam district has the total population of 32, 35,092 lakhs in that, the population of scheduled tribes were 4,68,886 lakhs constituting 14.27 percentage of the district total population (Census of India, 1991).

The tribal areas of Visakhapatnam district consists of hilly regions with an average altitude of about 900 meters. The agency area mostly consists of hilly regions covered by eastern ghats. The major tribal groups inhabiting the district are Bhagata, Kondadora, Valmiki, Konda Kammara, Porja, Gadaba, Muka-dora, Mannemdora, Yerukula and Mali.

In Visakhapatnam, ITDA covers 11 blocks out of which 2 mandals in agency area namely Paderu and Munchingput area were selected on the basis that they are relatively isolated and unaffected by the outside contacts. Paderu and Munchingput with an area of 484 and 561 km. and the population of 32,226 and 29,341 thousands respectively constitute the density of population of about 67 and 52 per sq. km. The inhabitants of the agency tract is demarcated as the tribal area in Visakhapatnam (Rani Gopal, 1996) Fig. 3(b).

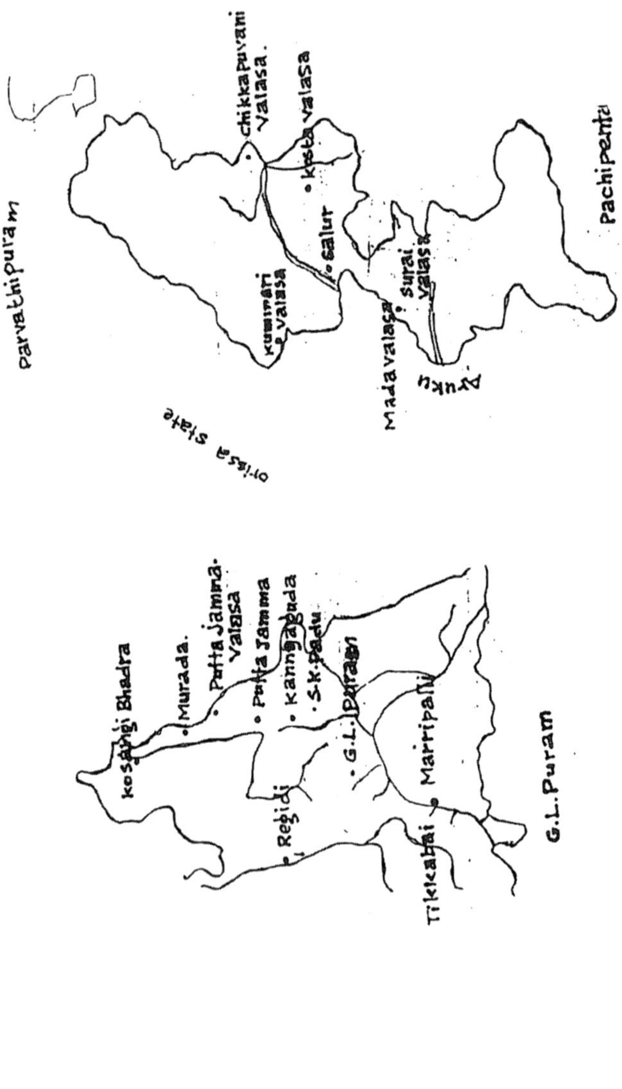

Fig. 3(a). Map showing selected villages in two mandals of Vizianagaram Dist. of A.P. India.

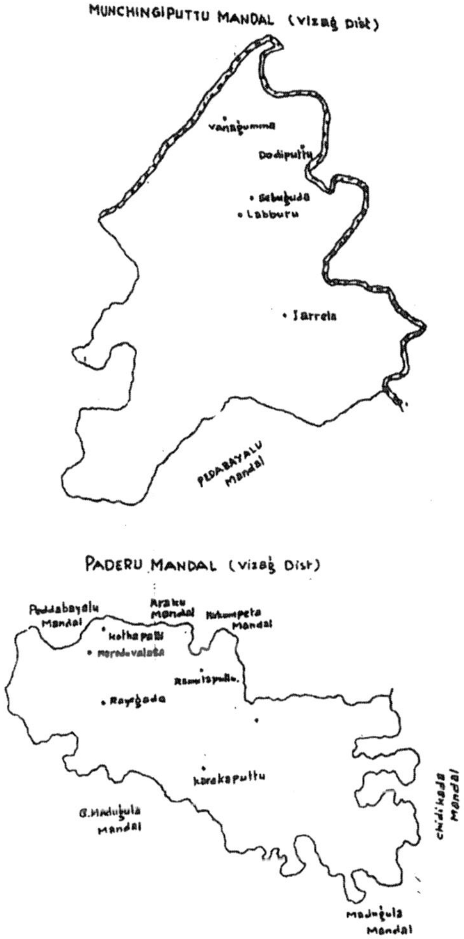

Fig. 3(b). Map showing selected villages of two mandals of Visakapatnam districts of Andhra Pradesh, India.

East Godavari district

East Godavari district is located between the northern latitudes of 16°30' and 82°30'. It occupies an area of 10,807 sq. kms. and has a population of 3,701,040. Out of which scheduled tribe population is 1,76,083 and constitute 3.88 per cent of the total population in the district (Census of India, 1991). The district lies on the north east coast of Andhra Pradesh and is bounded on the north by Visakhapatnam district and the state of Orissa on the east and south by the Bay of Bengal and on the west by Khammam and West Godavari district. Total forest area of the district is 2850 sq. kms. i.e., 26.4 per cent of the total geographical area of the district. Three fourth of the forest area is hilly and the rest is the plains (Census of India, 1991). The Kondareddi, Koya Dora, Kond Kammara and Valmiki are the major sub-tribes existing here.

In East Godavari district the two agency blocks namely Maredumilli and Y. Ramavaram having 83 and 100 kms. away from Rajahmandry and population of 17,532 and 23,776 thousand respectively were selected. The two mandals were relatively isolated and unaffected by the outside contacts Fig. 3(c).

Kurnool and Prakasam districts

Out of 30,274 total Chenchu population in Andhra Pradesh, nearly 50 per cent of them are found in Kurnool and Prakasam districts with the population of 4961 and 7291 thousands respectively (Integrated Tribal Development Agency (ITDA) Srisailam, 1994). Based on the concentration of the chenchu tribe population two districts namely Kurnool and Prakasam were selected for the study.

Kurnool district lies approximately between the north latitude of 14°54' and 16°18' and the eastern longitudes of 76°58' and 79°34'. It is bounded on the north by Tungabhadra and Krishna rivers as well as Mahaboobnagar district, on the south by Anantapur and Cuddapah districts. On the West by Karnataka state and on the east by Prakasam district. It occupies an area of 17,658 sq. km. and has a population of 2,973,024. The total forest area of the district is 3,535 sq. km. The major parts of the forest area are mainly confined to the Nallamalai including its extensions the Erramalai and a part of the Velikonda (Census of Kurnool district, 1991). Srisailam and Atmakur mandals having population of 20,891 and 28,311 thousand respectively were selected. The selected mandals come under Srisailam ITDA which constitutes 100 per cent Chenchus Fig. 3(d).

Fig. 3(c). Map showing selected villages in two mandals of East Godavari district, Andhra Pradesh, India.

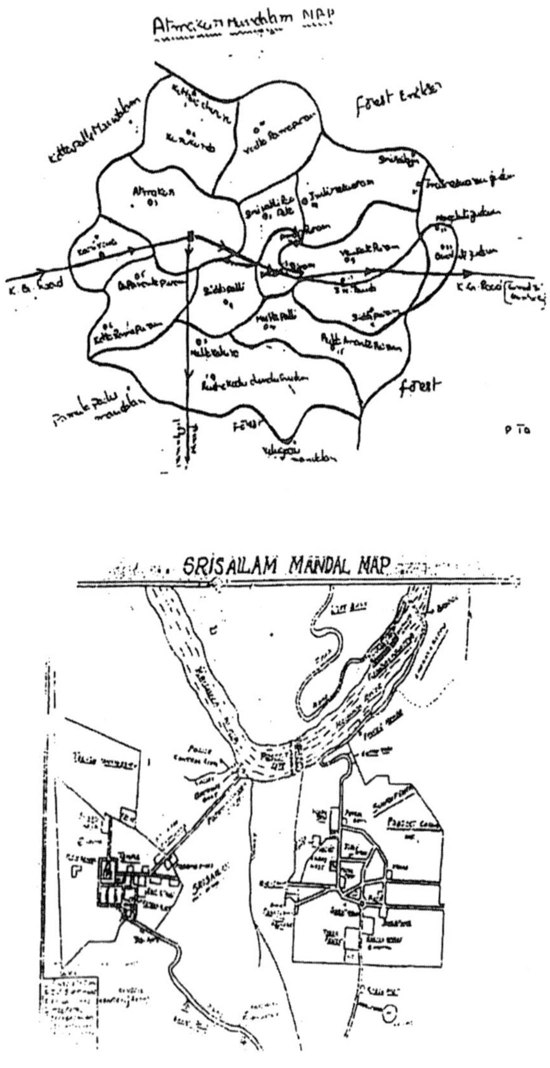

Fig. 3(d). Map showing selected villages in two mandals of Kurnool district, Andhra Pradesh, India

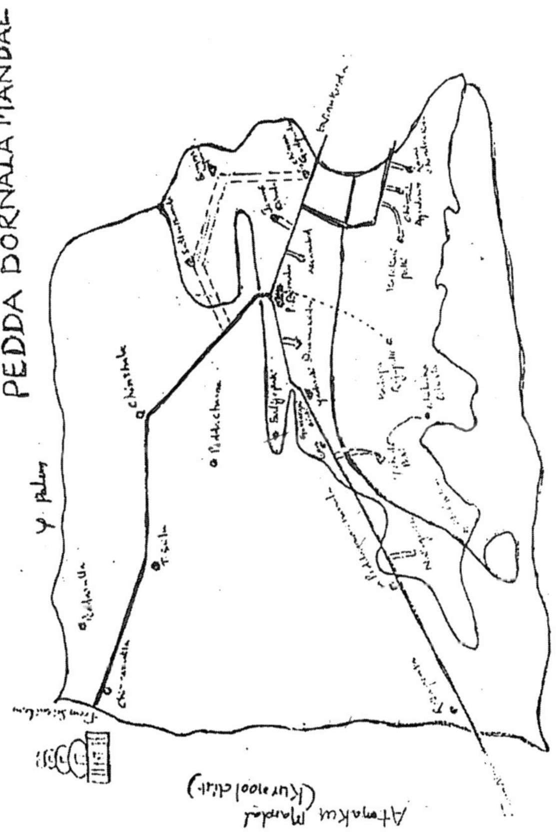

Fig. 3(e). Map showing selected villages in one mandal of Prakasam district, Andhra Pradesh, India

Prakasam district is a part of the Southern Andhra Coastal plains lying approximately between 15°30' and 16°0' longitude. It is bounded on the north by Mahaboobnagar and Guntur districts, on the West by Kurnool district, on the south by Cuddapah and Nellore districts and the Bay of Bengal on the east. The central portion of the district contains large tracts of low shrubs jungle diversified with rocky hills and stony plains which is a distinctive feature of the district.

It occupies an area of 17,629 sq. km. and has a population of 2,759,116. The total forest area in the district accounts for 4,42,499.00 hectares forming 25.11 per cent of the total geographic area (Census of Prakasam district, 1991).

The mandal namely Pedda dornala having 33,145 population was selected for study. The mandal comes under Srisailam ITDA constitutes 100 per cent chenchus Fig. 3(e).

Selection of Villages

From each mandal five interior villages adjacent to the forest were selected so as to get more information about the foods collected from forest and consumed by the tribals.

The villages that were selected from each mandal and the major tribes inhabiting the area are presented in Table 3.

TABLE 3

Particulars of the mandals and Tribal villages selected from the five districts of Andhra Pradesh, India

S. No.	*District*	*Mandal*	*Villages*	*Major tribes*
1.	Vizianagaram	G.L. Puram	Tikkabai	
			Savarakotapadu	
			Kannaiguda	Savara
			*Puttajemmu	
			*Puttajemmuvalasa muruda	
		Pachipenta	Kummarivalasa	
			Kostavalasa	Gadaba
			*Madavalasa	Mannemdora
			Suraivalasa	
			*Chokkapuvari valasa	
2.	Visakhapatnam	Paderu	*Rayegada	
			Korakaputtu	Bhagatha

S. No.	District	Mandal	Villages	Major tribes
			*Kothapalli	Kondadora
			Ramula puttu	Valmiki
			Mareduvalasa	
		Munching puttu	*Labburu	
			Dodiputtu	Bhagatha
			Jarrela	Porja
			*Vanagumma	Mali
			Sebuguda	
3.	East Godavari	Maredumilli	*Kundada	Kondareddy
			*Chatlavada	Koyadora
			Pullangi	Konda
			Tadepalli	Kammaras
			Chavidikota	Valmiki
		Y. Ramavaram	*Chintalapudi	
			*Kanivada	Kondareddy
			Chamagudda	Koyadoras
			Pathakota	Konda Kamaras
			Daragudda	Valmiki
4.	Kurnool	Srisailam	*Mekalabanda	
			Srisailam Project colony	Chenchus
		Atmakur	Sundipenta	
			*Bairlutu	Chenchus
			*Nagalutu	
5.	Prakasam	Peddadornala	*Thummala	
			Bailu	Chenchus
			Chinthala	

* Villages choosen for food colleciton.

Source: As per the records from ITDA Parvathipuram, ITDA Paderu, ITDA Rampachodavaram, ITDA Srisailam.

Collection of baseline information

Baseline information pertaining to food colleciton from the forest, period of availability, storage, consumption practices, processing procedures adopted and attitudes and preferences attached to forest foods etc. was collected Fig. 4. using a structured, pretested interview schedule (Appendix I). Also, information regarding deficiencies related to eye, plant material used and native treatment adopted by tribals for cure during illness also was gathered. The interview schedule was pretested before use. The total number of households thus covered from 5 districts were 400 comprising of 10 from each village.

Morbidity data was collected from the mandal PHC records for one year period 1997-98/99.

Collection of forest foods and estimation of carotene content:

Seasonal collection and analysis of forest foods for beta-carotene content (Raw and processed foods) was done using High performance liquid chromatography (Fig. 5) following the method of Nelis and Deleanher (1983) with modifications (Bhaskerchary, 1986). Vitamin A as Retinol Equivalents (RE) was calculated based on in vivo conversion factor given by WHO (1983).

Statistical analysis

Data processing statistical analysis using one way ANOVA (Snedecor and Cochran, 1965), were done.

CHAPTER 3

FINDINGS OF THE STUDY

General Information of the Tribals Surveyed

It was observed that the tribals inhabiting forest clad mountains and hills has cultural homogenity and unifying social organisation (Fig. 6). Their pattern of living, food and dietary practices, attitudes and beliefs related to various aspects found to be similar. Majority (80%) of the tribal groups studied were having family size between four to six members. Their literacy levels were very poor. Developmental programmes of ITDA and ICDS were observed to be implemented in some of the tribal villages surveyed.

Food and Agricultural Practices

The tribals practice podu cultivation and grow cereal and millet crops like maize (*Zea mays*), jowar (*Sorghum vulgare*), bajra (*Pennisetum typhoideum*), ragi (Eleusine coracana), korra (*Setaria italica*) and pulses like redgram (*Cajanus cajan*), horsegram (*Dolichos biflorus*) and blackgram (*Phaseolus aureus*) and commercial crops like chillies (*Capsicum frutisans*), cotton (*Gossypium herbaceaum*) and groundnut (*Arachis hypogea*). The crop yields were found to be very poor. Forestry thus forms a major source of food and economic activity among the tribals. So they largely depend on collection and selling of minor forest produce like gum, soapnuts, mniyrobalans, adda leaves, honey and hillbrooms etc. Tribals purchase or sell their forest foods in the nearest shandy (market) once in a week (Fig. 7). The generally purchased culinary items were onions, dried chillies, dry fish, salt, potatoes.

The tribals do not store any food grains for consumption, but store grains for seed purpose in gunny bags, bamboo baskets, earthern pots.

Food Consumption Practices

With regard to food consumption practices, the tribals consume two to three meals per day. Their diet was found to be monotonous, poor in quantity and quality. They consume thin millet ambali (porridge) as morning breakfast, prepared with left over rice of previous night. Lunch consists of millet (mostly ragi) ambali (porridge) with vegetable curry or dahl and tamarind extract. For dinner, plain rice (Canji drained off) with dhal/vegetable curry with tamarind extract are consumed.

Pickles made with tamarind, tomato, chillies are stored throughout the year for consumption by the tribals of East Godavari district.

Boiling is the most common method adopted by the tribals for cooking. They use large proportions of water to vegetable (1:10 and above) while boiling. The cooked vegetables are then seasoned with onions and dried chillies using one to two tea spoons of either palm oil or mahua (Bassia latifolia) oil. Boiling and draining off water is followed for some green leafy vegetables before the product preparation. Extracted tamarind juice is also added to certain preparations.

Their personal and environmental hygiene was obsrved to be very poor. Raw tobacco smoking is common among all the age groups.

CHAPTER 4

FOOD BELIEFS AND ATTITUDES OF THE TRIBALS

Beliefs, customs and traditions influence the general pattern of living in any community. Beliefs inherent and integral as they are in the cultural matrix act as invisible force in translating pre-set ideas into overt acts and customs (Randall and Sanjur, 1981; Cherian, 1981; Onuoha, 1982). Handed down from generation to generation, beliefs lend authority to customs leading one to accept traditional customs and practices on their face value. The cultural pattern of each community determines the nature and extent of food behaviour found in the area. Some of the traditions followed blindly by the tribals may be good and should be preserved. Knowledge of their attitudes, traditional food and dietary practices in general and in specific physiological conditions, etc., is essential in planning appropriate nutrition and health education programmes intended for the tribals. Information of this nature in the tribal population is very limited.

Superstitions and beliefs invariably influence the attitudes towards foods. Food habits and beliefs differ among the different tribes and even among the communities within the tribes. Certain foods are prohibited from consumption by all and in some cases, the food restrictions are determined by age, sex and physiological status and seasonal availability (Onuoha, 1982).

The Indian diet especially in the rural or tribal setting, is greatly influenced by the two established systems of medicine — Ayurvedic and Unani, both of which classify foods as hot or cold, according to the effect they are believed to create on body mechanisms (Gopaldas *et al.*, 1983). Some of the general food beliefs and attitudes of the tribals observed during pregnancy and lactation are given in Table 4.

TABLE 4

General food beliefs and attitudes of the tribals during pregnancy and lactation

Physiological condition	*Foods recommended*	*Reason*	*Foods avoided*	*Reason*
Pregnancy	Sama rice (Echinochloa fnumentacea) Podi kura (GLV) (Lipidium sativum)	Cooling effect Heal oedema	Papaya, sesame Eggs, coconut	Causes abortion Deliver bald head child
	All GLVs	Good health	Tubers, dhals, potatoes, peas, burnt tubers, jack fruit seeds, gingelly seeds	Cause blisters & tumours to the child to be born
	Thopa (product of ragi powder)	Good health	Pumkin, beans, sarukura (*Colacasia antiquorum*) brinjal, egg, groundnut, Jaggery, fish	Cause diarrhoea, skin allergies, cough & cold to mother and child considered as hot food
Lactation	Only rice, garlic and chilli powder upto one week after delivery. Only Redgram dhal, blackgram dhal crisps, Dondakai (Coccinia cordifolian) curry, Plain rice upto six months after after delivery	For good health of mother and child	All vegetables, fruits	Not good for the health of child and mother
			Pumpkin, Beans Curd	Cause Diarrhoea Cause cold to mother and Oil child Cause diseases to mother and child
			Fish and meat	Cause death of the mother
	Tender papaya	Galactogogue		
	White kura (*Cleome viscosa*) seeds, cumin seeds, salt and pepper made into paste & consumed	To prevent cough and cold for both mother and child	Saru kura (*Colacasia antiquorum*)	Causes Skin allergies, cough, and cold to child
			Banana, egg	Cause seizures in new born child, Stomach ache and cause sterility to the child to be born
	Vavilaku (*Vitex nigundo*) and bamboo leaves together put in hot water used for bath	Relieves body pains in delivered women		

CHAPTER 5

MORBIDITY INCIDENCE IN TRIBAL AREAS AND NATIVE TREATMENT ADOPTED FOR EYE RELATED DISEASES

Morbidity data available from the mandal PHC records for 1 year period 1997-98/99 (Table 5) indicated that fevers, respiratory problems and scabies are the major health problems of the tribal communities. Problems related to eye were found to be low and mostly non-nutritional.

Tribal generally were said to underutilize medical health facilities available and generally follow certain native treatment for common ailments (Table 6). Some of the native treatment adopted by the tribals under study for eye related problems are presented in Table 7.

TABLE 5

Morbidity incidence in the study area as obtained from PHC records (1997-98/99) (consolidated)

Ailments	*Per cent to the total population in the study area*
Fevers (mainly Malaria)	13.58
Respiratory organ infection including Tuberculosis	8.24
Scabies	8.02
Trauma (injuries)	1.28
Diarrhoea	1.18
Orthopaedic problems	1.58
Gynaecological problems	6.12
Eye diseases (non-nutritional)	0.95
Heart	0.09
General illness	3.04
Others	8.40

Clinical observations for nutritional deficiency symptoms revealed that 10% of preschool children were found to be suffering from Protein Energy Malnutrition (PEM) and anemia was observed to be prevalent in pregnant and lactating women of 5 districts studied. Angular stomatitis was observed in 10-20 per cent of school aged children in all the districts. Vitamin A deficiency symptoms in terms of night blindness and bitot spots were found to be scarce. However, conjunctivitis and symptoms of eye irritation, redness of eyes were found to be common among tribal adults and children. They follow certain native treatments for eye diseases and were believed to be effective in terms of cure.

The tribals have abundant traditional knowledge of some medicinal plants for use in general ailments.

TABLE 6

Forest plants used/avoided for certain ailments by the tribals

Plant name	*Therapeutic use*	*Plant name*	*Avoided in conditions*
Sesharaasi kura	Deworming		
Nelachettu (leaves and turmeric paste)	skin allergies		
Tender papaya curry	Galactogogue	Chittimitti fruits (*Polyalthia cerasoides*) Konkadi kura (*Pteridium aquilinum*)	Seizures
Gantikamma kura (*Cleome monophyllum*) Seeds made to paste and eaten with rice	Good digestion and healthy lungs	Sarukura (*Colacasia antiquomum*)	Respiratory Problems, wounds
		Brinjal, Beans	Wounds (For fear of pus formation)
Neelagiri leaves (Eucalyptus sp.) Balaraju chettu (seeds, leaves, roots)	Skin ailments	Mullu kura (Amaranthus spinosus)	Skin problems and eye irritation
Tridax (leaves made into paste)	Skin allergies and application on wounds	Mustard leaves, ferns sweet potato and pumpkin	Sore eyes
Mahua (*Bassia latifolia*) seed oil	Body pains and headache		
Pepper and ginger	Respiratory problems		
Guava and pomegranate (leaf extracts)	Gastritis		
Chittankundankura			
Oodika chiguru Balaraju chettu Reddiga chettu (leaf extracts)	Good eyesight		
Kiketha gingalu (leaf extract)	Eye irrigation		

TABLE 7

Native treatment adopted by tribal communities for eye related problems

Botanical Name	*Medicinal Value*
Aerva lanata	Leaf is wetted and the water is poured into the eye straight from leaves to prevent eye irritation.
Alangium salvifolium	Apply leaf juice with common salt (2:1) on eye lids as cure for eye disease like redness eyes.
Alternanthera sessilis	Apply fresh leaf juice as drops in treatment of eye diseases.
Alternanthera ficoidea	Fresh stem juice as drops in eye diseases.
Anthocephalus chinensis	Juice of stem bark with common salt (3:1) as cure for eye inflammation.
Argemone nexicana	Plant juice in the treatment of eye troubles like conjunctivitis.
Asparagus racemosus	Dried root powder with ghee clarified butter (5:2) to children for improving eye sight.
Boerhaavia diffusa	Plant extract with goat milk (3:2) to children as cure for night blindness.
Borreria articularis	Leaf extract in conjunctivitis.
Butea monosperma	Root decoction with hen's egg (1:1) to children as medicine in the treatment of night blindness.
Cardia spermum halicacabum	Fresh leaf juice as drop for curing eye diseases like conjunctivitis.

Botanical Name	*Medicinal Value*
Cassia fistula	Stem bark paste with paste of black pepper (3:1) to the patient as cure for night blindness.
Cardiospermum halicacabum common name: Ballon vine, Heartseed.	Apply fresh leaf juice as drop for curing eye diseases like conjunctivities.
Comretum roxburghii (combretaceae)	Fresh stem sap as drop in eye diseases.
Crinum asiatica	Extract is taken orally to cure night blindness and toothache.
Cuscuta reflexa (cuseutac· ae)	Plant juice as drop in the treatment of eye diseases.
Diospyros melanoxylone (Ebenaceae) (CN-coromandelebony persimmon)	Decoction of young leaves with unboiled egg and rice bran (3:2:2) for the treatment of night blindness.
Dipteracanthus prostratus (Acanthaceae)	Apply infusion of roots in eye diseases.
Clipta alba (Asteraceae) C.N. — Yerbadetaso	Fresh leaf juice with common salt (2:1) as drop in the treatment of eye troubles.
Emblica officinalis C.N. — Indian gooseberry/ Emblic myrobalan	Put fresh leaf juice with diluted solution of common salt (2:1) as drop in eyes for improving weak eye sight.
Euphoribia nerifolia (Euphorbiaceae) C.N. - Holy milk hedge, Dog's Tongue	Rub diluted latex with common salt (2:1) on eye lids, against dimners of sight.
Heliotropium indicum (Boraginaceae) Common name: Scorpion tall	Apply leaf juice with common salt (2:1) as drop for cure of conjunctivitis.

Botanical Name	*Medicinal Value*
Hemarthria compressa (Poaceae)	Use plant sap accumulated in the internode for eye diseases.
Hibiscus rosa - sinensis (Malvaceae) C.N. - shoe flowers, chinese hibiscus	Apply root paste with honey (1:1) in eye sore.
Ipomoea aquatica (convolulaceae) C.N. - swamp cabbage	Apply juice of fresh flowers as drop for treatment of eye diseases.
Kirganelia reticulata (Euphorbiaceae)	Diluted juice of fresh stem 2-3 drops at a time as cure for conjunctivitis.
Leonotis nepetifolia	Seed in eye for bringing out foreign particles from eyes.
Leucas plykeneti (Lamiaceae)	Fresh leaf juice with common salt (3:1) and prescribe it for treatment of Kir-Kir (a kind of eye diseases).
Mitragyna parvifolia (Rubiaceae) C.N. - Kaim	Take root bark decoction with egg (2:1) as cure for night blindness.
Moghania chapper (Fabaceae)	Put fresh young leaf juice with common salt diluted in water (3:1) as drop for treatment of eye diseases.
Momordica charantion (cucurbitaceae) C.N. - bitter gourd, carilla fruit, Balsam pear.	Stem juice with rice bran and fruit paste of amla (emblica officinalis) (3:1:1) in night blindness.
Nelumbo nucifera (Nelumbonaceae) C.N. - sacred lotus, Indian lotus chinere eater lily	Blower nectar for treatment of conjunctivitis.

Botanical Name	*Medicinal Value*
Nerium indicum (Apocynaceae) C.N. - Indian oleander sweet scanted oleander	Watery latex from fresh twigs in diluted form as drops in conjunctivitis.
Ocimum americanum (Lamiaceae) C.N. - Hoary basil	Put two seeds/extracts of seeds & 4 leaves in eyes for bringing out foreign particles if any and to improve eye sight.
Oryza rufipogan (poaceae) C.N. - Junglee rice	Water obtained in internodes, as drop in conjunctivitis.
Oxilis corniculata (oxalideceae) C.N. - Indian sorrel	Leaf juice in eyes as drops for treatment of opaque eye sight.
Paederia scandens (Rubialeae) C.N. - Chinese fervervine	Decoction with unboiled egg (3:2) for treatment of night blindness.
Plectranthus mollis (Lamiaceae) C.N. - Spurflower weed	2-3 seeds in eyes for bringing out foreign particles.
Ricinus communis (Euphorbiaceae) common name: castor, cartor seed.	Leaf decoction and unboiled eggs (3:2) to children for treatment of night blindness.
Rivea hypocrateri formis (convolvulaceae) C.N. - Midnapur creeper	Flower juice as drop in eye diseases.
Rubia cordifolia (Rubiaceae) C.N. - Indian madder	Root infusion with brassica oil (4:1) for treatment of eye and ear diseases.
Sesbania grandiflora (fabaceae) C.N. - Agathi, swamp pea, sesban	Leaf juice with honey (3:1) to children for treatment of night blindness. Petal juice as drops in eyes against inflammation.

Botanical Name	*Medicinal Value*
Shorea robusta (Diptero carpaceae) C. Name : Sal tree	Apply powder of resine charcoal (by burning resine) with mustard oil (2:1) against eye inflammation.
Sida acuta (Malvaceae)	Apply root bark paste with honey (2:1) for treatment of eye cataract.
Solena amplexicaulis	The juice of petals of male flowers as drop for cure of eye diseases.
Strychnos potatorum (Loganiaceae)	Apply seed paste with common salt (3:1) for treatment of conjunctivitis.
Symplocos racemosa (Symplocaceae) C.N. - sweet leaf tree, lodh tree	Apply infusion of stem bark as drop for treatment of conjunctivitis.
Tamarindus indica (Caesalpiniaceae)	Put stem bark decoction as eye lotion.
Tephrosia purpurea (Fabaceae) C.N. - wild indigo, purple tehrosia	Flower juice in eyes for treatment of eye inflammation.
Thespesia populnea (Malvaceae) C.N. - portia tree, Indian tulip tree, false rose wood	Juice of flower petals as cure for eye diseases.
Trapanatans (Trapaceae) C.N. - water chestnut, caltrops, singhara nut	Juice of petioles in eyes as cure for eye diseases like conjunctivitis.
Trianthema portulacastrum (Aizoaceae) C.N. - Desert horse pur slane	Plant decoction with yolk (2:1) to children for treatment of night blindness.

Botanical Name	*Medicinal Value*
Ventilago denticulata (Rhamnaceae)	Root bark decoction as cure for eye diseases like redness of eyes.
Vigna trilobata (fabaceae) C.N. - cow pea	Fresh seed decoction with paste of ginger (3:1) as cure for blindness.
Madhuca longifolia	Nectar (from flowers) in eyes as drop for treatment of any kind of eye infection.
Ervatamia coronaria (Apocynaceae) Local name: Nandivardhanamu	Flowers extract to remove foreign material from eyes
Terminalia chebula (Combretaceae) Local name: Karaka	Fruits are macerated in ginger juice along with 5 pepper fruits, one inflo-rescence of piper longum and administered orally

CN: Common name

Source: Pal DC, Jain S K 1998, Tribal Medicines Naya Prokash, Calcutta.

CHAPTER 6

PARTICULARS OF THE FOREST FOODS COLLECTED AND ANALYSED FOR BETA CAROTENE CONTENT

104 edible forest foods of the tribals including 70 green leafy vegetables, 22 fruits, 5 roots and tubers, 3 other vegetables were collected seasonally from forests of the selected villages in the five districts of Andhra Pradesh during the year March 1998 to September 1999 with the assistance of the tribals (Appendix II).

The list of the edible forest foods thus collected are presented in Table 8 with botanical description.

The carotene content of different foods with statistical analysis was represented in Tables 9-14. Among various carotenoids in nature beta-carotene is the most abundant in GLVs and has the maximum vitamin A activity.

Among the 70 GLVs analysed majority (36) were found to contain High vitamin A activity with TC ranging from 12.22 to 36.13 and BC content 5.21 to 14.05 mg% respectively. 30 GLV's showed moderate vitamin A activity with TC ranging from 10.60 to 31.33 and BC content 2.19 to 4.78 mg% respectively and remaining 4 GLV's found to have low vitamin A activity. Other vegetables, roots and tubers analysed showed negligible vitamin A activity with TC and BC content ranged from 0.01 to 0.61 and 0.14 to 0.23 mg% respectively.

Among the fruits, Canthium parviflorum contained very high TC (9.51 mg%) and BC (6.10 mg%) content, where as other fruits contained negligible content of TC (0.0015 to 1.32 mg%) and BC (0.004 to 0.49 mg%). The inedible orange colour fresh rind portion of canthium parviflorum analysed found to have the highest Beta-carotene content (6.8 mg%).

Another fruit Diosphros melanoxylon, the edible pulp portion of fruit contained no Beta-carotene. However, rind portion both fresh and dried analysed had good amounts of Beta-carotene 0.79 and 2.17 mg%, respectively.

Among the plant foods analysed, leafy vegetables had considerably more carotenoids than tubers, other vegetables and fruits. The carotenoids of a plant are mainly deposited in the leaves which in general, have a higher relative Beta-carotene content than stalk. Several factors like genetics, geographic location of the plant, interplant, diurnal, age of the plant, the position of the leaf on the stalk and enzymatic and photochemical processes during and after harvesting influence the carotenoid pattern and thereby vitamin A activity. Some of the forest GLVs analysed found to have high vitamin A activity (RE) and the amount needed to satisfy the recommended daily allowance (RDA) for vitamin A is less than half of the daily amount prescribed by ICMR for Indians (ICMR, 1992). Classification of GLVs as to the quantity needed to meet RDA for vitamin A is given in Table 15 (Fig. 8-10).

TABLE 8
Botanical Description of Edible Forest Foods Analysed for Carotene Content

S. No.	*Local Name*	*Botanical Name*	*Family*	*Habit*
Green leafy vegetables				
1*	Sikaya chiguru	Acacia concinna	Caesalpinaceae	Shrub
2*	Dukkina kura	Achyranthes aspera	Amaranthaceae	Herb
3.	Amsukura	Adiantum lunatum	Adiantaceae	Fern
4.	Pindi kura	Aerva Lanata	Amaranthaceae	Under shrub
5.	Pedda pindi kura	Aerva sanguinolenta	Amaranthaceae	Herb
6.	Nagali sarekura/ Pendlibeddi kura	Allmania nodiflora	Amaranthaceae	Herb
7.	Ponnaganti kura/ Simhadri kura	Alternanthera sessilis	Amaranthaceae	Herb
8.	Perugu thota kura	Amaranthus Gangeticus	Amaranthaceae	Herb
9*.	Tella thota kura	Amaranthus lividis	Amaranthaceae	Herb
10*.	Daggula kura	Amaranthus Polygamus	Amaranthaceae	Herb
11*.	Mullu kura	Amaranthus spinosus	Amaranthaceae	Herb
12*.	Puvuthota kura	Amaranthus viridis	Amaranthaceae	Herb
13.	Vurikanda Aku	Amorphophallus campanulatus	Araceae	Herb
14*.	Adavi kanda	Amorphophallus sylvaticus	Araceae	Herb

S. No.	Local Name	Botanical Name	Family	Habit
15.	Puleru kura	Antidesma acidus	Stilaginaceae	Shrub
16*.	Yerra bacchali	Basella rubra	Basellaceae	Twinning herb
17*.	Peddamakula/ Bodantan/Goddu/ Godrung kura.	Bauhinia purpurea	Caesalpinaceae	Tree
18.	Teddukamma kura	Boerhuvia diffusa	Nyctaginaceae	Herb
19*.	Garammasala Aku	Bryophyllum pinnatum	Crassulaceae	Herb
20*.	Balusu kura	Canthium Parviflorum	Rubiaceae	Shrub
21*.	Chirumirapakaya kura	Capsicum fruitesans linn	Solanaceae	Shrub
22*.	Peddatantem kura	Cassia occidentalis	Caesalpinaceae	Under shrub
23.	Chinnatantem/ Tantebu kura	Cassia tora	Caesalpinaceae	Herb
24.	Gurum kura	Celosia argentia	Amaranthaceae	Herb
25.	Chappi kura	Cissus Carnosa	Vitaceae	Herb
26.	Cheepuru kura	Cocculus hirsutus	Menispermaceae	Creeper shrub
27.	Venneduru/Dora kura	Commelina benghalensis	Commelinaceae	Herb
28*.	Sarukura/ Chamakura Rasisaru kura	Colacasia antiquorum	Araceae	Tuberous plant herb
29.	Gantikamma kura	Cleome monophyllum	Capparidaceae	Herb
30.	Gummadiaku/ gummadi Chiguru	Cucurbita maxima	Cucurbitaceae	Creeping Herb
31*.	Chenchel kura	Digera arvensis	Amaranthaceae	Herb
32.	Chilaka bappana kura	Digera murriculata	Amaranthaceae	Herb
33.	Garisa kura	Dryopteris Cochleata	Dryopteridaceae	Fern
34.	Devadari kura	Erythroxylum monogynum	Erythroylaceae	Shrub/ small tree
35.	Chitti kura	Ficus cunia	Moraceae	Tree
36*.	Dela kura	Ficus religiosa	Urticaceae/ Moraceae	Tree
37.	Isukarasi kura	Gisekia pharmaceoides	Aizoceae	Herb
38.	Sashap kura	Globba bulbifera	Zingiberaceae	Herb
39*.	Adavigummadi kura	Gmelina arborea	Verbanaceae	Herb

S. No.	Local Name	Botanical Name	Family	Habit
40.	White kura	Gynandropsis Pentaphylla.	Cruciferae	Herb
41*.	Chikka kura	Hevea brasiliensis	Euphorbiaceae	Tree
42.	Nela benda	Hibiscus abelmoschus	Malvaceae	Tree
43.	Janapa kura	Hibiscus cannabinus	Malvaceae	Herb
44*.	Korla kura	Ipomea sepiaria	Convolvulaceae	Creeping Herb
45.	Melli kura	Jasmine Augustifolium	Oleaceae	Shrub
46.	Podi kura	Lepidium sativum	Cruciferae	Creeping Herb
47.	Chinna Tummi kura	Leucas aspera	Libiateae	Herb
48.	Peddatummi kura	Leucas Cephalotes	Labiateae	Herb
49.	Kolem kura	Lygodium microphyllum	Schizaeaceae	Herb
50.	Elakachevula kura	Merremia emarginata	Convolvulaceae	Creeping Herb
51*.	Munaga kura	Moringa oleifera	Moringaceae	Tree
52*.	Konda karivepaku	Murraya ko-eingil	Rutaceae	Shrub/small tree
53*.	Pilliadugula kura	Oxalis Corniculata	Geraniacea	Creeping Herb
54.	Chintala kura	Phyllanthus Maderaspatensis	Euphorbiaceae	Herb' under shrub
55*.	Silleru kura	Physalis Minima	Solanaceae	Herb
56.	Pappu kura	Portulaca oleraceae	Portulacaceae	Herb
57.*	Doddanelli kura/ Nelli kura	Premna latifolia	Verbanaceae	Tree
58.	Konkadi kura	Pteridium aquilinum	Polypodiaceae	Herb
59.	Ghanta bharani kura	Pygmaeopremna herbacea	Verbanaceae	Herb
60'.	Beddi kura	Rivea hypocrateriformis	Convolvulaceae	Creeping Herb
61.	Gaju kura	Solanum nigrum	Solanaceae	Herb
62.	Tellabacchali kura	Talinum cuneiformis	Portulacaceae	Herb
63.	Ambalimadu	Trianthema Portulacastrum	Aizoceae	Herb
64.	Desara kura	Unidentified		
65.	Mandi kura	Unidentified		

S. No.	*Local Name*	*Botanical Name*	*Family*	*Habit*
Other Vegetables				
1.	Aradondakaya	Coccinia indica	Cucurbitaceae	Creeping Herb
2	Sweet pumpkin	Cucurbita Maxima	Cucurbitaceae	Creeping Herb
3.	Adavi Potla kaya	Tricosanthus dioica	Cucurbitaceae	Herb
Roots and Tubers				
1.	Chanda Gadda	Amorphophallus Paeonifolius	Araceae	Herb
2.	Chedu dumpa	Dioscorea bulbifera	Dioscoreaceae	Climbing Herb
3.	Pandi dumpa	Dioscorea Pentaphylla	Dioscoreaceae	Climbing Shrub
4.	Thega dumpa	Dioscorea Puber	Dioscoreaceae	Climbing Herb
5.	Karra Pendalamu	Manihot esculenta crantz	Euphorbiaceae	Shrub
Fruits				
1.	Udiki Pandu/ Ooduga Pandu	Alangium Salvifolia	Alangiaceae	Tree
2.	Jeedi Mamidi Pandu	Anacardium occidentale	Anacardiceae	Tree
3.	Rama phalam	Annona reticulate	Annonaceae	Tree
4.	Panasa Pandu	Artocarpus integrifolia	Moraceae	Tree
5.	Nakiri Pandu	Canthium parviflorum	Rubiaceae	Tree
6.	Papaya Pandu	Carica papaya	Caricaceae	Tree
7.	Banka Pandu	Cordia Myxa	Boraginaceae	Tree
8.	Banka neredu Pandu	Cordia obliqua	Boraginaceae	Tree
9.	Tummik Pandu	Diosphros Melanoxylon	Ebenaceae	Tree
10.	Neredu Pandu	Eugenia Jambolana	Mystaceae	Tree
11.	Elakkaya/velaga Pandu	Feroxia elephantum	Rutaceae	Tree
12.	Bodda Pandu	Ficus Glomerata	Moraceae	Tree
13.	Chittimiti pandu	Gardenia Turgide	Rubiaceae	Tree
14.	Chitti mamidi Pandu/ Adavi mamidi Pandu	Mangifera indica	Anacardiaceae	Tree

S. No.	Local Name	Botanical Name	Family	Habit
15.	Pala Pandu	Manilkara hexandra	Sapotaceae	Tree
16.	Golimi Pandu	Murraya Paniculata	Rutaceae	Shrub/ Small tree
17.	Chittietha Pandu	Phoenix humilis	Palmae bold	Tree palm
18.	Pedda etha Pandu	Phoenix sylvestris	Palmae	Tree palm
19.	Usiri Kayalu	Phyllanthus emblica	Euphorbiaceae	Tree
20.	Chiluka dudduru-pandu	Polyalthia cerasoides	Annonaceae	Tree
21.	Nalla jeedi Pandu	Semecarpus anacardium	Anacardiaceae	Tree
22.	Regu Pandu	Zizyphus jujuba	Rhamnaceae	Small tree
Others				
1.	Veduru Kommulu	Bambusa Arundinecea	Cyperaceae	Tree
2.	Bhimmudu vulli	Crinum asiaticum	Bromeliaceae	Herb
3.	Ippa flower/ Ippa fruit nut/ Ippa (Mahua oil)	Madhuca longifolia	Sapotaceae	Tree
4.	Thandra (stored product)	Mangifera indica	Anacardiaceae	

* GLV's are Perennials.

TABLE 9

Total carotenoids and Beta Carotene content of edible forest GLVs with High Vitamin A activity (5-14 mg per cent)

S. No.	Name of the GLVs	Moisture g %	T.C. mg %	B.C. mg %	% of B.C. in T.C.	Vit. A R.E. mg %
1.	Gaju kura (*Solanum nigrum*)	84.52	35.25	14.05	39.86	2.34
2.	Dela kura (*Ficus religiosa*)	65.71	22.75	12.62	55.47	2.10
3.	Pindi kura (*Aerva lanata*)	79.07	25.97	10.81	41.62	1.80
4.	Dukkina kura (*Achyranthes aspera*)	76.61	36.13	10.49	29.03	1.75
5.	Cheepuru kura (*Cocculus hirsutus*)	68.06	35.64	10.26	28.79	1.71

S. No.	Name of the GLVs	Moisture g %	T.C. mg %	B.C. mg %	% of B.C. in T.C.	Vit. A R.E. mg %
6.	Mullu kura (*Amaranthus spinosus*)	77.02	32.39	10.09	31.15	1.68
7.	Peddamakula kura (*Bauhinia purpura*)	68.17	32.88	9.26	28.16	1.54
8.	Daggula kura (*Amaranthus polygamus*)	76.83	32.75	9.13	27.88	1.52
9.	Chilka bapanna kura (*Digera murriculata*)	56.41	12.38	9.04	73.02	1.51
10.	Ghantikamma kura (*Cleome monophyllum*)	90.43	12.75	8.65	67.84	1.44
11.	Beddi kura (*Rivea hypocrateriformis*)	74.06	23.55	8.57	36.39	1.43
12.	Melli kura (*Jasmine augustifolium*)	68.46	25.69	8.45	32.89	1.41
13.	Adavi kanda kura (*Amorphophallus sylvaticus*)	80.02	30.14	8.41	27.90	1.40
14.	Devadaddiri kura (*Erythroxylon monogynum*)	51.85	24.89	8.26	33.19	1.38
15.	Ponnaganti kura (*Alternanthera sessilis*)	82.30	24.02	8.25	34.35	1.37
16.	Silleru kura (*Physalis minima*)	67.78	22.94	7.79	33.96	1.30
17.	Nela benda (*Hibiscus abelmoschus*)	82.31	25.72	7.77	30.21	1.29
18.	Peruguthota kura (*Amaranthus gangeticus*)	80.84	20.67	7.40	35.80	1.23
19.	Puvvuthota kura (*Amaranthus viridis*)	78.12	26.45	7.16	27.07	1.19
20.	Chenchel kura (*Digera arvensis*)	86.72	15.84	6.94	43.81	1.16
21.	Pilliadugula kura (*Oxalis corniculata*)	85.55	25.81	6.83	26.46	1.14
22.	Ambalimadu kura (*Trianthema portulacastrum*)	85.59	17.61	6.41	36.40	1.07

S. No.	Name of the GLVs	Moisture g %	T.C. mg %	B.C. mg %	% of B.C. in T.C.	Vit. A R.E. mg %
23.	Drumstick leaves *(Moringa oleifera)*	75.76	22.38	6.23	27.84	1.04
24.	Sikaya chiguru *(Acacia concinna)*	71.91	26.99	6.04	22.38	1.01
25.	Tellathota kura *(Amaranthus lividis)*	74.67	24.70	6.04	24.45	1.01
26.	Pedda tantem *(Cassia oxidentalis)*	83.56	21.69	6.01	27.71	1.00
27.	Gurum kura *(Celosia argentia)*	81.31	12.62	6.00	47.54	1.00
28.	Podi kura *(Lepidium sativum)*	83.53	16.43	5.77	35.12	0.96
29.	White kura *(Gynandropsis pentaphylla)*	87.09	14.52	5.75	39.60	0.96
30.	Nelli kura *(Premna latifolia)*	76.91	23.07	5.70	24.71	0.95
31.	Nagalisare kura *(Allmania nodiflora)*	87.14	18.55	5.57	30.03	0.93
32.	Sashap kura *(Globba ophioglossa)*	81.59	28.64	5.56	19.41	0.93
33.	Pendlibeddi kura *(Allmania nodiflora)*	80.73	15.45	5.46	35.34	0.91
34.	Amsu kura *(Adiantum lunatum)*	73.54	27.31	5.41	19.81	0.90
35.	Chinna tentem kura *(Cassia tora)*	80.42	18.28	5.29	28.94	0.88
36.	Gongura/Janapa kura *(Hibiscus cannabinus)*	83.99	12.22	5.21	46.63	0.87

Quantity of above vegetable required is 17 to 50 gm/day to meet the recommended dietary allowance

Results presented are mean of three independent determination

F-Calculated–17.84 SED = 0.715 CD = 1.45 at 0.05% level of signifidance

TABLE 10

Total Carotenoids and Beta Carotene content of edible Forest GLVs with Moderate Vitamin A Activity (2-5 mg per cent)

S. No.	*Name of the GLVs*	*Moisture g %*	*T.C. mg %*	*B.C. mg %*	*% of B.C. in T.C.*	*R.E. mg %*
1.	Garisa kura (*Dryopteris cochleata*)	75.56	31.33	4.78	15.26	0.80
2.	Chitti kura (*Ficus cunia*)	68.01	19.07	4.68	24.54	0.78
3.	Adavi Gummadi kura (*Gmelina arborea*)	88.44	11.71	4.29	36.63	0.71
4.	Balusu kura (*Canthium parviflorum*)	76.62	25.74	4.07	15.81	0.68
5.	Vuri kanda (*Amorpho phallus companulatus*)	86.63	21.19	4.05	19.11	0.67
6.	Tella bacchali (*Talinum cuneifolium*)	92.65	11.59	3.99	34.43	0.66
7.	Chikka kura (*Hevea brasiliensis*)	75.24	15.76	3.99	25.32	0.66
8.	Chintala kura (*Phyllanthus maderaspatensis*)	74.02	19.45	3.52	18.10	0.59
9.	Chama/Saru kura (*Colacasis antiquorum*)	85.53	8.35	3.50	41.92	0.58
10.	Elakachevula kura (*M erremia emarginata*)	77.39	17.96	3.48	19.38	0.58
11.	Isukarasi kura (*Gisekia pharmaceoides*)	90.72	7.53	3.48	46.21	0.58
12.	Kolem kura (*Lycodium microphyllum*)	75.24	19.26	3.47	18.02	0.58
13.	Chirumirapakaya kura (*Capsicum frutesans*)	80.79	14.30	3.25	22.73	0.54
14.	Desara kura	54.12	15.62	3.25	20.81	0.54
15.	Ghantabharani kura (*Pygmaeopremna herbacea*)	84.22	7.49	3.24	43.26	0.54

S. No.	Name of the GLVs	Moisture g %	T.C. mg %	B.C. mg %	% of B.C. in T.C	R.E. mg %
16.	Veneduru/Doraga kura *(Commelina benghalensis)*	90.09	13.52	3.20	23.67	0.53
17.	Doddanelli kura *(Premna latifolia)*	60.67	18.40	3.00	16.30	0.50
18.	Bodantan kura *(Bauhinia purpurea)*	80.49	9.20	2.96	32.17	0.49
19.	Mandi kura	73.11	16.05	2.80	17.44	0.47
20.	Teddu kamma kura *(Boerhuvia diffusa)*	87.99	11.61	2.65	22.82	0.44
21.	Pedda Pindi kura *(Aerva sanguinolenta)*	83.06	8.32	2.62	31.49	0.44
22.	Pedd- Tummi kura *(Leucas cephalotes)*	90.05	7.71	2.59	33.59	0.43
23.	Gummadi Aku *(Cucurbita maxima)*	86.28	13.04	2.55	19.55	0.42
24.	Pulleru kura *(Antidesma acidus)*	73.77	9.25	2.48	26.81	0.41
25.	Kondakarivepaku *(Murraya koeingii)*	70.15	10.24	2.45	23.92	0.41
26.	Konkadi kura *(Pteridium aquilinum)*	68.74	21.78	2.42	11.11	0.40
27.	Chinnatummi kura *(Leucas aspera)*	87.84	6.36	2.32	36.48	0.39
28.	Simhadri kura *(Alternanthera sessilis)*	87.80	6.71	2.29	34.13	0.38
29.	Yerra bacchali *(Basella rubra)*	89.67	17.31	2.27	13.11	0.38
30.	Korla kura *(Ipomea sepieria)*	75.95	10.60	2.19	20.66	0.36

Quantity of above vegetable required is 50-100 gm/day to meet the recommended dietary allowance.

Results presented are mean of three indendent determination

F-calculated – 701.818 SED = 0.036 CD = 0.073 at 0.05 per cent level of significance

TABLE 11
Total Carotenoids and Beta Carotene content of Edible forest GLVs with Low Vitamin A Activity (Below 2 mg per cent)

S. No.	*Food Stuff*	*Moisture g /100 gm*	*Total carotenoids (mg/100g)*	*Beta Caroten (mg/100g)*	*% Beta Carotene in total carotenoids*	*Retinol equiva-lents*
1.	Chappi kura *(Cissus carnosa)*	89.68	13.13	1.94	14.77	0.32
2.	Garam masala Aku *(Bryophyllum pinnatum)*	91.47	5.12	1.90	37.11	0.32
3.	Rasi saru kura *(Colacasia antiquorum)*	87.85	5.97	1.45	24.29	0.24
4.	Pappu kura *(Portulaca oleraceae)*	88.50	6.69	0.40	5.98	0.07

Results presented are mean of three independent determination
F-calculated = 2499.98; SED = 0.02; CD = 0.056 at 0.05% level of significance

TABLE 12
Total Carotenoids and Beta Carotene Content of Edible other Vegetables, Roots and Tubers Collected from Forest

S. No.	*Food Stuff*	*Moisture g /100 gm*	*Total carotenoids (mg/100g)*	*Beta Caroten (mg/100g)*	*% Beta Carotene in total carotenoids*	*Retinol equiva-lents*
Other Vegetables						
1.	Sweet pumpkin *(Curcurbita maxima)*	94.05	0.61	0.23	37.70	0.038
2.	Aradonda kaya *(Coccinia indica)*	63.10	1.96	0.13	6.63	0.216
3.	Adavipotla kaya *(Trisanthus dioica)*	59.47	0.30	0.12	40.00	0.020
Roots and Tubers						
4.	Chanda gadda *(Amorphophallus paeonifolius)*	80.21	0.23	0.14	60.87	0.023
5.	Chedu dumpa *(Dioscorea bulbifera)*	85.40	0.05	–	–	–
6.	Karra pendalam *(Manihot esculenta Crantz)*	65.52	0.03	–	–	–
7.	Pandi dumpa *(Dioscorea pentaphylla)*	86.95	0.01	–	–	–
8.	Thega dumpa *(Dioscorea puber)*	88.33	0.01	–	–	–

Results presented are mean of three independent determination
F-calculated = 11583.09; SED = 0.03; CD = 0.06 at 0.05% level of significance

TABLE 13
Total Carotenoids and Beta Carotene Content of Edible Forest Fruits

S. No.	Food Stuff	Moisture g /100 gm	Total carotenoids (mg/100 g)	Beta Caroten (mg/100 g)	% Beta Carotene in total carotenoids	Retinol equiva-lents mg%
1.	Nakiri pandu *(Canthium parviflorum)*	62.85	9.51	6.10	64.14	1.02
2.	Chilukadudduru pandlu *(Polyalthia cerasoides)*	60.75	1.32	0.49	37.12	0.08
3.	Pala pandlu *(Manilkara hexandra)*	66.04	0.55	0.44	80.00	0.07
4.	Papaya pandu *(Carica papaya)*	86.54	3.11	0.36	11.57	0.06
5.	Chitti mamidi pandu *(Mangifera indica)*	83.50	0.93	0.27	29.03	0.045
6.	Adavi mamidi pandu *(Mangifera indica)*	84.58	0.76	0.21	27.63	0.035
7.	Elakkaya/velaga *(Feroxia elephantum)*	62.31	0.30	0.15	50.00	0.025
8.	Pedda Etha pandlu *(Phoenix sylvestris)*	30.82	0.38	0.11	28.95	0.018
9.	Nalla Teedi pandlu *(Semecarpus anacardium)*	64.46	0.85	0.02	2.35	0.003
10.	Banka pandlu *(Cordia myxa)*	62.71	0.02	0.01	50.00	0.002
11.	Panasa pandu *(Artocarpus integrifolia)*	64.73	0.04	0.004	10.00	0.001
12.	Banka neredu pandu *(Cordia obliqua)*	54.55	0.18	–	–	–
13.	Neredu pandu *(Eugenia jambolana)*	78.47	0.11	–	–	–
14.	Tummik pandu *(Diosphros melanoxylon* Roxb*)*	69.75	0.10	–	–	–
15.	Chitti etha pandu *(Phoenix humilis)*	37.92	0.097	–	–	–
16.	Jeedi mamidi pandu *(Anacardium occidentale)*	84.86	0.07	–	–	–

S. No.	Food Stuff	Moisture g/100 gm	Total carotenoids (mg/100g)	Beta Carotene (mg/100g)	% Beta Carotene in total carotenoids	Retinol equiva-lents mg%
17.	Chittimiti pandu *(Gardenia turgida)*	69.41	0.04	–	–	–
18.	Usiri kayalu *(Phyllanthus emblica)*	80.39	0.032	–	–	–
19.	Regu pandu *(Zizyphus jujuba)*	70.11	0.028	–	–	–
20.	Bodda pandu *(Ficus glomerata)*	87.47	0.016	–	–	–
21.	Rama phalamu *(Annona reticulata)*	57.69	0.015	–	–	–
22.	Golimi pandu *(Murraya paniculata)*	59.64	0.0015	–	–	–
23.	Udiki pandu *(Alangium salvifolium)*	67.65	–	–	–	–

Results presented are mean of three independent determination
F-calculated = 47637.47; SED = 0.008; CD = 0.016 at 0.05 per cent level of significance

TABLE 14
Stored Products of Tribals Analysed

S. No.	Food Stuff	Total carotenoids (mg%)	Beta Carotene (mg%)	% Beta Carotene in total carotenoids	Vit. A Retinol equiva-lents
1.	Mamidi thandra *(Mangifera indica)*	1.89	1.09	57.67	0.18
2.	Ippa oil *(Madhuca longifolia)*	–	–	–	–
3.	Processed veduru kommulu *(Bambusa arundinecea)*	–	–	–	–
4.	Bhimmudu vulli *(Crinum asiaticum)*			Not analysed	

Results presented are mean of three independent determination

TABLE 15

Classification of GLVs based on Quantity Needed to Meet Daily Vitamin A Requirement

17-50 gms

1. Gaju kura *(Solanum nigrum)*
2. Dela kura *(Ficus religiosa)*
3. Pindi kura *(Aerva lanata)*
4. Dukkina kura *(Achyranthes aspera)*
5. Cheepuru kura *(Cocculus hirsutus)*
6. Mullu kura *(Amaranthus spinosus)*
7. Peddamakula kura *(Bauhinia purpura)*
8. Daggula kura *(Amaranthus polygamus)*
9. Chilka bapanna kura *(Digera murriculata)*
10. Ghantikamma kura *(Cleome monophyllum)*
11. Beddi kura *(Rivea hypocrateriformis)*
12. Melli kura *(Jasmine augustifolium)*
13. Adavi kanda kura *(Amorphophallus sylvaticus)*
14. Devadaddiri kura *(Erythroxylon monogynum)*
15. Ponnaganti kura *(Atternanthera sessilis)*
16. Silleru kura *(Physalis minima)*
17. Nela benda *(Hibiscus abelmoschus)*
18. Peruguthota kura *(Amaranthus gangeticus)*
19. Puvvuthota kura *(Amaranthus viridis)*
20. Chenchel kura *(Digera arvensis)*
21. Pilliadugula kura *(Oxalis corniculata)*
22. Ambalimadu kura *(Trianthema portulacastrum)*
23. Munaga kura *(Moringa oleifera)*
24. Sikaya chiguru *(Acacia concinna)*
25. Tellathota kura *(Amaranthus lividis)*
26. Pedda tantem *(Cassia oxidentalis)*
27. Gurum kura *(Celosia argentia)*
28. Podi kura *(Lepidium sativum)*
29. White kura *(Gynandropsis pentaphylla)*
30. Nelli kura *(Premna latifolia)*
31. Nagalisare kura *(Allmania nodiflora)*
32. Sashap kura *(Globba bulbifera)*
33. Pendlibeddi kura *(Allmania nodiflora)*
34. Amsu kura *(Adiantum lunatum)*
35. Chinna tentem kura *(Cassia tora)*
36. Gongura/Janapa kura *(Hibiscus cannabinus)*

50-100 gms

1. Garisa kura
   (Dryopteris cochleata)
2. Chitti kura
   (Ficus cunia)
3. Adavi Gummadi kura
   (Gmelina arborea)
4. Balusu kura
   (Canthium parviflorum)
5. Vuri kanda
   (Amorphophallus companulatus)
6. Tella bacchali
   (Talinum cuneifolium)
7. Chikka kura
   (Hevea brasilensis)
8. Chintala kura
   (Phyllanthus maderaspatensis)
9. Chama/Saru kura
   (Colacasia antiquorum)
10. Elakachevula kura
    (Merremia emarginata)
11. Isukarasi kura
    (Gisekia pharmaceoides)
12. Kolem kura
    (Lycodium microphyllum)
13. Chirumirapakaya kura
    (Capsicum frutesans)
14. Desara kura
15. Ghantabharani kura
    (Pygmaeopremna herbacea)
16. Veneduru/Doraga kura
    (Commelina benghalensis)
17. Doddanelli kura
    (Premna latifolia)
18. Bodantan kura
    (Bauhinia purpurec
19. Mandi kura
20. Teddu kamma kura
    (Boerhuvia diffusa)
21. Pedda Pindi kura
    (Aerva sanguinolenta)
22. Pedda Tummi kura
    (Leucas cephalotes)
23. Gummadi Aku
    (Cucurbita maxima)
24. Pulleru kura
    (Antidesma acidus)
25. Kondakarivepaku
    (Murraya koeingii)
26. Konkadi kura
    (Pteridium aquilinum)

Above 100 gms

1. Chinnatummi kura
   (Leucas aspera)
2. Simhadri kura
   (Alternanthera sessilis)
3. Yerra bacchali
   (Basella rubra)
4. Korla kura
   (Ipomea sepieria)
5. Garammasala Aku
   (Bryophyllum pinnatum)
6. Chappi kura
   (Cissus carnosa)
7. Rasi saru kura
   (Colacasia antiquorum)
8. Pappu kura
   (Portulaca oleraceae)

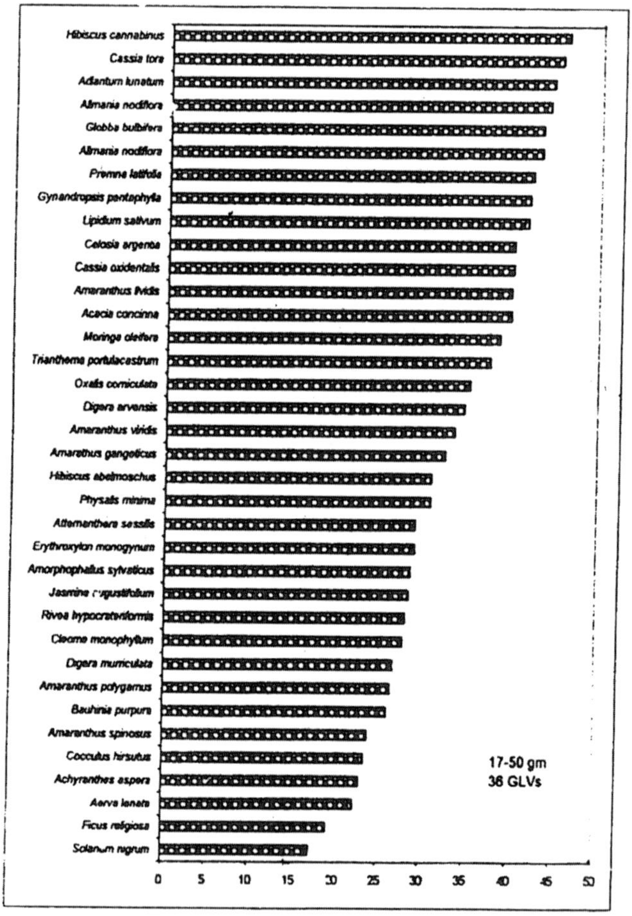

Fig. 8 : High vitamin A activity GLVs require 17-50 g to meet daily vitamin A requirement

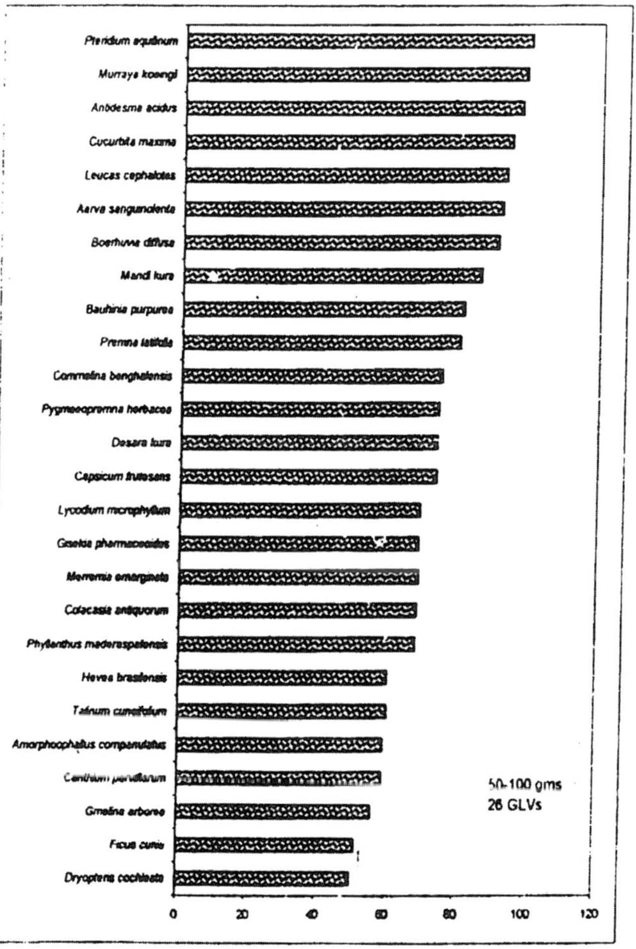

Fig. 9 : Moderate vitamin A activity GLVs require 50-100 g to meet daily vitamin A requirement

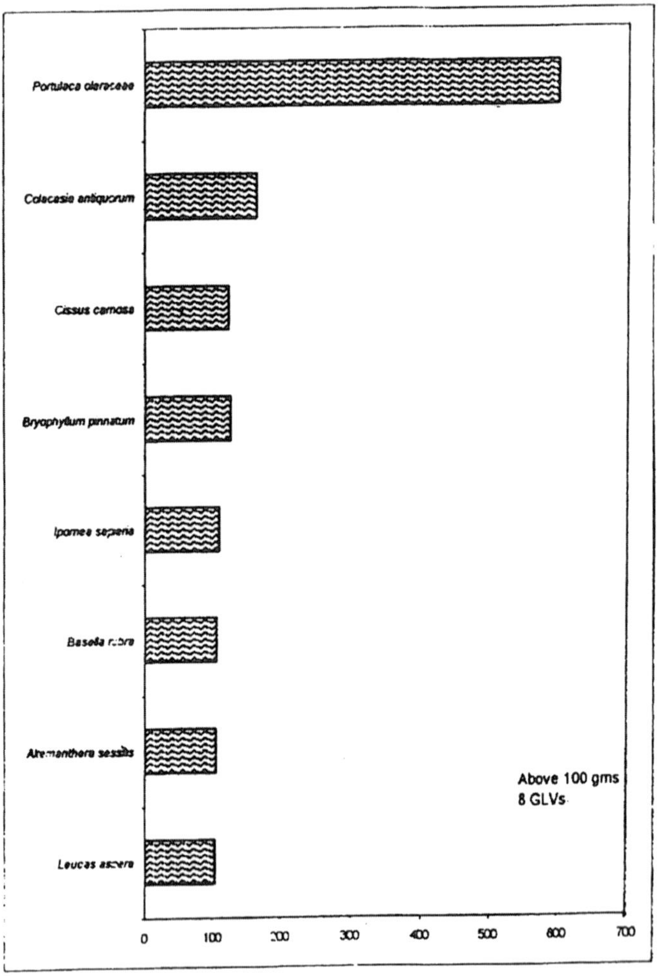

Fig. 10 : GLVs which require above 100 g to meet daily vitamin A requirement

CHAPTER 7

CULINARY METHODS AND EFFECT ON CAROTENE CONTENT

Food processing practices, in general, said to differ depending on various factors like tradition and culture. The possibility of processing of foods for preparing diverse food products is therefore essential and should be explored.

The common cooking method adopted by tribals for cooking of vegetables is boiling. The other methods include combination with dhal or broken rice, addition of tamarind extract. Frying of the vegetable is not common with the tribals. Occassionally they make chutney where the GLVs are shallow fried with a little oil and ground to paste. The effect of boiling on per cent retention of carotene in forest GLVs is presented in Table 16-19 (Fig. 11).

For making curries, generally GLVs are boiled in water (1:10 proportion) and to which ground paste of chillies and salt are added and seasoned (option) with curry leaves, red chillies and mustard seeds.

The culinary products were prepared in the laboratory following exactly the methods of the tribals. The processed samples were analysed for carotene content using HPLC. The results are presented in Table 20.

Among the various cooking procedures adopted by tribals, GLV's with cooking water retained found to have maximum Beta carotene retention followed by GLV's shallow fried. GLV's cooked with tamarind extract showed least retention of Beta carotene. (Fig. 12)

Beta carotene is known to be heat labile. Certain processing methods used prior to consumption of foods also affect vitamin A activity of carotenoids. Green leafy vegetables when boiled in water, the water becomes some what green. This might be due to migration of green chloroplasts from the leaves into the water. Loss of carotenoids is obvious as both chloroplasts and carotenoids occur in the parenchyma of the leaves. Cooking in acid medium, high temperature and prolonged exposure have been shown to adversely affect pro-vitamin A content.

Cooking converts the trans to cis isomers resulting in lowering of the Vitamin A activity. However, the losses in total carotene need not reflect the losses in B-carotene (BC). Some of the forest GLVs found to be more stable to heat in that they retained higher per cent of carotene even after heat processing as compared to others. Among them Cassia occidentalis, Cassia tora, Amaranthus lividis, Cleome monophyllum, Digeria murriculata, Rivea hypocrateriformis needs special mention with maximum (75 to 98%) retention of β-carotene on processing and having high vitamin A activity.

Tribals generally do not store perishable for long or even for short duration. However, mangoes when available in plenty, the juice is extracted and spread on bamboo mat evenly and when semi dried another layer is spread on it. The process goes on till the required thickness is obtained. The sundried layered mango product locally known as *mamidi tandra* is stored for nearly one year.

TABLE 16

Effect of boiling on per cent retention of carotene in forest GLVs (5-25%)

S. No.	*Name of the GLVs*	*Fresh*		*Boiled*		*% Retention*	
		T.C. *mg%*	*B.C.* *mg%*	*T.C.* *mg %*	*B.C.* *mg %*	*T.C.* *mg %*	*B.C.* *mg %*
1.	Chikka kura *(Hevea brasiliensis)*	15.76	3.99	6.60	0.93	41.88	23.31
2.	Cheepuru kura *(Cocculus hirstus)*	35.64	10.26	5.65	1.95	15.85	19.01
3.	Ambalimadu kura *(Trianthema portulacastrum)*	17.61	6.41	6.81	1.17	38.67	18.25
4.	Silleru kura *(Physalis minima)*	22.94	7.79	3.91	1.42	17.05	18.23
5.	Elukachevula kura *(Merremia emerginata)*	17.96	3.48	5.14	0.62	28.62	17.82
6.	Adavi kanda *(Amorphophallus sylvaticus)*	30.14	8.41	8.73	1.47	28.97	17.48

Contd...

S. No.	Name of the GLVs	Fresh		Boiled		% Retention	
		T.C. mg%	B.C. mg%	T.C. mg %	B.C. mg %	T.C. mg %	B.C. mg %
7.	Peddamakula kura *(Bauhinia purpurea)*	32.88	9.26	9.27	1.49	28.19	16.09
8.	Garisa kura *(Dryopteris cochleata)*	31.33	4.78	5.25	0.66	16.76	13.81
9.	Chinnatummi kura *(Leucas aspera)*	6.36	2.32	2.17	0.29	34.12	12.50
10.	Adavi Gummadi Kura *(Gmelina arborea)*	11.71	4.29	2.00	0.33	17.08	7.69
11.	Ghantabharani kura *(Pygmaeopremna herbacea)*	7.49	3.24	1.63	0.20	21.76	6.17
12.	Isukarasi kura *(Gisekia pharceiodes)*	7.53	3.48	3.50	0.21	46.48	6.04

Results presented are mean of three different determination

F-calculated = 30128.17; SED = 0.045; CD = 0.098 at 0.05 per cent level of significance

TABLE 17

Effect of Boiling on per cent Retention of Carotene in Forest GLVs (25-50 per cent)

S.No.	*Name of the GLVs*	*Fresh*		*Boiled*		*% Retention*	
		T.C. mg%	*B.C. mg%*	*T.C. mg %*	*B.C. mg %*	*T.C. mg %*	*B.C. mg %*
1.	Bodantan kura *(Bauhinia purpurea)*	9.20	2.96	5.09	1.51	55.35	48.61
2.	Nagalisare kura *(Allmania nodiflora)*.	18.55	5.57	8.80	2.67	47.44	47.94
3.	Pilliadugula kura *(Oxalis corniculata)*	25.81	6.83	13.97	3.06	54.13	44.80
4.	Amsu kura *(Adiantum lunatum)*	27.31	5.41	10.87	2.37	39.80	43.81
5.	Perugutota kura *(Amaranthus gangeticus)*	20.67	7.40	9.62	3.10	46.54	41.89
6.	Gaju kura *(Solanum nigrum)*	35.25	14.05	15.90	5.63	45.11	40.07

Contd....

S. No.	Name of the GLVs	Fresh		Boiled		% Retention	
		T.C. mg%	B.C. mg%	T.C. mg %	B.C. mg %	T.C. mg %	B.C. mg %
7.	Melli kura (*Jasmine augustifolium*)	25.69	8.45	17.02	3.22	66.25	38.11
8.	Simhadri kura (*Alternanthera sessilis*)	6.71	2.24	6.32	0.82	94.19	36.61
9.	Pindi kura (*Aerva lanata*)	25.97	10.81	14.53	3.36	55.95	31.08
10.	Pulleru kura (*Antidesma acidus*)	9.25	2.48	4.43	0.69	47.89	27.82
11.	Chitti kura (*Ficus cunia*)	19.07	4.68	5.50	1.21	28.84	25.86

Results presented are mean of three different determination.
F-calculated = 809937; SED = 0.054; CD = 0.115 at 0.05 per cent

TABLE 18

Effect of Boiling on per cent Retention of Carotene in Forest GLVs (50-60 per cent)

S. No.	Name of the GLVs	Fresh		Boiled		% Retention	
		T.C. mg%	B.C. mg%	T.C. mg %	B.C. mg %	T.C. mg %	B.C. mg %
1.	Ponnaganti kura *(Alternanthera sessilis)*	24.02	8.25	11.08	3.60	65.39	60.87
2.	Desara kura	15.62	3.25	10.15	1.96	64.98	60.31
3.	Munaga kura *(Moringa oleifera)*	22.38	6.23	13.01	3.30	49.42	57.65
4.	Nelli kura *(Premna latifolia)*	23.07	5.70	17.17	3.28	74.44	57.60
5.	Podi kura *(Lepidium sativum)*	16.43	5.77	13.01	3.30	79.10	56.96
6.	Daggula kura *(Amaranthus polygamus)*	32.75	9.13	16.11	5.18	49.23	56.77
7.	Gurum kura *(Celosia argentia)*	12.62	6.00	10.55	3.39	83.44	56.56

S. No.	Name of the GLVs	Fresh		Boiled		% Retention	
		T.C. mg%	B.C. mg%	T.C. mg %	B.C. mg %	T.C. mg %	B.C. mg %
8.	Mullu kura (*Amaranthus spinosus*)	32.39	10.09	17.36	6.05	53.60	55.42
9.	Nela benda (*Hibiscus abelmoschus*)	25.72	7.77	13.76	4.29	53.42	55.11
10.	Dela kura (*Ficus religiosa*)	22.75	12.62	20.64	6.86	90.73	54.36
11.	White kura (*Gynandropsis pentaphylla*)	14.52	5.75	5.97	3.12	40.93	54.05
12.	Sikaya chiguru (*Acacia concinna*)	26.99	6.04	15.40	3.13	57.00	51.57
13.	Gongura/Janapkura (*Hibiscus cannabinus*)	12.22	5.21	7.13	2.65	58.35	50.87
14.	Devadaddiri kura (*Erythroxylon monogynum*)	24.89	8.26	15.79	4.17	63.44	50.49
15.	Puvvuthota kura (*Amaranthus viridis*)	26.45	7.16	16.89	3.56	63.72	49.55

Results presented are mean of three different determination

F - calculated = 8099.37; SED = 0.054; CD = 0.115 at 0.05 per cent level of significance

TABLE 19

Effect of Boiling on per cent Retention of Carotene in Forest GLVs (75-100%)

S. No.	*Name of the GLVs*	*Fresh*		*Boiled*		*% Retention*	
		T.C. *mg%*	*B.C.* *mg%*	*T.C.* *mg %*	*B.C.* *mg %*	*T.C.* *mg %*	*B.C.* *mg %*
1.	Kolem kura *(Lycodium microphyllum)*	19.26	3.47	15.89	3.39	82.53	97.67
2.	Pedda tantem *(Cassia oxidentalis)*	21.69	6.01	17.30	5.86	79.57	97.31
3.	Tellatota kura *(Amaranthus lividis)*	24.70	6.04	20.17	5.86	81.55	97.15
4.	Vennedura kura *(Commelina benghalensis)*	13.52	3.20	7.20	2.94	53.14	91.26
5.	Beddi kura *(Rivea hypocrateriformis)*	23.55	8.57	18.99	7.73	80.64	90.20
6.	Ghantikamma kura *(Cleome monophyllum)*	12.75	8.65	10.65	7.28	83.53	84.16
7.	Chinna tantem *(Cassia tora)*	18.28	5.29	9.87	4.04	53.87	76.49
8.	Chilka bapanna kura *(Digera murriculata)*	12.38	9.04	10.08	6.85	81.42	75.78

Results presented are mean of three different determination

F calculated = 1674.47; SED = 0.98; CD = 2.27 at 0.05 per cent level of significance

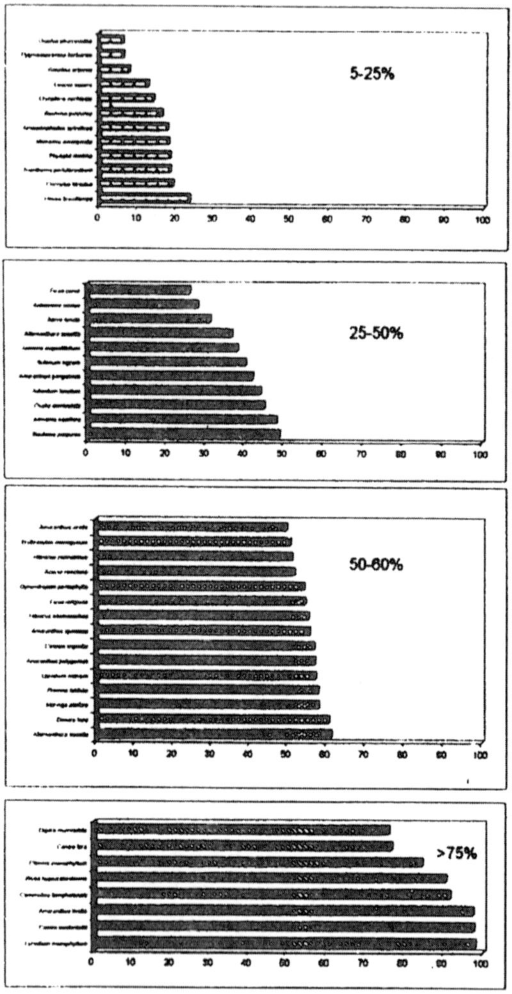

Fig. 11 : Effect of boiling on per cent retention of Beta-carotene in forest green leafy vegetables

TABLE 20

Carotene Content and per cent Retention in Common Tribal Recipes

S. No.	Cooking condition adopted for the GLV's	Ncme of the GLVs	Botanical name	Carotene content in (mg %)		% Retention	
				T.C.	B.C.	T.C.	B.C.
1.	Curry	Beddi kura	*Rivea hypocrateriformis*	17.82	8.07	75.67	94.17d
	GLV's boiled	Dela kura	*Ficus Religiosa*	15.56	9.16	68.40	72.58c
	(water drained off)	Melli kura	*Jasmine augustifolium*	13.24	5.92	51.54	70.06c
	and seasoned	Desara kura	*Cocculus hirsuus*	8.28	2.01	53.01	61.85c
		Chikka kura	*Hevea brasiliensis*	7.51	1.15	96.86	59.53c
		Peddamakula kura	*Bauhinia purpurea*	20.63	3.89	62.74	42.01b
		Devadadiri kura	*Erythroxylon monogynum*	12.32	0.81	49.50	9.81a
2.	Curry	Simhadri kura	*Alternanthera sessilis*	5.99	2.26	89.27	98.69c
	GLV's boiled	Balusu kura	*Canthium parviflorum*	15.25	4.81	59.17	98.01d
	(water retained)	Venedura kura	*Commelina benghalensis*	6.66	3.04	49.26	95.00d
	and seasoned	Elakachevula kura	*Merremia emerginata*	8.55	3.14	47.61	90.23d
		Chilakabapanna kura	*Digeria murriculata*	8.56	4.19	69.14	46.35b
		Mulluthota kura	*Amaranthus spinosus*	10.04	4.26	31.00	42.72b
3.	Dhal with GLV's	Chama kura	*Colacasia antiquorum*	8.96	1.72	81.76	55.55b
		Kolem kura	*Lycodium microphyllum*	14.10	1.69	73.23	48.60b

4.	Fry	Peruguthota kura	*Amaranthus gangeticus*	7.72	7.29	30.36	98.64d
	GLV's	Janapa kura	*Hibiscus cannabinus*	9.37	4.88	76.68	93.67d
	Shallow fried	Ghantikamma kura	*Cleome monophyllum*	10.57	3.43	82.91	39.65b
		Dukkina kura	*Achyranthes aspera*	10.24	1.99	28.26	18.82a
5.	Pulusu	Simhadri kura	*Alternanthera sessilis*	5.39	1.52	80.33	66.38d
	GLV's cooked with	Nukalatummi kura	*Leucas aspera*	5.37	1.42	84.43	61.21c
	broken rice and	Chitti kura	*Ficus cunia*	1.61	0.17	8.42	3.52a
	tamarind extract	Isukarasi kura	*Gisekia pharmaceoides*	1.38	0.09	18.24	2.65a
		Ghantabharani kura	*Pygmaeopremna herbacea*	0.18	0.015	2.35	0.42a
6.	Chutney	Janapa kura	*Hibiscus cannabinus*	7.56	2.75	61.87	52.78b
	GLV's fried in						
	little oil and ground to paste						

Results presented are mean of three independent determinations

(a) : 0-20% retention; b : 40-60% retention;

(c) : 60-75% retention; d : 90-100% retention.

Statistical significance

	F cal value	S.Ed.	CD	
(a)	51372.25	0.046	0.12	At 0.05% level of significance
(b)	25351.64	0.052	0.12	
(c)	24483.51	0.047	0.12	
(d)	11191.60	0.042	0.099	

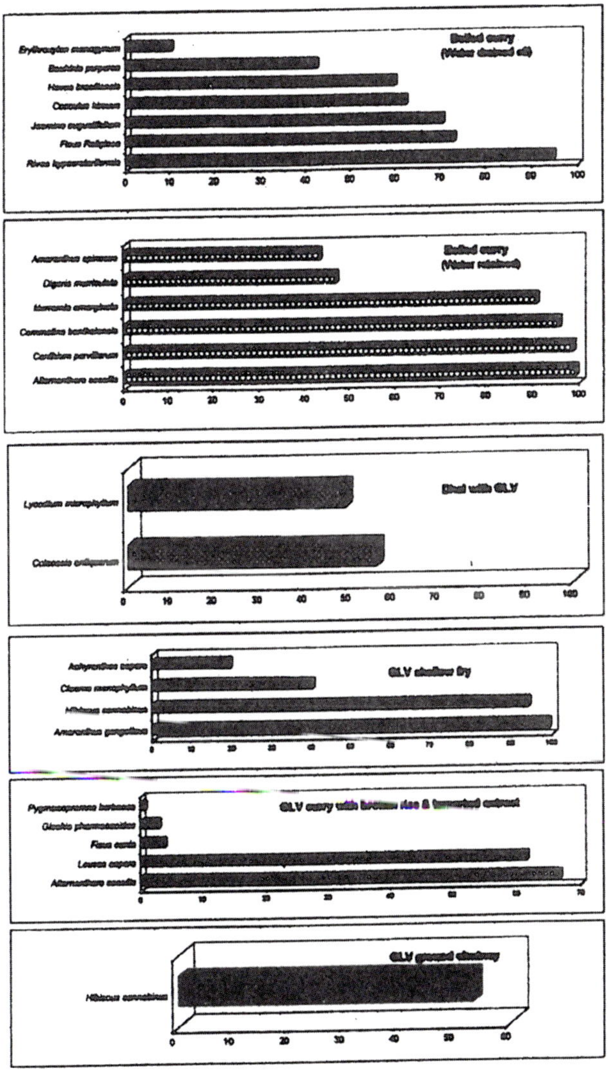

Fig. 12 :Per cent beta carotene retention in common tribal recipes

CHAPTER 8

BOTANICAL DESCRIPTION OF EDIBLE FOREST FOODS WITH ILLUSTRATIONS

ACACIA CONCINNA

Family : Caesalpinaceae

English/Trade name : Soap pod

Vernacular names : H. Kochi, Ritha; Kan. Sige; Mal. chikka; San. Amala, Bhuriphena, Charmakasha, Patraghana, Phena, Svarnapushpi, Vidula, Vimala, Vishanika; Tam. Shikai, Siyakkay; Tel. Chikayi, Manjisikaya, Sikaya chiguru.

Acacia concinna

Description: A climbing shrub with prickles on stems and leaves. Leaves compound, branched twice in the manner of a feather. Leaflets 5-14 pairs on each branch, oblong, unequal sized, pin pointed, 1-1.5 cm long. Flowers small in yellow round masses. Fruit a pod, fleshy, soapy 7.5-10 × 2-3 cm, depressed between 6-10 seeds.

Distribution: Occurs in tropical jungles and hotter parts of India.

Propagation: By seeds

Parts used for consumption: Tender leaves are acidic, used in chutneys. Seeds roasted and eaten.

Season of availability: July to November.

Medicinal value: The leaves are cathartic and cure biliousness. An infusion of leaves is used in malarial fever.

The pod is bitter, pungent; cooling, digestible, deobstruent, detergent, purgative, anthelmintic, anti diarrhoeal; improves appetite, cures kapha, biliousness, burning sensation, diseases of the blood, erysepelas, leucoderma, stomatitis; ascites, piles; cardiotonic.

In China and Japan, the pods are considered emetic, diuretic and laxative; they are used in constipation, and in troubles of kidneys and the bladder. The seeds are said to facilitate delivery in child birth. (WI Vol. I : 1948, 45, CSIR and IMP (KKR) Vol. II - 1988, 931).

Estimated
Carotene value (mg/100g)

Total carotenoids	:	26.99
Beta carotene	:	6.04
Retinol equivalents	:	1.01

ACHYRANTHES ASPERA Linn

Family : Amaranthaceae

English/Trade Name : Prickly chaff-flower plant

Vernacular names : H. circita, Cicimda; Kan. uttarani; Mal. Katalati, Vankatalali, Valiya Katalate; San. Apamargah; Tam. Katalati, Nayuruvi; Tel. Uttareni, Antisa, Apamargamu, Dukkina kura.

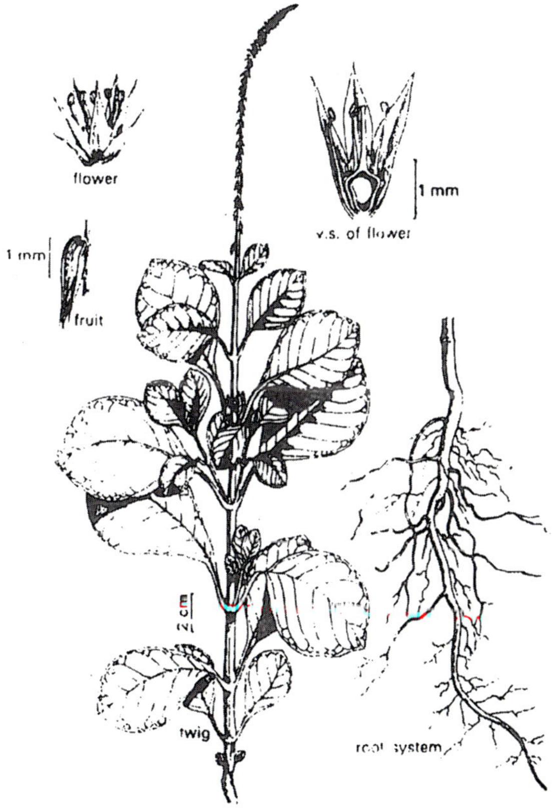

Achyranthes aspera linn

Description: An erect or procumbent, annual or perennial herb, 1-2 m. in height, often with a woody base. Stems angular, ribbed, simple or branched from the base, often tinged with reddish purple colour, leaves thick, ovate-elliptic or obovate - rounded, but variable in shape and size, flowers greenish white, numerous in axillary or tarminal spikes, upto 75 cm long, seeds subcylindric, truncate at apex, rounded at the base, reddish brown.

Distribution: Found as a weed of road sides, waste places, through out India, upto an attitude of 2,100 m, and in South Andaman Islands.

Propagation: Natural regeneration by seeds.

Parts used for consumption: Young leaves are served like spinach.

Season of availability: Almost found through out the year, mainly in July to November.

Medicinal value: The plant possess valuable medicinal properties as a pungent and laxative, and is considered useful in dropsy, piles, boils, eruptions of the skin etc. The dried plant is given to children for colic, and also as an astringent in gonorrhoea. Water, in which the crushed plant has been boiled is given in pneumonia.

The infusion of root is given as a mild astringent. The seeds and leaves are considered ematic, and are useful in hydrophobia.

In Sind it is used by foresters as an application to wounds caused by Babool thorns.

In Las Bala, the plant is used as a cure for coughs and rhuematisms.

In Ceylon, the juice of leaves is taken for dysentery. In Bihar, the flowering spike made into pills with a little sugar is a popular preventive medicine for persons bitten by rabies dogs.

In Mauritius and La Reunion, the herb is commonly used as a depurative, astringent, diuretic and pectoral. In Madagascar, the root is given in puerperal, pulmonary, syphilitic and rheumatismal troubles. It is used in opthalmia, dropsy, and cutaneous diseases (IMP (KKR and BBD) Vol. III-1988, 2066).

Estimated
Carotene value (mg/100g)

Total carotenoids	:	36.13
Beta carotene	:	10.49
Retinol equivalents	:	1.75.

ADIANTUM LUNULATUM

Family : Adiantaceae

English/Trade name : Walking Maiden Hair fern.

Vernacular names : H. Kalijhant; Raja Hamsa,
Mar. Raja Hans; Tel. Amsu kura.

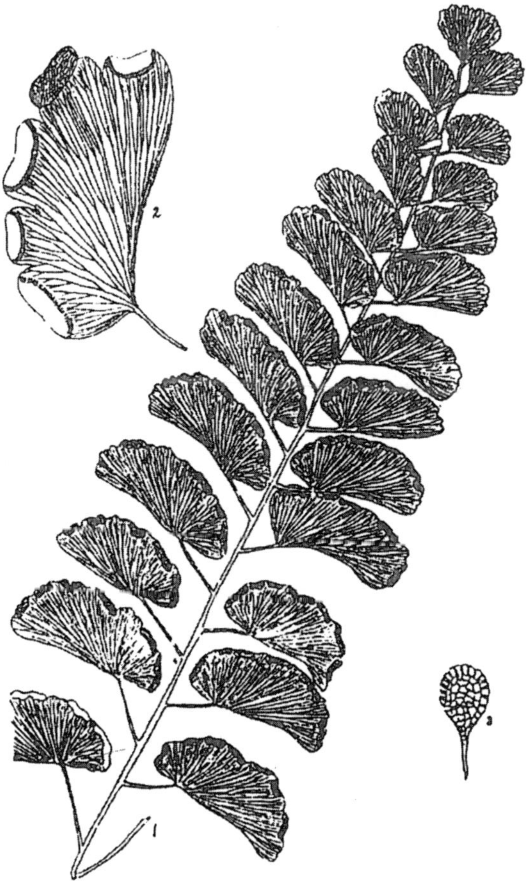

Adiantum lunatum

Description: A graceful fern, stipes 6-15 cm. long, tufted, wiry, glabrous, polished, dark chest nut brown, fronds 15-30 cm. long, simply pinnate, often elongated and rooting at the apex, pinnae distinctly stalked, half-moon shaped, frequently lobed. Rachis on both surfaces naked. Texture herbaceous. Sori linear in continuous line along the edge.

Distribution: Found on rocks and slopes of the lower hills throughout the greater part of India upto an attitude of 1,200 m. It is also found on brown laterite soil or under shade near swamps.

Propagation: Natural regeneration by seeds.

Parts used for consumption: The leaves of the fern are used as vegetable.

Season of availability: July to November.

Medicinal value: The plant is pungent and alexiteric. It is used in blood diseases, burning sensation, epileptic fits and dysentery and as a cooling lotion in cases of erysipelas. The fronds are used in leprosy and fever. In Bihar, the fern is used in rabies. A decoction of the rhizome is given in throat infections, it is also used for febril conditions in children. The rhizome is prescribed for strangury and for fever due to elephantiasis. The fronds made into a plaster are applied to chronic gouty and other swellings, also to chronic tumours. Burnt with oil, they are used as an application for itch (WI Vol. I-1948, 80 CSIR).

Estimated

Carotene value (mg/100g)

Total carotenoids	:	27.31
Beta carotene	:	5.41
Retinol equivalents	:	0.90.

AERVA LANATA JUSS

Family : Amaranthaceae

English/Trade name : —

Vernacular names : H. Chaya, Gorakhganja; Kan. Bilihindisoppu; Mal. Cerula, Cerupula; San. Bhadra; Tam. Cerupulai, Sirukkanpoolai; Tel. Pindi kura, Thelaga Pindi kura.

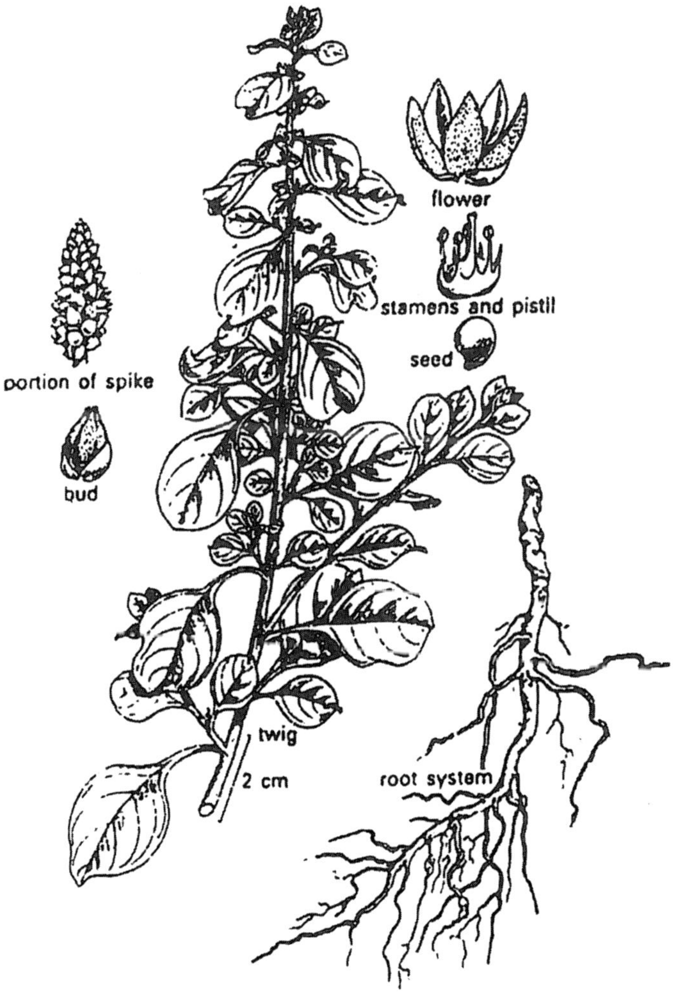

Aerva lanata

Description: An erect or prostrate, many branched under shrub, 30-60 cm in height, woolly, tomentose throughout; leaves simple alternate, short petioled, densely tomentose, usually smaller in the flowering branches; flowers very small, sessile, bisexual, greenish or hoary white, often clustered in spikes, perianth calycine membranous, five and free filaments of the five stamens connate at the base with alternating linear staminodes; fruits greenish, roundish, compressed utricle; seeds kidney shaped with shining black, coriaceous testa.

Distribution: Throughout India, Ceylon-Arabia, Tropical Africa, Java, Phillippines.

Propagation: Natural regeneration by seeds.

Parts used for consumption: Leaves are used as a vegetable.

Season of availability: July to February.

Medicinal value: The plant is astringent, bitter, cooling, mollient, vermifuge, suppurative, diuretic, and lithontriptic. It is useful to treat boils cephalalgia, cough, strangury and lithiasis. The roots are used as a treatment for headache. The plant is regarded as a demulcent on the Malabar coast. It is valued for cough in Ceylon; also as a vermifuge for children (IMP (OL) Vol. I, 1948, 67; and IMP (KKR, BBD) Vol. III-1988, 2064).

Estimated

Carotene value (mg/100g)

Total carotenoids	:	25.97
Beta carotene	:	10.81
Retinol equivalents	:	1.80.

AERVA TOMENTOSA FORSK

(Aerva sanquinolenta)

Family : Amaranthaceae

English/Trade name : Javanese wool plant

Vernacular names : Tam : Poolan keerai; Tel : Pedda Pindi kura.

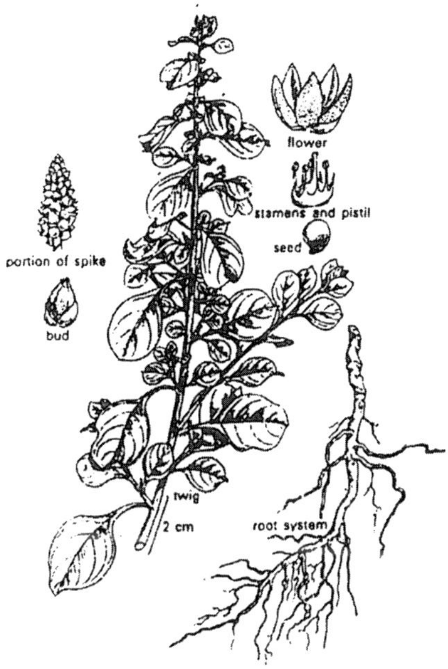

Aerva lanata

Description : The plant is very conspicuous on account of it's white tomentose nature. It grows to a height of 3 1/2 ft. or more and is much branched. The stem is round, striate and thickly white tomentose. Leaves are simple, alternate, sub sessile, oblong spatulate and obtuse. Flowers are small, white, woolly and numerous in dense terminals penicles of simple or branched spikes 1—6 inches long. The plant being dioecious, the male and female flowers occur on different individuals. Female plants are very common and males are extremely rare. Bracts and bracteoles are broadly ovate, membranous and white. Perianth consists of five white sepals. All the sepals are densely woolly at the back. Ovary is superior 1 celled, and 1ovuled and surrounded at the base by a small toothed ring of staminodes style is short. Fruit is a membraneous utricle. Seed is small, round, biconvex and shining brownish black in colour (WI, 1948, CSIR).

Distribution : The Deccan and Carnatic as also in Coimbatore.

Propagation : Natural regeneration by seeds.

Parts used for consumption : Leaves.

Medicinal value: --

Estimated
Carotene value (mg/100 g)

Total carotenoids	:	8.32
Beta carotene	:	2.62
Retinol equivalents	:	0.44.

ALTERNANTHERA SESSILS (Linn.) R.Br.Ex.DC

Family : Amaranthaceae

English/Trade name : —

Vernacular names : H. Gudri Sag; Kan. Honugonesoppu; Mal. Minannani, Ponnannani, Ponnankannikkira; San. Mạtsyaksi, Patturah; Tam. Ponnannkannikkirai; Tel. Ponnagantikura, Simhadrikura (Vizianagaram dt).

Description: A much branched prostrate herb, branches often purplish, frequently rooting at the lower nodes; leaves simple, opposite, somewhat fleshy, lanceolate, oblanceolate or linear-oblong,obtuse or subacute, sometimes obscurely denticulate, glabrous, shortly petiolate; flowers small, white, in axillary clusters; fruits compressed obcordate utricles, seeds suborbicular.

Distribution: Throughout India, in most places upto 2,100 m, often cultivated.

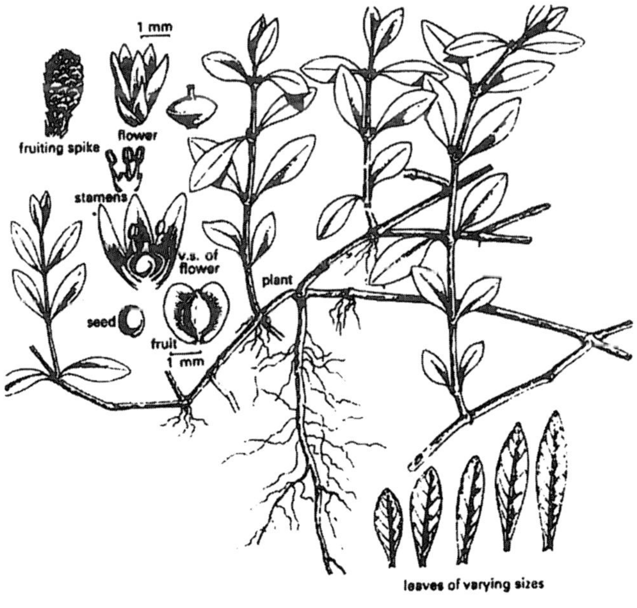

Alternathera sessilis

Propagation: By rooted stem cuttings, also by seeds.

Parts used for consumption: Tender shoots and leaves are eaten as vegetable or in soup, also eaten with fish or rice. Young shoots are nutritious. Boiled leaves mixed with condiments are eaten as vegetable.

Season of availability: Flowering from August to May and fruiting from July to January.

Medicinal value: The plant is bitter, sweet, astringent, acrid, cooling, constipating, depurative, digestive, cholagogue, galactagogue and febrifuge and is useful in vitiated conditions of kapha and pitta, burning sensation, diarrhoea, leprosy, skin disease, dyspepsia, haemorrhoids, agalactia, splenomegaly and fever (IMP-Vol. I-118, 199,) (OL).

In some parts of Bihar, the plant is used for hazy vision, night blindness, diarrhoea, dysentery and post natal complaints (WI Vol. I-206, 1948).

In Ceylon, it is used as a lactogogue, also as a wash for eyes.

In Malaya, it is valued as a febrifuge.

In Madagascar, the plant is much used as a galactogogue. It is given in baths for pruritis and phlyctena of young children (IMP (KKR & BBD) Vol. III, 1988, 2069).

Estimated
Carotene value (mg/100g)

		Ponnagantikura (from East Godavari)	Simhadrikura (From Vizianagaram district)
Total carotenoids	:	24.02	6.71
Beta carotene	:	8.25	2.29
Retinol equivalents	:	1.37	0.38

AMARANTHUS GANGETICUS LINN

Family : Amaranthaceae

English/Trade name : Love-lies bleeding, Red cocks-Comb.

Vernacular names : H. : Rajkiri; San : Harish, Sinhalese, Sudutampala; Kan : Dantu; Tam : Kirai; Tel : Perugu totakura.

Amaranthus gangeticus linn

Description : An erect herb 0.6-1.2 m. high, stem stout branching above the middle, often tinged with purple grooved and striate, glabrous or nearly so. Leaves variable, 5-15 by 2.5-10 cm, rhomboid-ovate or lanceolate, or deltoid-ovate, obtuse, finely apiculate, often noched at the tip, glabrous, base long-tapering decurrent on the petiole, main nerves numerous, prominent beneath, petioles 2.5-7.5 cm long. Flowers clustered in the axils and forming a long terminal more or less interrupted spike, bracteoles 3 mm long narrowly lanceolate, subulate, with a slender awn, membranous. Perianth 4 mm long sepals 3, lanceolate, with a long capillary awn membranous, stemens 3 capsules 2-5 inch long, avoid, suddenly narrowed at the apex, curcumseissile about the middle, rugose, membranous, styless 3 distinct. Seed 1.5 mm diam. lenticular, smooth and shining black.

Distribution : Throughout India, Ceylon, Tropical Asia, Africa and America.

Propagation : Natural regeneration by seeds.

Parts used for consumption : Leaves and tender shoots.

Season of availability : July to December.

Medicinal value : The leaves are sweetish, expectorant, vulnerary, antipyretic, emmenagogue, emetic, stop suppuration, useful in biliousness, flashy tumours, toothache, burning sensations, liver complaints, inflammations, decoction a good gargle in stomatitis (Yunani).

The plant is astringent, and highly recommended in menorrhagia, diarrhoea, dysentery and heamorrhages from the bowels (IMP (KKR & BBD) IV, 1988, 2060).

Estimated

Carotene value (mg/100g).

Total carotenoids	:	20.67
Beta carotene	:	7.40
Retinol equivalents	:	1.23.

AMARANTHUS LIVIDUS

Family : Amaranthaceae

English/Trade name : Trailing Amaranth, wild blite.

Vernacular names : H. chholi, chaulai, Sadamatiya; San. Alpamarisha, bashpaka; Tam. Aarumatha thandu, Kiraitandu; Tel. Pedda tota kura, Tella tota kura.

Description : An erect, ascending or prostrate annual herb, stem slender to stout, simple or considerably branched, green to reddish or yellow, leaves mostly glabrous, long petioled, lamina ovate to rhomboid ovate, 1.0-8.0 cm x 0.6-6.0 cm; flowers green, in slender or stout terminal spikes and axillary cymose clusters.

Distribution : It is found as a common weed and also cultivated extensively all over India.

Propagation: Natural regeneration by seeds.

Parts used for consumption : The tender leaves and shoots are boiled and used in curries or as a substitute for spinach. The soft succulent stem is sliced into small pieces and dressed in the manner of french beans and sometimes substitute to asparagus.

Season of availability : Almost throughout the year, found mostly during July to November.

Medicinal value: The bushmen of south West Africa make an intoxicating drink from this plant. The herb is cooling, stomachic emollient and slightly astringent, useful in biliousness and haemorrhagic diathesis. It is used as a tonic. It is good remedy for round worm (WI, Vol. I, 1948, 277-78, CSIR).

Estimated
Carotene value (mg/100g)

Total carotenoids	:	24.70
Beta carotene	:	6.04
Retinol equivalents	:	1.01.

AMARANTHUS POLYGAMOUS Willd

Family : Amaranthaceae

English/Trade Name : —

Vernacular names : H. Chowlaikabhaji, Chumli sag; Sanskrit, Ganna, Mekanada, Tanduliya; Tam. Kappikkirri, Kuruvikkirai, Shirukirai, Sirrukirai; Tel. Doggali kura, Koyyatota kura, Sirakura, Daggula kura.

Description : Erect, very ramous near the ground. Leaves rhomboid-oval, emarginate. Clusters axillary and in terminal spikes. Sepals subulate ending in an awaled joint, longer than the utricle.

Distribution : Commonly found in waste places, road sides and cultivated as a pot plant.

Propagation : Natural regeneration by seeds.

Daggula kura
(Amaranthus polygamus)

Parts used for consumption : The leaves are eaten as pot herb.

Season of availability : Almost found throughout the year, mainly during July to December.

Medicinal value : The roots are considered demulcent. The herb is used as diuretic in form of decoction in combination with some other medicine. In Annam, the whole herb is used as an ascaricide (IMP (KKR & BBD) Vol. III, 1988, 2061).

Estimated

Carotene value (mg/100g)

Total carotenoids	:	32.75
Beta carotene	:	9.13
Retinol equivalents	:	1.52.

AMARANTHUS SPINOSUS Linn

Family : Amaranthaceae

English/Trade Name : Spiny Amaranth, Spiny pigweed, Thorny Amaranth

Vernacular names : H. Goja, Kantemat, Kantewali-Chaulal; Kan. Mullu dantu, Mullu harive soppu; Mal. Mullancheru-Cheera, Kattumullen keera; San. Tanduliya; Tam. Mulluk-keerai; Tel. Yerra Mullu-Gorinta, Mullatota kura, Nalla Doggali, Mullukura.

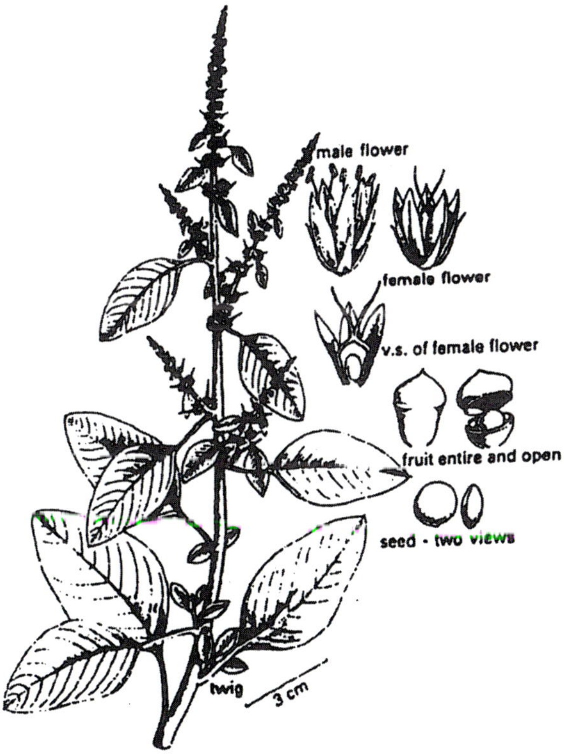

Amaranthus spinosus linn

Description : An erect glabrous herb 30-60 cm high; stems hard, often reddish, with many grooved branches and with sharp divaricate spines, often exceeding 1.3 cm long, in the leaf axils. Leaves ovate or lanceolate, obtuse, spinous–apiculate, entire, glabrous above, sometimes scrufy beneath; flowers very numerous, sessile, in dense axillary clusters and in terminal and axillary dense or interrupted spikes; bracteoles linear, capsule 1.5 mm. long, ovoid, thickened at the top, circumscissile about the middle, membranous, rugore; styles 2, divaricate, pubescent.

Distribution: Throughout India, ceylon - Many tropical countries.

Propagation : By seeds.

Parts used for consumption : The plant in times of scarcity used as pot herb. It is wholesome and aggreable. The plant has considerable food value and contain moisture 84.5; protein 3.0; fat 0.5; carbohydrates 8.1; mineral matter 3.6, Ca 560.0, P 15.0, Fe 30.5 (WI Vol. I, 1948, 219).

Season of availability : Almost throughout the year but mainly from July to December.

Medicinal value : The plant is cooling; digestible, alexiteric, laxative, diuretic, stomachic, antipyretic; improves the appetite; useful in "Kapha", and biliousness, blood diseases, burning sensation, hallucination, leprosy, bronchitis, rat-bite, piles, leucorrhoea. The root is heating, expectorant; lessens the menustral flow; useful in leucorrhoea and leprosy. The root is considered specific in gonorrhoea. It is used in menorrhagia and eczema. A decoction of plant improves digestion is used in kidney complaints and as mouth wash for toothache. The boiled leaves and roots are given to children as a laxative. They are applied as an emollient poultice to obsecesses, boils and burns. In combodia, the root is used internally as a diuretic sudorific and febrifuge.

In the Goldcoast, it is used as an enema for stomach trouble and the krobos use it for curing piles. In Medagaskes, the root is considered diuretic, laxative and galactogogue. The decoction is given for retention of urine and gonorrhoea. The root ground in water is applied ezematous skin. The ash of the plant is applied topically to fumigating chancre (IMP (KKR) Vol. 111, 1988, 2057—2059).

Estimated

Carotene value (mg/100 g)

Total carotenoids	:	32.39
Beta carotene	:	10.09
Retinol equivalents	:	1.68.

AMARANTHUS VIRIDIS

Family : Amaranthaceae

English/Trade name : —

Vernacular names : Kan. Chilikirae suppy, Daglisoppu; San. Tanduliya; Tam. Kuppaikeerai, Sinna keerai pullu; Tel. Chilaka tota kura, Puvvu tota kura.

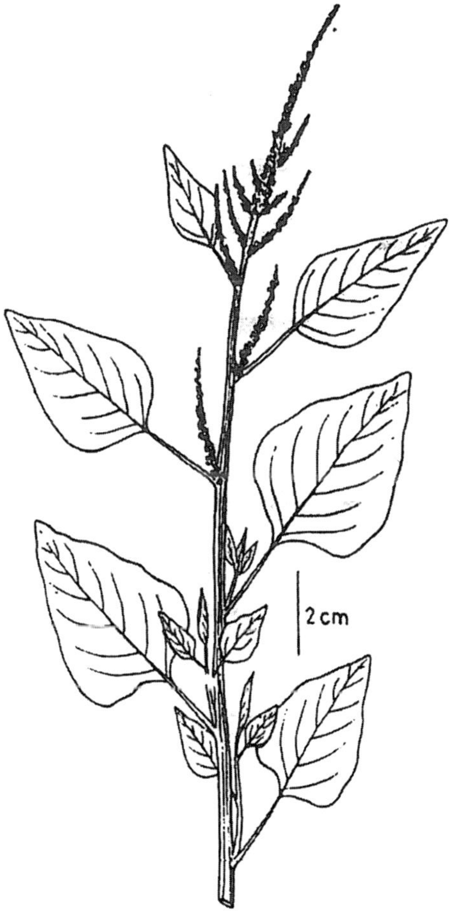

Amaranthus viridis

Description : An erect much branched glabrous herb 30-60 cm high; branches grooved, glabrous, often purplish. Leaves 2.5-7.5 by 1.3.-5 cm, ovate or deltoid-ovate, obtuse, usually notched at the apex, glabrous, base truncate or cuneate; petioles 1.3-5 cm long. Flowers shortly pedicellate, pale green, in small axillary clusters and in slender tapering terminal and axillary paniculate spikes—like racemes. Seed 1 mm. diameter, tenticular, smooth shining black.

Distribution : Throughout India.

Propagation : Natural regeneration by seeds.

Parts used for consumption : The leaves and tender shoots are edible and use as a vegetable.

Season of availability : Available almost throughout the year.

Medicinal value : The plant is cooling, digestible, alexiteric, laxative, diuretic, stomachic, antipyretic, improves the appetite, useful in kapha and biliousness, blood diseases, burning sensation, hallucination, leprosy, bronchitis, piles, leucorrhoea.

The root is heating expectorant; lessens the menstrual flow, useful in leucorrhoea and leprosy (IMP) (KKR) Vol.III, 1988, 2061).

Estimated

Carotene value (mg/100g)

Total carotenoids	:	26.45
Beta carotene	:	7.16
Retinaol equivalents	:	1.19.

AMORPHOPHALLUS CAMPANULATUS

Family : Araceae

English/Trade name : —

Vernacular names : H. Zamin-kand; Kan. Nansikanda; Mal. Chenakarona Krizhanna; San. Arsaghna; Tam. Karunaik, Kizhangu; Tel. Vurikanda akulu.

Description : A stout 1.0-1.5 m high herb with an underground depressed globose corns of 20-30 cm diameter. Leaf single (rarely two) 30-90 cm across, 3-partite with the lateral segments bifurcate and pinnatified with oblong lobes. Petiole dark green with pale blotches. Spathe 15-25 cm long with a campanulate tube, suddenly widening, spadix as long as the spathe, and very stout.

Distribution : Throughout India and also extensively cultivated throughout India.

Party used for consumption : Leaves.

Season of availability : —

Medicinal value : The acrid roots are used medicinally in boils and opthalmia.

Estimated
Carotene value (mg/100 g)

Total carotenoids	:	21.19
Beta carotene	:	4.05
Retinol equivatents	:	0.67.

Amorphophallus paeoniifolius var. campanulatus

AMORPHPHALLUS SYLVATICUS

Family : Araceae

English/Trade name : —

Vernacular names : Tam. Kattu; Tel. Adavi kanda, Vanakanda, Adavi dumpa aku.

Description : A stout 1.0-1.5 m high herb with an underground depressed globose corn. Tuber sub globore, leaves one or two, 45-75 cm diameter, bipinnatified, leaflets lanceolate, long accuminate. Petiole and peduncle 30-60 cm high above the ground. Spathe clouded, barred and streaked with green and pale pink, enclosing a 15-30 cm long stipitate spadix.

Distribution : Occurs throughout the Deccan peninsula.

Parts used for consumption : Leaves and roots.

Season of availability : Almost found throughout the year.

Medicinal value : The tuber is dry, acrid, pungent, increases both appetite and taste, stomachic, constipating, useful in piles, enlargement of the spleen, tumours, asthma, bronchitis, vomiting, abdominal pains, blood diseases, elephantasis, causes itching sensation, harmful in kapha leprosy, leucoderma (Ayurveda).

The corns and the seeds are used as irritants and relieve the pains of rheumatic swellings when applied externally. The root is used in opthalmia and applied to boils. It is also used as an emmengogue.

The raw tuber, well ground, is rubbed on swellings of the extremities by the Mundas of chota Nagapur (IMP (KKR & BBD) IV, 1988, 2609-2610).

Estimated

Carotene value (mg/100g)

Total carotenoids	:	30.14
Beta carotene	:	8.41
Retional equivalents	:	1.40.

ANTIDESMA ACIDUS

Family : Stilaginaceae

English/Trade name : Carpenters tamarind

Vernacular names : H. Amari, Amta, dhakki, katma; Kan. Bilikoomme, Karrihulipa, Sannagooge; Mal. Areepazham; Tam. Ariporian; Tel. Pellagumudu, Pulleru kura.

Description : A decidous shrub or small tree with spreading branches, upto 6 m. in height and 60 cm. in girth, bark smooth, grey, pale, red inside, leaves variable, elliptic, obovate, oblong to lanceolate, turning deep red before fall, 2.5-5.0 cm × 1.25-4 cm. male and female flowers greenish yellow, terminal or lateral racemes, drupes ovoid, smooth, purplish red when ripe.

Distribution : Distributed in the tropical Himalayas from Kumaun eastwards to North Bengal and Sikkim, and also common throughout Eastern India and in Peninsular India ascending to an altitude of 1,200 m.

Propagation : By seeds.

Parts used for consumption : The leaves and fruits are pleasantly acidic and are eaten. The leaves are cooked as vegetable and made into preserves in Assam. They are used as shampoo in Kerala.

Season of availability : June to December.

Medicinal value: —

Estimated

Carotene value (mg/100g)

Total carotenoids	:	9.25
Beta carotene	:	2.48
Retinol equivalents	:	0.41.

BASELLA RUBRA

Family : Basellaceae

English/Trade name : Indian spinach

Vernacular names : H. Poi; Kan. Basale; Mal. Basala; Tam. Sivappu Salakkeerai; Tel. Yerra bacchali.

Description : A perennial twining herb, with leaves upto 5" × 3". They are broadly ovate and pointed at apex. Flowers greenish white in axillary peduncled spikes. Fruit an utricle, 4-7 × 5-10 mm depressed globose, dark violet or blackish with violet juice when ripe.

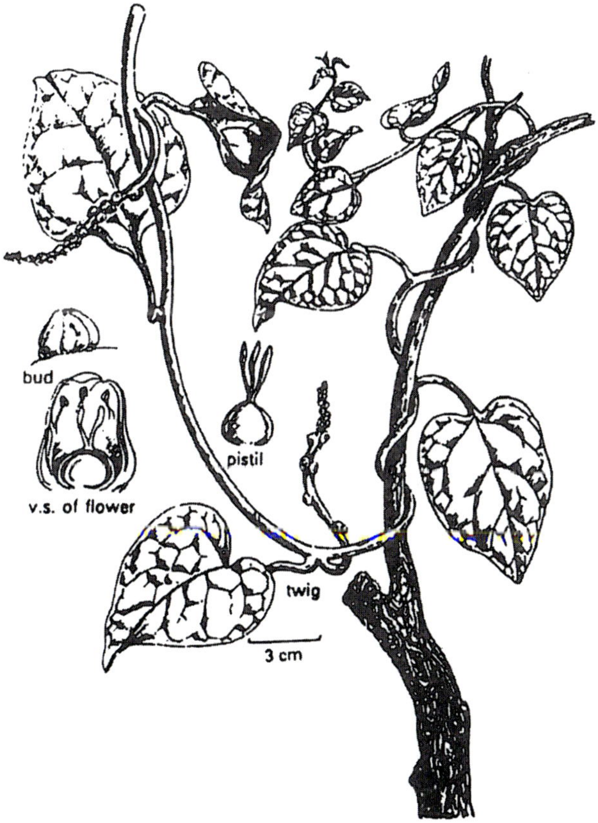

Basella alba var. rubra

Destribution : The plant is grown as pot herb in almost every part of India.

Propagation : Seedling are raised in nursery and then transplanted and also stem cutting.

Parts used for consumption : The tender stems and leaves make a very wholesome spinach.

Season of availability : Available throughout the year.

Medicinal value : The pulped or bruised leaves; on account of the presence of mucilage, are used a poultice. The juice of leaves is prescribed in cases of constipation particularly in children and pregnant women and in utricari-.

Estimated

Carotene value (mg/100 g)

Total carotenoids	:	17.31
Beta carotene	:	2.27
Retinol equivalents	:	0.38.

BAUHINIA PURPUREA

Family : Caesalpinaceae

English/Trade name : Butterfly, Orchid tree

Vernacular names : H. Lal Kachnar, Kaliar, Kandan, Khairwal, Sona; Kan. Kanchivala, Baswanapada; Mal. Chuvannamandaram; Tam. Mandarai; Tel. Deva Kasia, Peddari, Kanchanam, Bodantankura.

Bauhinia purpurea

Description : A tree 9-15 m high, leaves notched both at the tip and base into two lobes. Flowers showy, rosy purple, rarely white. Pod strap like 15-25 cm long. Seed 12-15, flat roundish, 1.3 cm across dark brown.

Distribution : Occurs throughout the country upto an altitude of 1600m and also cultivated.

Propagation : This species comes up easily from seeds and by natural regeneration.

Parts used for consumption : The tender leaves are eaten as vegetables. The seeds are eaten raw and roasted.

Season of availability : Found throughout the year.

Medicinal value : Roots carminative, bark used in diarrhoea, also yields a fibre. Flower buds are laxative, anthelmintic.

Estimated
Carotene value (mg/100 g)

		Peddamakula kura (Prakasam district)	Bodantankura (Vizianagaram district)
Total carotenoids	:	32.88	9.20
Beta carotene	:	9.26	2.96
Retinol equivalents	:	1.54	0.49

BOERHAVIA DIFFUSA Linn

Family : Nyctaginaceae

English/Trade name : Hogweed, Pigweed

Vernacular names : H. Punarnava, Sant, Santhi; Kan. Thami-zhama; Mal. Tavilama, Talutama; San. Punarnava, Sophaghni; Tam. Mukkurattai, Mukkurattai-Kirai; Tel. Atakamamidi, Teddukamma kura.

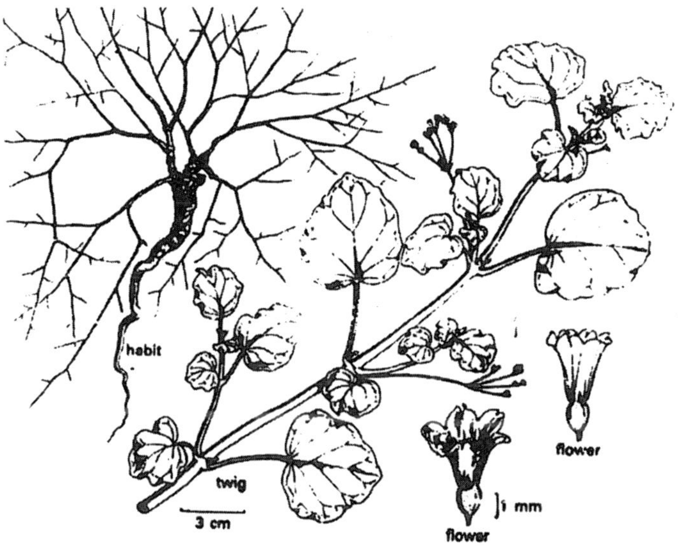

Boerhaavia diffusa

Description : A perennial diffuse herb with stout root stock and many procumbent branches; leaves simple, opposite, short-petioled in unequal pairs, ovate oblong, acute or obtuse, rounded or sub cordate at base, glabrous above, and whitish beneath; flowers pale rose coloured, small, short walked, in irregular clusters of terminal panicles at the ends of branches; fruits highly viscid, easily detachable, one seeded, indehiscent with a thin pericarp.

Distribution : Throughout India, as a weed in waste lands and road sides.

Propagation : Natural regeneration by seeds, can also be done by cuttings.

Parts used for consumption : Leaves are collected and used as a vegetable.

Season of availability : July to November.

Medicinal value : The plant is highly prized in Hindu medicine. It is bitter, astringent, cooling, anthelmintic, diuretic, aphrodisiac, cardiac stimulant, diaphoretic, emetic, expectorant, anti-inflammatory, febrifuge, laxative and tonic. It is useful in all types of inflammations, strangury, leucorrhoea, opthalmia, lumbago, myalgia, scabies, cardiac disorders, jaundice, anaemia, dyspepsia, constipation, cough, bronchitis and general debility (IMP (OL) Vol. I, 1995, 281).

Estimated

Carotene value (mg/100g)

Total carotenoids	:	11.61
Beta carotene	:	2.65
Retinol equivalents	:	0.44.

BRYOPHYLLUM PINNATUM

Family : Crassulaceae

English/Trade name : —

Vernacular names : H. Zakhm-haigat; Beng. Patharkunchi, Tamil. Runakalli, Sans: Pashanabheda. Tel. Sima Jamudu, Garam masala aku.

Description : A perinnial herb with thick fleshy leaves, the plants spread by vegetative propagation, and new plants arise from crenulations of any leaf that comes into contact with the soil.

Distribution : Found throughout the hot and moist parts of India and Ceylon.

Propagation : The plants spread by vegetative propagation, and new plants arise from the crenulations of any leaf that comes into contact with soil.

Garam masala aku
(Bryophyllus pinnatum)

Parts used for consumption : Thick, fleshy leaves are used as vegetable.

Season of availability : Available throughout the year mostly during July to January. Flowers in winter and fruits in summer.

Medicinal value : Slightly toasted leaves are a very good application for wounds, bruises, boils and bites of venomous insects. Beneficial effects follow their application to contused wounds, swelling and discoloration are prevented and the union of the cut parts takes place rapidly (Kirt and Basu II, 1988, 999). In the form of poultice and powder they are used for ulcers (WI Vol. I, 1948, 233 CSIR). It cures polyuria allay, thirst, alleviates burning sensation and dysuria sheetala (sheetaveerya) heals urinary calculi (Asima Chatterjee *et al.*, 1994, Vol. 1-3).

Estimated

Carotene value (mg/100 g)

Total carotenoids	:	5.12
Beta carotene	:	1.90
Retinol equivalents	:	0.32.

CANTHIAM PARVIFLORUM

Family : Rubiaceae

English/Trade name : —

Vernacular names : Kan. Karai, Therane, Achchumullu; Tam. Theranaikarai, karaychedi, Nallakarai, Mullukarai, Sengarai; Tel. Balusukura.

Description : A rigid shrub with 2.5-5 cm. long, stout, straight spines. Leaves usually crowded on shortened lateral shoots. 1.5-2.5 cm. long, ovate, orbicular or obovate. Flowers very small Ca 0.8-1.5 cm. cymes. Fruit Ca 1.5 cm. diameter, subquadrate or oboval.

Distribution : From Konkan southwards upto Kanniyakumari.

Propagation : By seeds and stem cuttings.

Parts used for consumption : Leaves are used as vegetable. The fruits of the plant are also edible.

Season of availability : Throughout the year.

Medicinal value : The roots and leaves are astringent, sweet, thermogenic diuretic, febrifuge, constipating, anthelmentic and tonic. They are useful in vitiated conditions of Kapha, diarrhoea, strangury, fever, leu corrhoea, intestinal worms and general debility (Imp (OL) Vol. I, 1995, 336).

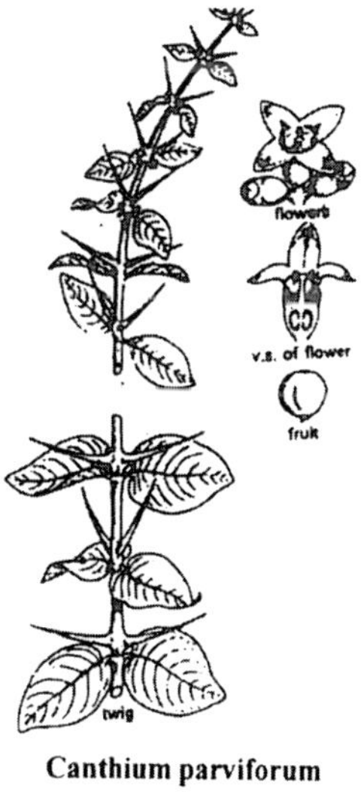

Canthium parviforum

Estimated

Carotene value (mg/100 g)

Total carotenoids	:	25.74
Beta carotene	:	4.07
Retinol equivalents	:	0.68.

CAPSICUM FRUITESANS Linn

Family : Solanaceae

English/Trade name : Golconda-chillies, pod pepper, goat pepper.

Vernacular names : Tel. Chittimirapa, Chirumirapakaya kura, H. mirchi, Kan. menasu, Tam. milakai mulagai.

Description : It is a shrubby perennial plant 3-4 ft. high, bearing small, conical fruits, 12-25 mm. long which are extremely pungent. The plants degenerate under cultivation in one or two years.

Distribution : It occurs wild or semi-wild in the tropics.

Propagation : Natural regeneration by seeds.

Parts used for consumption : The leaves and fruits are used for consumption.

Season of availability : Available throughout the year.

Medicinal value : The leaves are used as a green vegetable in some countries. They form an ingredient in remedies for head stroke, inflammation and boils, for cuts and wounds. The leaves are chewed and the juice is swallowed as a remedy for tuberculosis. The leaves and bark are employed in breathlessness. The decoction of leaves is used for pains in the throat and paralysis (WI, 1955, Vol. III, 263-64, CSIR).

Estimated
Carotene value (mg/100 g)

Total carotenoids	: 14.30
Beta carotene	: 3.25
Retinol equivalents	: 0.54.

Capsium fruitesans linn

CASSIA OCCIDENTALIS Linn

Family : Caesalpinaceae

English/Trade name : Negro coffee, stinking weed

Vernacular names : H. Kasaumdi, Barikasaumdi; Kan. Doddaagace; Mal. Ponnaviram; San. Kasamardah; Tam. Ponnavirai, Peravirai, Nattam takarai;, Tel. Kasinda, Kasivinda, Peddatantem kura.

Description : A diffuse under shrub, with furrowed, subglabrous branches; leaftlets 3-5 pairs; flowers yellow, in short peduncled, few flowered racemes; fruits cylindrical or compressed, transversely septate glabrous pods containing 20-30 seeds, seeds ovoid, compressed, hard, smooth and shiny dark olive-green or pale brown.

Distribution : Throughout India, growing abundantly on waste lands immediately after rains.

Parts used for consumption : Leaves of the plant are used as vegetable.

Propagation : Natural regeneration by seeds.

Season of availability : Throughout the year, but mostly during July to November.

Medicinal value : The plant is bitter, sweet, thermogenic, purgative, expectorant, and febrifuge, and is useful in vitiated conditions of vata and kapha, cough, bronchitis, constipation, fever, epilepsy and convulsions. The roots are bitter, acrid, thermogenic, diuretic, anti inflammatory, digestive, stomachic, and tonic. They are useful in vitiated condition of vata, inflammation, diabetes, strangury, elephantiasis, ring worm, colic, flatulence, dyspepsia, epilepsy, convulsions and scorpion sting. The leaves are bitter, acrid, sweet, thermogenic, depurative, vulnerary, anodyne, expectorant, alexeteric, and aphrodisiac, and are useful in vitiated conditions of vata and kapha, leprosy, erysipelas, wounds, ulcers, cough, bronchitis, liccough, asthma, pharyngodynia, fever and hydrophobia. The root is a cure for snake-bite, the juice when fresh is useful in ring worm; heals wounds; cures ascites. The fruit is a cure for scorpion sting.

The seeds are bitter; they are used in heat of the blood, for winter cough and for cough in animals.

In the Konkan, the seeds are used as a cure for the convulsions of children.

At Kotra, in Kachhi the plant is considered a cure for sore eyes.

In La Reunion, the root is considered bitter, tonic and stomachic; the leaves, depurant and febrifuge; the seeds, tonic and febrifuge.

In Madagascar, the whole plant is considered febrifuge.

In West Indies, the root is considered diuretic and the leaves taken internally and applied externally are given in cases of itch and other cutaneous diseases.

In Brazil, an infusion of the root bark is used as a tonic and diuretic.

In Guinea, every part of the plant is considered tonic and febrifuge.

The plant is much used in native medicines of Gold coast. The diuretic properties of the root are recognised not only in India but also in Tahiti, Martinique, Guadelocyse, Senegal, Nossi-Be, La Reunion.

Estimated

Carotene value (mg/100 g)

Total carotenoids	:	21.69
Beta carotene	:	6.01
Retinol equivalents	:	1.00.

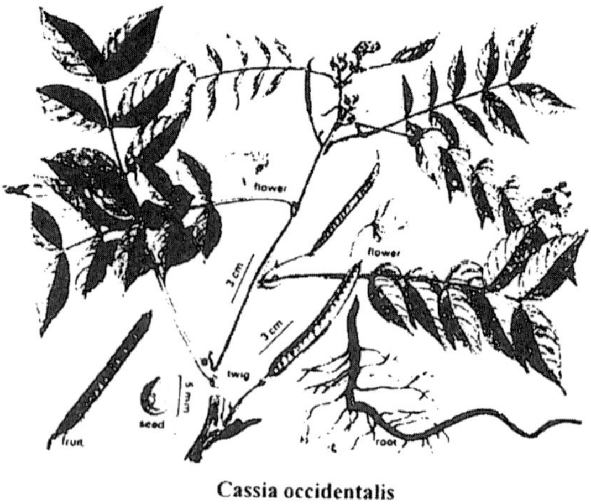

Cassia occidentalis

CASSIA TORA Linn

Family : Caesalpinaceae

English/Trade name : Foetid cassia

Vernacular names : H. Chakavat, Chakunda, Parmad, Panevar; Kan. Vanavarika, Tagaci; Mal. Chakramandrakam, Takara; San. Ayudham, Chakramarda, Dadamandan; Dadamari; Prishnaparni, Tam. Tagarai, Usittagaraj, Senavaa; Tel. Tagirise, Tantiyama, Tantemu, Tentebu Kura, Chinna Tantem kura.

Description : A herbaceous foetid annual weed, almost an undershrub, upto 90 cm in height; leaves pinnately compound, rachis grooved with a conical gland between each of the two lowest pairs of leaflets, leaflets three pairs, obovate-oblong, membranous, base somewhat oblique, main nerves 8-10 pairs; flowers yellow, in subsessile pairs, in the axils of the leaves, the upper ones crowded, stamens seven, perfect and three staminodes; fruit subtetragonous obliquely septate pods, 15-23 cm long, the sutures very broad; rhombohedral 25-30 per pod.

Propagation : Natural regeneration by seeds.

Parts used for consumption : Young leaves and twigs are cooked and eaten as vegetable. Mature seeds are boiled with tea as an ingredient and consumed to keep the body warm in winter. Young fruits are also used as a vegetable.

Season of availability : July to December.

Medicinal value : The leaves and seeds are acrid, thermogenic, laxative, depurative, antiperiodic anthelmintic, liver tonic, opthalmic, expectorant and cardiotonic and are useful in ringworm, pruritus, leprosy, skin diseases, hepatopathy, helminthiasis, flatulence, colic, dyspepsia, intermittent fevers, constipation, opthalmopathy, cough, bronchitis, cardiac disorders, and haemorrhoids.

In China, the seeds are used externally and internally for all sorts of eye diseases; preparations are also given for liver complaints and boils.

In Indochina, the pods are used in dysentery and in diseases of the eye.

In Nigeria, the leaves are used as a mild laxative. In Gold Coast, it is chiefly used as a purgative. In Madagascar and La Reunion, the root is considered bitter, tonic, stomachic.

Estimated

Carotene value (mg/100 g)

Total carotenoids	:	18.28
Beta carotene	:	5.29
Retinol equivalents	:	0.88.

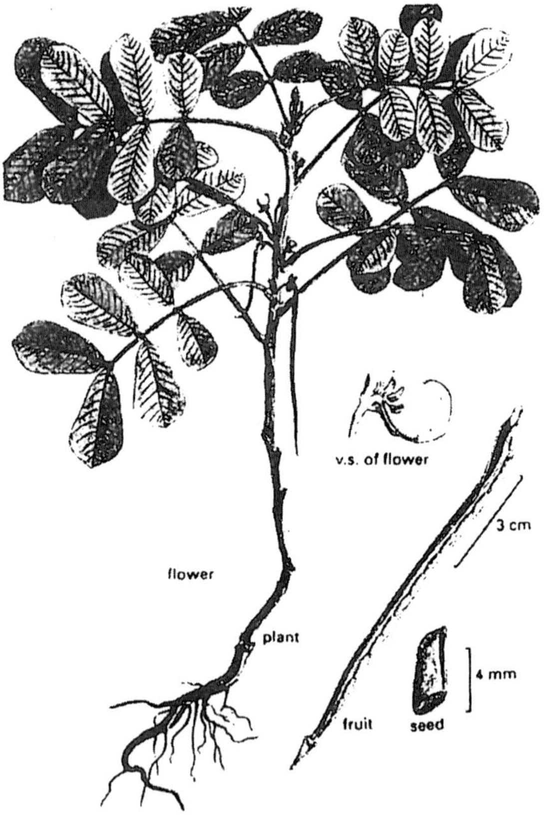

Cassia tora linn

CELOSIA ARGENTEA Linn

Family : Amaranthaceae

English/Trade name : Quail grass

Vernacular names : A. Safed Murgha, Debkoti; San. Vitunna; Tel. Gunugu, Gurugu, Panchechettu, Gurum kura.

Description : Annual, 0.3-0.9 m high, glabrous; stem erect, simple or ascending; branches grooved. Leaves variable, 2.5-10 by 0.6-3.2 cm, linear or linear-lanceolate, acute, entire, glabrous, base much tapering into a short petiole or leaves sessile. Flowers at first pinkish, afterwards glistening white, crowded and imbricate, in close cylindric blunt or acuminate terminal spikes 2.5-1.5 by 2-2.5 cm, sometimes branching at the apex in a cock's comb form; bracteoles 4-5 mm. long, linear-lanceolate, scarious. Perianth 8 mm. long or more; Sepals linear-lanceolate; acute scarious, with 3 close parallel slender striae on the back. Stamens short; filaments connate into a cup. Style filiform, elongate after flowering. Sometimes exserted in fruit, capsules 3-4 mm. long, ellipsoid, tapering at the apex into the style, circum sessile about the middle. Seeds 4-8, subreniform, compressed. 1.5 mm diameter, black polished, shining.

Distribution : It is a common weed in cultivated fields, hedges, river banks, and open places throughout India. Occasionally ascending upto 1800 mt in Himalayas.

Propagation : Natural regeneration by seeds.

Parts used for consumption : Tender leaves are cooked and eaten as sag, aids in digestion. Leaves are used as spinach.

Season of availability : July to December.

Medicinal value : The plant has heating properties; the seeds are useful in diarrhoea. The seeds are bitter; aphrodisiac, vulnerary; useful in diarrhoea, blood diseases, mouth sores. The leaves are antipyretic, aphrodisiac; reduce inflammations, strengthen the liver; useful in gonorrhoea; burnt leaves are styptic.

In China, the dried plant is considered antiscorbatic and cooling. The seeds have a reputation of clearing the vision and healing the diseases of the eye.

Estimated

Carotene value (mg/100g)

Total carotenoids	:	12.62
Beta carotene	:	6.00
Retinol equivalents	:	1.00.

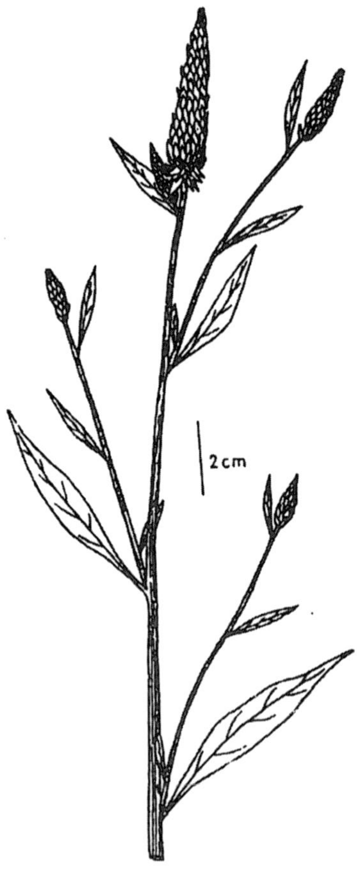

Celosia argentea linn

CISSUS CARNOSA

Family : Vitaceae

English/Trade name : Fleshy wild vine, fox grape

Vernacular names : Urdu. ·Amalabel; Hindi. Amlat bel, Kadamadrvalli; Malayalam. Sorivalli; Tamil. Sanskrit. Aranyavasini, Atyamlaparni Balli surana, Banastha, Kandura, Tikshna. Telugu: Kadepatige, Kamputige, Kaniyapatige, Kurudinne, Mandulamaritige, Mekamettani, Pulimada, Chappi Kura.

Description : Scandent, stems herbaceous or woody at the base only, compressed, densely pubescent when young, tendrils short, slender, usually branched leaves 3-foliolate, common petioles 2-4.5 cm. long, leaflets thick, 3.8—5.7 by 2.2—3.2 cm. (The middle one the largest) round—ovate, ovate–lanceolate or obovate, acute or obtuse, crenate–serrate or subinciso–dentate, more or less pubescent on both surfaces; main nerves 5-6 pairs; petiolules of the lateral leaf lets 3-6 mm. Long those of the terminal leaflets twice as long; stipules small, ovate, acute, flowers in branched divaricate. Pubescent long, penduncled cymes, buds globose; pedicels about 3 mm. long. calyx pubescent outside, funnel-shaped, truncate or obscurely 4–lobed. Petals 4 oblong, rounded at the apex, 2.5 mm long, hooded, pubescent outside. Disk cup shaped with a plicate margin style conical, berry turbinate, fleshy 1.2–2 cm long, 2-4 seeded seeds triangular, rounded and rugose on the back, cuneate on the face.

Distribution : Throughout India and Ceylon, Malaysia, Peninsula–Java. A climber in outskirts of the forests.

Season of availability : October-January.

Propagation : Natural regeneration by seeds.

Parts used for consumption : Leaves.

Medicinal value : The root has a sharp sour taste; cures "vata" and "kapha" tumours, pains and spleen complaints (Ayurveda).

The root is sour with a sharp taste, purifies the blood and lessens biliousness, good for liver and heart troubles, and for inflammation of the spleen; tonic, stomachic; produces cough (Yunani). The names given to it in many parts of India denote one of its most general uses, viz. the treatment of yoke sores on the necks of bullocks. For that purpose, a poultice of the leaves is employed (Elliot). According to Irvine the seeds and also leaves are employed as an embrocation. Stewart remarks that the root, ground with black pepper, is applied to boils.

The root is used as an astringent medicine (Kirtikar K R, Basu B D 1988 Indian medicinal plants, 2nd edition Vol. I, 611-12).

Estimated

Carotene value (mg/100 g)

Total Carotene	:	13.13
Beta Carotene	:	1.94
Retinol equivalent	:	0.32.

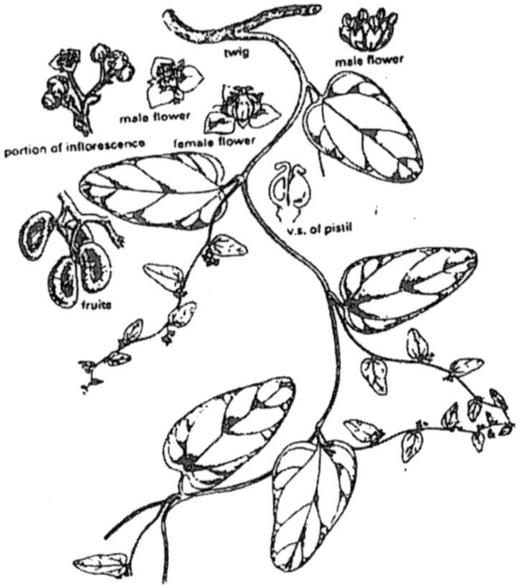

Cocculus hirsutus

COCCULUS HIRSUTUS (Linn.) Diels
(C. villosus Lam.)

Family : Menispermaceae

English/Trade name : Broom creeper, Ink berry

Vernacular names : Hind — Patalagarudi, Jalisamni
San — Patalagarudah, Chitihindah
Tam — Katlukkoti
Kan — Sagadiballi, Dusariball
Tel — Dusaratiga, Cheepurukura

Description : A straggling scandent shrub with softly villous young parts; leaves simple, alternate, ovate-ablong, obtuse, apiculate, subcordate or truncate at the base, softly villous on both surfaces, petioles densely villous; male flowers small, in axillary cymose panicles, female flowers 2-3 together in axillary clusters, petals thick and fleshy, divided at the apex into two triangular lobes, claw hairy, fruits transversely rugose, purplish black drupes.

Distribution : Throughout India in dry localities.

Parts used for consumption : leaves

Seasonal availability : September-November

Medicinal value : The roots are bitter, acrid, thermogenic, laxative, alterant, emollient, alexeteric, depurative, demulcent, digestive, carminative, diuretic, aphrodisiac, expectorant, anodyne, antipyretic and tonic and are useful in vitiated conditions of kapha and vata, poisonous bites, leprosy, skin diseases, pruritus, dyspepsia, flatulence, colic, strangury, cough, bronchitis, gout, cephalagia, intermittent fever, spermatorrhoea, urethrorrhea, burning sensation, tubercular glands, fractures, hypertension and general debility.

The leaves are mycilaginous, cooling demulcent, anodyne and expectorant, and are useful in eczema, gonorrhoea, prurigo, impetigo cough opthalmia, cephalalgia and neuralgia [IMP (OL), 1995, 2, 138].

Estimated
Carotene value (mg/100 g)

Total carotenoids	:	35.64
Beta carotene	:	10.26
Retinol equivalents	:	1.71.

COMMELINA BENGHALENSIS

Family : Commelinaceae

English/Trade name : —

Vernacular names : H. Kandhara; Mal. Vazhapadathi; San. Kanchata; Tam. Kanarazhai; Tel. Amruthakada, Vennadevikura, Venneduru kura, Doraga kura.

Description : A herb, 60–90 cm high, leaves ovate or oblong, flower bluish or bluish white, 2–3 together, fruit a capsule, pear shaped mostly 5-seeded.

Distribution : Thoughout India in moist regions upto an attitude of 2000 mts. in Himalayas.

Propagation : Mainly by stem cuttings, also by seeds.

Parts used for consumption : Tender shoots are eaten as vegetable after cooking. Young leaves are fried with spiced gram flour and eaten as 'pakodas'. Starchy underground shoots are cooked and eaten.

Season of availability : July to November.

Medicinal value : The plant is bitter, useful in leprosy and vata (Ayurveda) In La Reumon, the plant is considered as an emollient and Mucilaginous. It is much used in the form of decoction as drink, lotion, bath. The sutos prepare a medicine from the plant in treating bareness in women (IMP (KKR) IV, 1988, 2536) (WI, II, 1950, CSIR, 2533).

Estimated

Carotene value (mg/100 g)

Total carotenoids	:	13.52
Beta carotene	:	3.20
Retinol equivalents	:	0.53

Commelina benghalensis

COLACASIA ANTIQUORUM

Family : Araceae

English/Trade name : Coco Yam, Dasheen, Eddo, Taro

Vernacular names : H. Arvi-ka-Sag; Kan. Shamangaddeyele; Mal. Chembuilagar; San. Kachu; Tam. Seppamilaigal; Tel. Chama akulu. Sarekura, sarukura, Rasisaru kura.

Description : A perennial tuberous plant, with large, heart shaped leaf blades, borne on long petioles, $1^{1}/_{2}$—7 ft. high, arising from a group of underground farinaceous corns, flower in spadix in 30—40 cm long, yellow spathe which is peduncled.

Distribution : Grows wild on the banks of streams, ponds and marshes and in moist shady situations inside forests in India. Different varieties are commonly cultivated in many parts of country upto an attitude of 2500 mt.

Propagation : By tubers and suckers.

Parts used for consumption : Young leaves and stalks are edible and can be cooked and used like spinach or sag. They are cooked in the same way as other greens, but a pinch of baking soda is added to remove the acridity which increases with age. Leaves which are unopened or just to open are more satisfactory than older leaves. The leaves and petioles are said to be good sources of provitamin A and vitamin C.

Season of availability : June to October.

Medicinal value : The pressed juice of the petioles is used as a styptic or astringent.

Estimated
Carotene value (mg/100 g)

		Sarukura/ Chemakura (mature leaves)	Rasisaru kura (tender leaves)
Total carotenoids	:	8.35	5.97
Beta carotene	:	3.50	1.45
Retinol equivalents	:	0.58	0.24.

CLEOME MONOPHYLLA

Family : Capparidaceae

English/Trade name : —

Vernacular names : Kolami : Chamani

Mundari : Carmani ara, carmari ara

Sadani : Hurhuriasag

Santali : Hurhura, Kedar jhawar

Telugu : Ghantikammakura

Description : Erect branched 30—60 cm high, more or less hairy or pubescent; stems striate, leaves simple, 2.5—7.5 by 1.8—2.2 cm. Passing gradually into bracts above, oblong–lanceolate, base truncate rounded or cordate; petioles slender, 2.5—3.8 long flowers pink, solitary in the axils of stalked, leafy bracts, in a long erect raceme; pedicels slender; bracts ovate or sub deltoid, cordate, strongly pubescent stamens 6, sepals linear, acute, ciliate with gland tipped hairs, petals oblong, rounded at top, clawed capsules 6.3—9 cm by 2-3 mm, subcylindric, pointed straiate, clothed with short shout hairs. Gynophore very short or 0. Seeds transversely rugose.

Distribution : From Bihar and Orissa to Gujarat, the deccan, the Konkan, South Maratha country and Ceylon in fields and waste places of tropical Africa.

Season of availability : July-December.

Propagation : It is grown in field as weed.

Parts used for consumption : Leaves.

Medicinal value : The pounded root is put on the lips by the santals to restore consciousness when in a faint (IMP Kirtikar, and Basu, Vol-I, 1988, 182-183).

Estimated

Carotene content (mg/100 g)

Total carotenoids	:	12.75
Beta carotene	:	8.65
Retinol equivalents	:	1.44.

CUCURBITA MAXIMA DUCHESNE

Family : Cucurbitaceae

English/Trade name : Melon pumpkin, Red gourd, Red pumpkin

Vernacular names : H. Kumhra Sag; Kan. Kumbale Soppu, Mal. Mathanelakal, Tam. Parangi ilai; Tel. Gummadi akulu.

Description : A trailing annual herb, with long running, somewhat prickly or hairy stem, bearing large flaccid leaves, orbicular-reniform in outline, with rounded lobes. The fruits are variable in size with soft spongy peduncle, which is neither ridged nor prominently enlarged near the attachment. The fruits are rounded or oval bluntly ribbed, brownish yellow in colour, and contain a sweet fine grained yellowish or reddish flesh when ripe. Seeds are numerous, white or brown to bronze in colour with margin of same colour and texture of body.

Distribution : Cultivated throughout India and in most warm regions of the world.

Propagation : Natural regeneration by seeds.

Parts used for consumption : All parts of the plant are edible. Tender shoots and leaves eaten as salads, flowers and fruits cooked as a vegetable.

Season of availability : July to September.

Medicinal value : The fruit has flavour; diuretic, tonic; allays thirst; cures "kapha", indigestible; increases "vata"; causes biliousness and loss of appetite. The pulp of fruit is used as a poultice on boils, burns and inflammations. The seeds are used as a taeniacide.

In Malta, the seeds are an old popular remedy for tapeworm. In Guinea, the fruit is considered sedative, emollient, and refrigerant (IMP KKR & BBD Vol. II, 1988, 1155).

Estimated

Carotene value (mg/100 g)

Total carotenoids	:	13.04
Beta carotene	:	2.55
Retinol equivalents	:	0.42.

DIGERA ARVENSIS Forsk

Family : Amaranthaceae

English/Trade name : —

Vernacular names : H. Latmahuria, Lisava; S. Aranyavastuka, Kunanjara, Manjarika; Tel. Chenchal kura.

Description : An annual herb (becoming perennial), 30—60 cm high; branches glabrous, spreading. Leaves 2—7.5 by 1.3—4.5 cm, variable, thin, ovate or elliptic, acute or rounded at the apex, sometimes with reddish margins, glabrous; petioles 1.3—2.5 cm long. Flowers sessile, in threes in lax axillary pedunculate spikes 2.5—12.5 cm. long; bracts and bracteolates 2.5 mm. long, ovate-lanceolate, acute; submembranous, persistent. Perianth 4 mm long, rose-coloured; sepals ovate-oblong, acute. Fruit 2.5—3 mm. diameter, globose, somewhat compressed, margined muriculate. Seed yellowish brown.

Distribution : A common weed of cultivated fields, pastures and waste lands.

Propagation : By seeds.

Parts used for consumption : The leaves and shoots are eaten as pot herb.

Season of availability : July to November.

Medicinal value : The herb is sweetish, acrid; cooling; astringent to the bowels at first and then laxative in large doses; useful in "Kapha", biliousness, "tridosha". The flowers and seeds are given for urinary discharges (IMP (KKR & BBD) Vol. III, 1988, 2055).

Estimated

Carotene value (mg/100 g)

Total carotenoids	:	15.84
Beta carotene	:	6.94
Retinol equivalents	:	1.16.

DIGERA MURRICULATA/DIGERA ATLERNIFOLIA/ ACHYRANTHAS MURICATE

Family : Amaranthaceae

English/Trade name : —

Vernacular names : Hindi — Lesua, Gangatiya, Latmahuria

Telugu — Chilaka bappana kura

Description : An erect herb about 25—40 cm high, glabrous, slender leaves variable, thin, ovate, elliptic, 3.5—6.2 x 2.1—4.2 cm; flowers in axillary spikes about 10 cm long, perianth rose pinkish coloured, fruit minute, globose, compressed, muriculate, seeds yellowish brown.

Distribution : A frequent weed in cultivated fields and occasionally observed in forest outskirts.

Season of availability. October-January.

Propagation : Propagated as weed in cultivated fields by natural regeneration.

Parts used for consumption : Leaves.

Medicinal value : Seeds are given for urinary disorders. The plant is laxative in large doses. Flora of east Godavari district by Seshagiri *et al.* 1999 594.

Estimated
Carotene content (mg/100 g)

Total carotene	:	12.38
Beta carotene	:	9.04
Retinol equivalents	:	1.51.

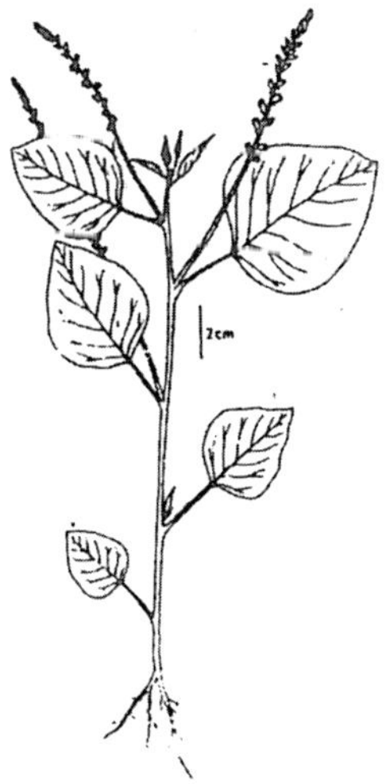

Digera murriculata/digera atlernifolia/achyranthas muricate

DRYOPTERIS COCHLEATA C. Chr.

Family : Dryopteridaceae

English/Trade name : —

Vernacular names : Tel: Garisa kura

Description : Caudex stout, erect, paleaceous, stripes and rachis sealy or often quite glabrous fronds 30 to 50 cm long, broad, ovate, lanceolate with pinnae. Panuatified to nearly the base, pinnules incised with sharp teeth to the lobes below the serrations; fertile fronds contracted, lower pinnae again pinnated, upper ones pinnatified sori very large, closely packed perfectly covering the under-surface of the fronds.

Distribution : Tirumala forests, and Eastern Coast of Andhra Pradesh.

Propagation:

Parts used for consumption : Leaves.

Season of availability : Throughout year.

Medicinal value: —

Estimated
Carotene value (mg/100 g)

Total carotenoids	:	31.33
Beta carotene	:	4.78
Retinol equivalents	:	0.80.

Dryopteris cochleata c. chr.

ERYTHROXYLUM MONOGYNUM

Family : Erythroxylaceae

English/Trade name : Bastard sandal, Deccany Deodar, Red Cedar.

Vernacular names : Kan. Adavigorante, Devadaru, Jivadane, Kuruvakumara, Sambulikayi; Tam. Dasa daram, Devaḍaram, Devadari, Simpulicham, Tavadaram; Tel. Adavigoranta, Devadari, Devadaru, Gadara Gatiri, Gatrinta, Pagadapukatta, Paribhadrakamu.

Description : A shrub or small tree with dark rough brown bark. Leaves 2.5—5 cm by 1.5—2.5 cm cuneate, obovate, or elliptic or cuneate, obovate with the tip rounded, dull not shining, glaucous-brown, beneath when dry nerves oblique, much reticulated, stipules triangular, long acuminate. Peduncles 6—8 mm long, flowers axillary, generally in fascicles of 1—4 style 3 fid at top. Drupe oblong, apiculate, bright scarlet, supported by the persistent sepals and stamens 1-celled, 1 seeded.

Distribution : Madras Presidency, N. Circars, Deccan and Carnatic in dry evergreen forests, W. Ghats in dry hill forests of Travencore upto 3000 ft., Ceylon.

Propagation : Natural regeneration by seeds.

Parts used for consumption : Leaves.

Season of availability : Throughtout year.

Medicinal value : According to modern sheriff an infusion of the wood and bark in stomachic diaphoretic and stimulant diuretic, useful in some slight cases of dyspepsia and continued fever and also in dropsy as an adyuvan to some other more active medicines. The leaves are refrigerant. Small quantities of alkaloids have been found in the leaves (IMP (KKR & BBD) I, 1988, 415).

Estimated
Carotene value (mg/100 g)

Total carotenoids	:	24.89
Beta carotene	:	8.26
Retinol equivalents	:	1.38.

Erythroxylum monogynum

FICUS CUNIA

Family : Moraceae

English/Trade name : Rough leaf fig. large brahmas banyan.

Vernacular names : H. Jahrphali, khain, khenan; Tam. Taragadi; Kan: Garagasa; Tel. Bommamarri, chitti kura.

Description : A moderate sized tree with elliptic or oblong lanceolate, entire or serrate leaves, fruits globose on long leafless, scaly branches borne from the trunk near the base, often ripening under ground.

Distribution : The tree is found in the sub Himalayan tract, from Chenab eastward to Bhutan ascending to 4000 ft. and in Assam, Bengal, Orissa and the Circars. It is common on the banks of streams or in ravines.

Propagation : Natural regeneration by seeds.

Parts used for consumption : Leaves and fruits.

Season of availability : May to December.

Medicinal value : The fruit is reported to be used for aphthous complaints. The juice of the roots is given in bladder ailments (WI, IV, 1956, 32).

Estimated

Carotene value (mg/100 g)

Total carotenoids	:	19.07
Beta carotene	:	4.68
Retinol equivalents	:	0.78.

Ficus cunia

FICUS RELIGIOSA

Family : Urticaceae/Moraceae

English/Trade name : Peepal tree, Sacred fig

Vernacular names : Hind: Pippal, Pipli, Pipar; San. Pippalah Asvatthah; Tam. Arasu, Asvattam; Kan. Aswaththa; Tel. Ravi, Delakura.

Description : A large deciduous tree with few or no aerial roots, often epiphytic, the drooping branchlets bear long petioled ovate, cordate, string leaves which produce a characteristic rusting sound when the wind blows. Leaves bright green, the apex produced into a linear lanceolate tail about half as long as the main portion of the blade. The receptacles occurring in pairs, axillary, depressed globose, smooth, purplish when ripe.

The bark is grey or ash-coloured with thin or membraneous flakes and are often covered with crutose lichen paches, the outer bark is not of uniform thickness, the middle bark in sections appears as brownish or light reddish brown. The inner part consists of layers of light yellowish or orange brown granular tissue.

Distribution : Throughout India, Sub-Himalayan forests, Bengal, Central India, planted elsewhere.

Propagation : Natural regeneration by seeds, and fruits.

Parts used for consumption : Leaves, tender shoots, and fruits.

Season of availability : Throughout year.

Medicinal value : The bark is astringent, sweet cooling and aphrodisiac and an aqueous extract of it has an antibacterial activity against staphylococcus aureus and Escherichia coli. It is used in the treatment of gonorrhoea, diarrhoea, dysentery, haemorrhoids and gastrohelcosis. A paste of the powdered bark is good absorbent for inflammatory swellings and good for burns. Leaves and tender shoots have purgative properties and are also recommended for wounds and skin diseases. Fruits are laxative and digestive, the dried fruit pulverised and taken in water cures asthma, seeds are refrigerant and laxative. The latex is good for neuralgia inflammations and haemorrhages.

In Ceylon, the juice of the bark is used as mouth wash for toothache and for strengthening the gums (IMP (OL) III, 1995, 38) (IMP (KKR & BBD) III, 1988, 2317—2319).

Estimated

Carotene value (mg/10 0g)

Total carotenoids	:	22.75
Beta carotene	:	12.62
Retinol equivalents	:	2.10.

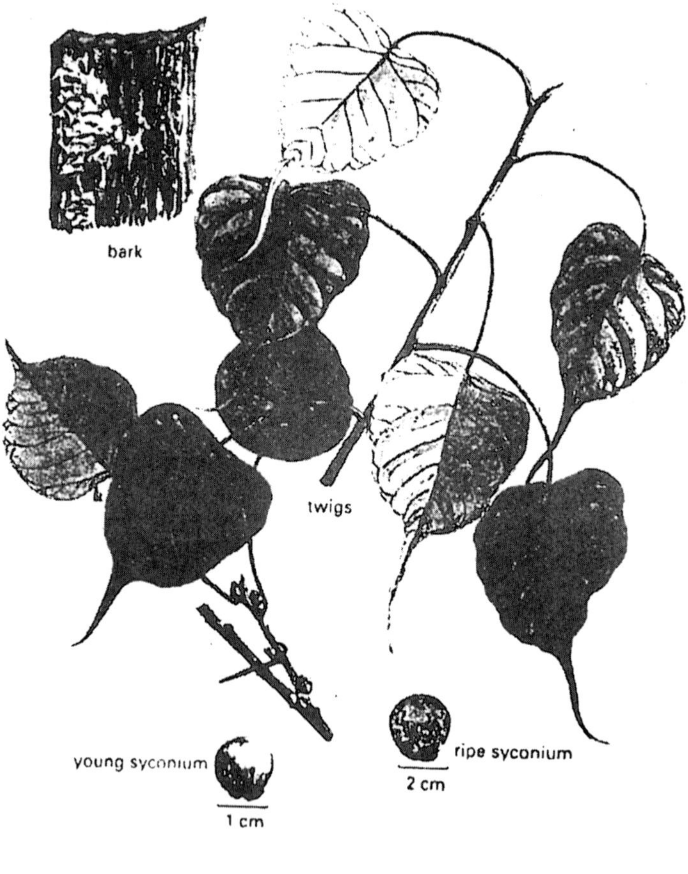

Ficus religiosa

GISEKIA PHARMACEOIDES

Family : Aizoaceae

English/Trade name : —

Vernacular names : H: Balu-ka-sag; Tel. Isukdasari-kura, Isuka dantu kura, Isukarasi kura; Tam. Manal keera's; Mal. Mandal keera.

Description : A diffuse, somewhat succulent, glabrous herb with prostrate or ascending branches. Leaves sub opposite, spathulate-oblong or elliptic-lanceolate. Flowers small numerous in almost sessile, axillary umbellate cymes. Fruit of five in dehiscent achenes, seeds blackish subreinform grandular.

Distribution : In drier parts of northern and western India and Deccan Peninsula.

Propagation : Natural regeneration by seeds.

Parts used for consumption : Whole plant.

Season of availability : May to June.

Medicinal value : The herb is aromatic, apparent and anthelmintic. The fresh herb, including leaves, stalks and capsules ground with water and employed in cases of Taenia (WI, IV, 130, 1956 CSIR).

Estimated

Carotene value (mg/100 g)

Total carotenoids	:	7.53
Beta carotene	:	3.48
Retinol equivalents	:	0.58.

Gisekia pharmaceoides

GLOBBA OPHIOGLOSSA

Family : Zingiberaceae

English/Trade name : —

Vernacular names : Tel. Sashap kura.

Description : An erect herb, 30—50 cm long with creeping rhizome, roots fleshy. Leaves linear to elliptic or oblong-lanceolate, 10-15 x 4-6 cm usually conspicously and finely candate and pubescent below. Racemose panicles narrow, lowest branches 4—6 flowered, sometimes few bulbils present in the lower axils, flowers orange yellow, about 2 cm across, bracts small, deciduous catyx broadly funnel shaped, pale green, teeth broad ovate, corolla orange-yellow, corolla tube, thrice the length of the calyx. Petals ovate, shorter then the lanceolate staminodes. Tip twice the length of the corolla, very deeply bifid, segments narrow, stamens very deeply bifid, segments narrow, stamen with a long 2-appendaged filament, anther oblong, connective produced beyond the cells, simple, winged staminodes petaloid, ovary globose 1-celled, ovules arranged on pariatal placentae, style filiform, 1-2 cm stigma turbinate, capsules globose, dehiscent smooth, seed ovoid, white and tomentose.

Distribution : In damp localities in Vizianagaram and East Godavari districts.

Propagation : Natural regeneration by seeds.

Parts used for consumption : The leaves of the plant are used as a vegetable.

Season of availability : July to December.

Medicinal value : —

Estimated
Carotene value (mg/100 g)

Total carotenoids	:	28.64
Beta carotene	:	5.56
Retinol equivalents	:	0.93.

GMELINA ARBOREA Roxb.

Family : Verbenaceae

English/Trade name : Coomb teak

Vernacular names : San. Ashveta, Bhadra, Gramdhari, Gristi, Subhadra; H. Gamari, Gamhar, Kambar, Khammara, Sewan, Shiwan; Tam. Arisa, Kalarbadi, Kattanam Kumil, Perungumil, Umitekku; Kan. Kumbalamara; Tel. Adavigummudu, Challagummudu, Gummadi, Gumteku, Kasmiri, Teggummnolu.

Description : A moderate sized unarmed deciduous tree, reaching 18 m high bark greyish yellow rather corky, branchlets and young parts clothed with fine white mealy pubescence. Leaves 10-20 by 7.5-1.5 cm broadly ovate, acuminate entire, glabrous above when mature, stellately fulvous-tomentose, beneath base cordate or sometimes truncate and shortly cuneate, petioles 5.7— 7 cm long cylindric, puberulous, glandular at the top. Flowers appearing with or sometimes before the young leaves, usually in small cymes of about 3 flowers arranged along the branches of a densely fulvous-hairy panicle reaching 30 cm long, buds elavate, augular bracts 8 mm long, linear-lanceolate, calyx 5 mm long, broadly campanulate densely fulvous hairy, teeth 5, small, triangular acute, corolla brownish yellow, densely hairy outside, reaching 3.8 cm long 5 lobes 2 lipped, upper lip rather more than 1 cm long deeply divided into 2 oblong, obtase lobes. Lower lip nearly 2.5 cm long 3 lobed, the middle lobe projecting forward, ovate, subobtuse with irregularly crenulate margin, much longer and broader than the obovate rounded lateral lobes. Drupe 2-2.5 cm long ovoid or pyriform smooth, orange yellow when ripe.

Distribution : Throughout India, Ceylon–Malayan and Philippine Islands.

Propagation : Natural regeneration by seeds.

Parts used for Consumption: Leaves.

Season of availability : Throughout year.

Medicinal value : The root in acrid, bitter, sweet, heating, indigestable, stomachic, laxative anthelmintic, improves the appetite, useful in hallucinations, thirst, piles, abdominal pains, burning sensations, fevers

"Tridosha", urinary discharges. The flowers are sweet, cooling bitter acrid, astringent, useful in leprosy and blood diseases. The fruit is acrid, sour, bitter, sweet, cooling, diuretic, tonic, aphrodisiac, alternative, astringent to the bowels, promotes the growth of hair, useful in vata; thirst, anaemia, leprosy, ulcers, consumption, strangury, vaginal discharges (Ayurveda).

The juice of the leaves is used to remove fetid discharges and worms from ulcers.

In Bombay, the juice of the young leaves is used as a demulcent in gonorrhoea, cough etc. either alone, or combined with other drugs of similar properties (IMP (KKR & BBD) III, 1988, pp. 1932-33).

Estimated

Carotene value (mg/100 g)

Total carotenoids	:	11.71
Beta carotene	:	4.29
Retinol equivalents	:	0.71.

Gmelina arborea

GYNANDROPSIS PENTAPHYLLA

Family : Cruciferae

English/Trade name : —

Vernacular names : H. Churota, Hulhul; Mal. Karvela; Tam. Kattu Kadugu, Naivelai, Tel. Vanicuta, Vainta, Veta Kura, White kura.

Description : An erect rather showy, glandular, pubescent, annual, 1—3 ft high. Leaves long stalked, digitately 3-5 foliate, leaflets unequal. sub-sessile, obovate or elliptic–oblong; flowers white or purple in corymbose racemes; capsules 2-4 inches long, striated, containing reniform, rugose, brown or black seeds.

Distribution : Waste places of all plain districts and at low elevations.

Propagation : Natural regeneration by seeds.

Parts used for consumption : The leaves are used as vegetable.

Season of availability : July to December.

Medicinal value : The leaves and the seeds are used in indigenous medicine in the same as mustard. Bruised leaves are rubefacient and vesicant, and used as counter-irritant in headache, neuralagia, rheumatism and other local pains, being merely rubbed on the part or applied as a poultice. Care being taken to remove the application before it causes blisters. The leaves are also applied to boils to prevent the formation of pus. The seeds are anthelmintic and rubefacient given internally for the expulsion of round worms and applied externally as counter-irritant. Decoction of seeds and leaves is given in typhoid fever. Oil expressed from the seeds is useful in the treatment of leprosy and skin diseases, it is also a vermifuge (WI. IV, 1956 CSIR).

Estimated

Carotene value (mg/100 g)

Total carotenoids	:	14.52
Beta carotene	:	5.75
Retinol equivalents	:	0.96.

Gynandropsis pentaphylla

HEVEA BRASELIANSIS

Family : Euphorbiaceae

English/Trade name : Para rubber tree
Caoutchouc tree
Hevea rubber

Vernacular names : Kannada – Rabbaru
Telugu – Rubber, Chikkakura

Description : A large tree, attaining a height of 60—100 ft or more and a girth of 8—12 ft; stem smooth and straight generally unbranched up to an considerable height, with a much branched leafy canopy; bark greyish; leaves trifoliolate with petiole 3.0-4.0 in long; leaflets glabrous, 4.0-6.0 inch long and 1.5-2.5 inch broad, elliptical-lanceolate, acuminate (tapering at both ends); flowers monoecious, small, creamy yellow or green, sweet scented in large pubescent panicles fruits ellipsoidal, capsular, tricarpellary, each carpel containing one seed; seeds ellipsoidal, variable in size, 1.0-1.5 inch long, mottled brown and shining.

Distribution : Hevea brasiliensis is considered indigenous to the amazon valley of Brazil, Venezuela Peru, Ecuador and Colombia. It exhibits large variability in morphological features, habitat preferences, altitudinal range, dry season tolerance, disease resistance, latex yield, rubber quality and other features.

Hevea brasiliensis thrives best in deep, well drained loamy soils. The soils in the rubber plantations of South India are red lateritic or clayey loams covered by natural undergrowth or leguminous cover crop and protected from erosion. The soils are generally deep and well drained.

Availability

Rubber is a long duration tree crop which stays on the ground for several years. The economic life of rubber tree is reckoned at 30—35 years. New opened jungle is considered to be the most suitable for rubber cultivation.

Propagation : Propagation is done by seeds or vegetatively by buddings or as is more common by a combination of both in tree flowers and fruits profusely. The fruits burst open when ripe and the seeds are scattered, sometimes 70—100 ft away from the tree. The seeds are gathered and as they lose viability rapidly, are sown fresh or as soon as possible. Under proper storage, the seeds retain viability for about a week to 10 days; seeds collected from seedling trees are sown only to raise stocks for budding. In S. India, the seeds are obtainable from July to September.

Seedlings are raised in nurseries or in the baskets, they may also be planted directly at stake in the field. Germination takes 1-3 weeks depending upon the freshness of the seed and favourable ecological conditions. With due attention to watering, shading etc. The seedlings attain a height of 3-4 ft in 6 months. They are transplanted in the field during the monsoon.

Medicinal value : The seeds of Hevea brasiliensis resemble castor seeds in appearance. The seeds contain a cyanogenetic glucoside, linamarin or phaseolunatin (acetone – cyanohydrin – B-glucoside) and a specific enzyme linase, which hydrolyses it to glucose and acetone – cyanohydrin; hydrolysis by emulsion yields glucose, acetone and hydrocyanic acid. The seeds contain an active lipase. The oil is chiefly used in soap making. It may be used as a partial substitute for linseed oil in paints and varnishes (WI, V, 1959, 45-74, CSIR).

Estimated

Carotene value (mg/100 g)

Total carotenoids	:	15.76
Beta carotene	:	3.99
Retinol equivalents	:	0.66

HIBISCUS ABELMOSCHUS Linn.

Family : Malvaceae

English/Trade name : Musk Mallow

Vernacular names : H. Mushkdana, Mishkolana; San. Ratakasturika; Tam . Kasturi vendai, Kattukkasturi; Kan . Kasturi bende; Tel. Karpura benda, Kasturi benda, Nela benda.

Description : A tall annual, stems clothed with long defluxed hairs. Leaves polymorphous, more or less cordate, the lower ovate, acute or roundish-angled, the upper palmately 3-7 lobed divided nearly to the base, lobes narrow-acute or oblong-ovate, crenate, serrate, or irregularly toothed, hairy on both surfaces, petioles 2.5 cm long, hairy, stipules 12 mm long, subulute hairy. Pedicles stout, equalling or shorter than the petioles. Involucral bracts 8-12, fulvous-hairy, 15 mm long shorter than the calyx caducous. Calyx 3.2 cm long, hairy, ovoid, cuspidate in bud, sepals connate, except at the tips 5 toothed at the apex, splitting down one side. Corolla 7.5 cm across, yellow with purple centre. Capsules fulvous-hairy, oblong-lauceolate, acute. Seeds subreinform, blackish, with a few raised striae.

Distribution : Cultivated in the hotter parts of India, tropics of the old world.

Propagation : Natural regeneration by seeds.

Parts used for consumption : Leaves.

Season of availability : July to December.

Medicinal value : Seeds with bitter and sharp taste, cooling-tonic, carminative, aphrodisiac, cure diseases due to kapha and vata, intestinal complaints, stomatitis, good in diseases of the heart, allay thirst and check vomiting (Ayurveda).

The roots and leaves are a cure for gonorrhoea (Yunani). In Bombay the seeds are rubbed to a paste with milk and used to cure itch.

The seeds are stimulants, tonic, and antispasmodic. In Manila they are given for urinary calculus. In America they are considered a specific antidote for the venom of the rattlesnake.

In West Indies, they are given in the cure of snakebite, being administered both internally and externally. In Guinea the seeds are considered stomachic and tonic. In Brazil the herb is used as a fermentation and an enema (IMP (KKR & BBD) I. 1988. 331-332).

Estimated

Carotene value (mg/100 g)

Total carotenoids	:	25.72
Beta carotene	:	7.77
Retinol equivalents	:	1.29.

Hibiscus abelmoschus linn

HIBISCUS CANNABINUS

Family : Malvaceae

English/Trade name : Bimlipatnam jute/Ambari hemp.

Vernacular names : H. Patsan, Ambari, Pitwa; Kan. Pundi; Mal. Kanjaru; San. Nalita; Tam. Pulichaikeerai, Kasini; Tel. Gongura, Janapakura.

Description : An erect, upto 3.5 m tall herbaceous annual with prickly stem. Leaves denticulate, upper deeply palmately 5-7 lobed, lower cordate 7-10 cm. diameter. Flowers 7-10 cm. diameter, yellow with crimson centre. Fruit a globore capsule, seeds brown.

Distribution : Indigenous to India. Largely cultivated in drier tracts of Deccan, also found wild in different parts of India. Usually ascending upto 800 mts. altitude.

Propagation : Natural regeneration by seeds.

Parts used for consumption : Leaves are used as vegetable.

Season of availability : Almost throughout the year.

Medicinal value : Seeds acrid and sour stomachic, appetiser, removes diseases due to Kapha and Vata, cures earache. Leaves used in dysentery, cure diseases of blood, bile and throat (Ayurveda). The seeds are used as an external application to pains and bruises and are said to be aphrodisiac and flattening. One tula of the juice of the flower with sugar and black pepper is a popular remedy for biliousness with acidity. The leaves are purgative.

The Gambia an infusion of the leaves is administered in coughs (IMP (KKR & BBD) I, 1988, 328).

Estimated

Carotene value (mg/100 g)

Total carotenoids	:	12.22
Beta carotene	:	5.21
Retinol equivalents	:	0.87.

Hibiscus cannabius

IPOMOEA SEPIARIA

Family : Convolvulaceae

English/Trade name : —

Vernacular names : H. Baukalni; San. Lakshmana; Kan. Lakshmana; Tam. Talikkirai talikkoli; Mal. Tirutali; Tel. Lakshmana, korla kura.

Description : A slender twinning perennial with usually villous stems and slightly tuberous roots, leaves simple, alternate, petiolate, ovate-cordate with wide sinus and rounded basal lobes, bloched with brownish or purplish patches towards the centre. Flowers pale purple or pink, large, funnel shaped in umbellate or subumbellate, oxillary cymes, fruits ovoid capsules 8 mm. long, 4 or 2 seeded, seeds grey covered over with silky puberscence.

Distribution : Throughout India in hedges near streams and tanks upto an elevation of 150 m.

Parts used for consumption : Leaves.

Propagation : Natural regeneration by seeds.

Season of availability : June to December.

Medicinal value : The plant is sweet, cooling resunevating, diuretic, aphrodisiac, laxative, deobstruant, uterotonic and tonic. It is useful in vitiated conditions of pitta, burning sensation, strangury, hyperdypsia, general debility and sterility in woman (IMP (OL) III, 1995, 237).

Estimated
Carotene value (mg/100 g)

Total carotenoids	:	10.60
Beta carotene	:	2.19
Retinol equivalents	:	0.36.

Ipomoea sepiaria

JASMINUM ANGUSTIFOLIUM

Family : Oleaceae

English/Trade name : Wild Jasmine

Vernacular names : Hindi — Banmallica, niwari
Sans. — Asphota, Kananamallica Vanamalli
Kan. — Kadumallige, Vanamallige
Mal. — Kattumalliga
Tam. — Kattumalligei, Kattumullai
Tel. — Adavimalli, Chirumalle, Mellikura Srimalli, Garuda malli

Description : A small scandent shrub with stem glabrous branchlets minutely pubescent, leaves simple very variable even on the same plant, acute base obtuse or almost rounded, glabrous, flowers exquisitely fragrant, white and star like either solitary or more usually in threes; corolla lobes 7 or 8, linear obtuse, very acute, carpels two usually well developed.

It bears bright, shining and deep green showy foliage and is particularly well adapted for screening windows and for arbours. It flowers in profusion during the hot weather and is a delightful plant for perfuming the verandah.

Distribution : Found in the lower hills of South India commonly in the circars, deccan and carnatic down to Tranvancore.

Propagation : The plant grows easily in every soil and situation and regeneration through stem cuttings.

Parts used for consumption: Leaves.

Season of availability : Throughout the year mainly July to November.

Medicinal value : The bitter root is used in external applications for ring worms. The juice of leaves is given as an emetic in case of poisoning (KKR and BBD II, 1988, 1520) (W.O.I., 1959, Vol. V Page 280-281).

Estimated
Carotene value (mg/100 g)

Total carotenoids	:	25.69
Beta carotene	:	8.45
Retinol equivalents	:	1.41.

LEPIDIUM SATIVUM Linn

Family : Cruciferae

English/Trade name : Garden cress

Vernacular names : H. Halim, hurf; Tam. Aliverai; Kan. Allibiza, Karutige; Tel. Adalavitulu, adeli, adityalu, podi kura.

Description : A small herbaceous, glabrous annual, 15-45 cm high, cultivated as a salad plant throughout India. It is found as an escape. Leaves variable, entire or variously lobed or pinatisect, radial leaves long petioled, twice pinatisect, cauline leaves sessile, linear, linear-oblong or pinnatified, flowers small, white, in long recemes, pods small, orbicular-ovate, notched at apex, winged, seeds solitary in each cell.

Distribution : Polymorphous species, considered to have originated primarily in the highland region of Ethiopia and Eritrea. Europe and Western Asia are regarded as secondary centres of form origination.

Propagation : Natural regeneration by seeds.

Parts used for consumption : Leaves and tender shoots.

Season of availability : July to December.

Medicinal value : The plant is medicinal and used in the treatment of asthma, coughs and bleeding piles. Leaves are mildly stimulant and diuretic, and useful in scorbatic diseases, and liver complaints. The root is used in secondary syphillis and tenesmus. The seeds of the plant are rubefacient, galactogogue, emmenagogue, laxative, tonic, aphrodisiac and diuretic. They are used in poultices for hurts and sprains (WI, VI, 1962, 71).

Estimated
Carotene value (mg/100g)

Total carotenoids	:	16.43
Beta carotene	:	5.77
Retinol equivalents	:	0.96.

Lepidium sativum

LEUCAS ASPERA

Family : Labiateae

English/Trade name : —

Vernacular names : H. chotahalkkusa; Kan. Tumbe; Mal. Tumpa; San. Dronapuspi; Tam. Tummi; Tel. Tumma chettu; Chinna tummi kura.

Description : An erect or diffuse much branched herbaceous annual, 15—60 cm in height with hispid or scabrid quadrangular stems and branches, leaves subsersile, linear or linear-oblong or linear-lanceolate, obtuse, entire or crenate, pubescent upto 7.5 cm long and 1.25 cm broad, flowers pure white, small, in dense terminal or axillary whorls, fruits nutlets, 2.5 mm long, oblong, brown, smooth, innerface angular and other face rounded.

Distributionn : More or less throughout India, as a weed found in cultivated fields, wastelands and roadsides.

Propagation : Natural regeneration by seeds.

Parts used for consumption : Fragrant plant, employed as a pot herb, in times of scarcity.

Season of availability : June to December.

Medicinal value : The leaves and flowers are acrid, thermogenic, carminative, digestive, anthelmintic, anti-inflammatory, emmenagogue, sudorific, antipyretic, expectorant, anti-bacterial and depurative. They are useful in colic, dyspepsia, verminosis, anthralgia, chronic skin eruptions, psoriasis, cough, and catarrh in children, amenorrhoea, dysmenorrhoea, intermittent fevers and ulcers. The juice of the leaves is highly recommendable as an eyedrop in encephalopathy due to worm infestation in children and is useful as a nasal drop in catarrh and cephalalgia (IMP (OL) Vol. III, 1995, 316).

Estimated

Carotene value (mg/100 g)

Total carotenoids	:	6.36
Beta carotene	:	2.32
Retinol equivalents	:	0.39.

Leucas aspera

LEUCAS CEPHALOTES

Family : Labiateae

English/Trade name : —

Vernacular names : H. Dhurpi Sag, deldona, gotna; San. Dronapushpi; Tel. Pedda tummi kura.

Description : An erect, scaberulous or pubescent, stout annual, 30—100 cm high. Leaves shortly petiolated, narrowly ovate or ovate lanceolate, crenate-serrate, flowers small, white, in dense terminal, globose whorls, nutlets small, smooth, brown about the middle; upper lip 4 mm long, white, wooly lower lip nearly twice as long as the upper and the middle lobe large, trunate nutlets 3 mm long abovoid–oblong rounded at the apex, the inner face angular, the dorsal face rounded smooth brown.

Distribution : Common weed in cultivated fields and waste lands through out the greater part of India.

Propagation : Natural regeneration by seeds.

Parts used for consumption : The plant is pungent to taste and is used as pot herb.

Season of availability : July to December.

Medicinal value : It is considered stimulant, diphoretic, laxative, anthelmintic, antiseptic and insecticidal. A syrup of the flowers is used as domestic remedy for cough and colds. The leaves are also useful in fevers and urinary discharges. The fresh juice is used in certain localities as an external application in scabies.

Estimated
Carotene value (mg/100 g)

Total carotenoids	:	7.71
Beta carotene	:	2.59
Retinol equivalents	:	0.43.

Leucas cephalotes

LYGODIUM MICROPHYLLUM/LYGODIUM SCANDENS OPHIOGLOSSUM SCANDENS

Family : Schizaeaceae/lygodiaceae

English/Trade name : —

Vernacular names : Telugu — Kolem kura.

Description : A slender graceful fern, rhizomes are cylindrical, creeping and slender. The indeterminate fronds are twining to a considerable extent to a height of 15 to 20 mts. The pinnules are arranged in opposite pairs. The pinnae petiolate, pubescent, glabrous. When the leaves are dried, they appear translucent. The pinnules 8-10 from orate cordate to oblong-lanceolate or hastate, 1.0 cm to 3.0 cm long, often shortly lobed at the base, articulate on a slight thickening of the apex of the petiole, sori short, protruding from the margin of segments usually shorter and broader than barren ones.

Sporangia in a sori are solitary with zygomorphic lateral flap of inducium covering each sporangia. The sporangia are oval with apical annulus.

Distribution : Distributed in Bengal, Bihar, Orissa, Bombay and South India up to 900 m in the hills. It is also cultivated in gardens to cover pillars and bowers.

Propagation : Propagated through seeds by natural regeneration.

Parts used for consumption : Leaves.

Season of availability : July to September.

Medicinal value : The young leaves are eaten in Java. A decoction of the leaves is given in dysentery, it also enters into many lotions. Leaves are applied in the form of poultices for skin diseases and swellings (WI, Vol VI 1962, 200, CSIR)

Estimated
Carotene value (mg/100 g)

Total carotenoids	:	19.26
Beta carotene	:	3.47
Retinol equivalents	:	0.58.

Kolem kura

MERREMIA EMARGINATA

Family : Convolvulaceae

English/Trade name : —

Vernacuiar names : H. Musakarni; San. Mushakarns; Tel. Elukage-mudu; Tam. Elikathukeerai, elakachevulakura.

Description : A creeping perennial herb rooting at the nodes, leaves simple, long stalked, reinform or ovate-cordate, flowers yellow, axillary an 1-3 flowered, very short peduncles which are shorter than the petioles, fruits subglobose capsules with 2-4 glabrous light brown seeds.

Distribution : Found in damp laces in Northern Circars, the Deccan and Kanatic, Coimbatore upto 3000 feet in the hills, in upper Gangetic plain, Bihar and in West Bengal.

Propagation : By seeds and bits of branches.

Parts used for consumption : Leaves and young shoots.

Season of availability : July to December.

Medicinal value : The plant is bitter, acrid, refrigerant, deobstrunent, diuretic, alterant, anthelminitic, carminative and digestive. It is useful in nephropathy, uropathy pnemonosis, cardiac diseases, gastropathy, metropathy, fever, anaemia, leucoderma, strangury otalgia, cephalagia and rate bite (IMP (OL) IV, 1995, 18).

Estimated

Carotene value (mg/100 g) Total carotenoids : 17.96

Beta carotene : 3.48

Retinol equivalents : 0.58.

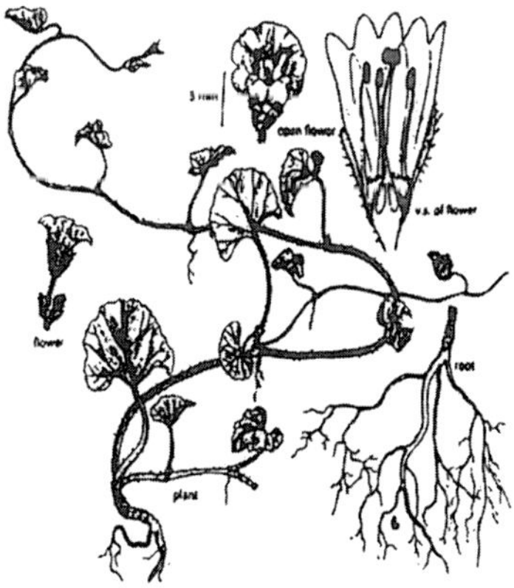

Merremia emarginata

MORINGA OLEIFERA

Family : Moringaceae

English/Trade name : Drum stick

Vernacular names : H. Sahijan, Sainjana, Mungana; Kan. Nuggi, Nuggeyele, Murunga; Mal. Murinna; San. Sigruh, Sobhanjanah; Tam. Murungai kurai; Tel. Munaga, Mulaga kura.

Description : An unarmed middle sized graceful tree, about 10 m. high, bark, thick soft, corky, deeply fissured, leaves usually tripinnate, leaflets elliptic, flowers white, fragrant in large panicle, pods pendulous, greenish 22.5-50 cm or more in length, triangular, ribbed, seeds trigonus, angles winged.

Distribution : Throughout India, also cultivated.

Parts used for consumption : Flowers and tender leaves are eaten as pot herb. Tender pods are cut into slices and used in culinary preparations.

Propagation : Natural regeneration by seeds.

Season of availability : Throughout the year.

Medicinal value : The roots are bitter, acrid, thermogenic, digestive, carminative, anthelmintic, constipating, anodyne, anti-inflammatory, emmenagogue, sudorific, diuretic, opthalmic, rubefacient, expectorant, haematinic, antilithic, alexipharmic, stimulant and vesicant. They are useful in vitiated conditions of vata and kapha, dyspepsia, anorexia, verminosis, diarrhoea, colic, flatulence, otalgia, paralysis, inflammations, amenorrhoea, dysmenorrhoea, fever, strangury, vesical and renal calculi, opthalmopathy, cough, asthma, bronchitis, pectoral diseases, cardiopathy, abscess and pharmyagodynia. The bark is acrid, bitter, thermogenic, abortifacient, antifungal, cardiac and circulatory stimulant.

The leaves are anti-inflammatory, anodyne, anthelmintic, opthalmic and rich in vitamins A and C. They are useful in scurvy and catarrhal infections.

The seeds are acrid, bitter, anti-inflammatory, purgative, antipyretic and opthalmic (IMP (OL) 1995 Vol. 4, 59; WI Vol. VI 1962, 426).

Estimated

Carotene value (mg/100 g)

Total carotenoids	:	22.38
Beta carotene	:	6.23
Retinol equivalents	:	1.04.

Moringa oleifera

MURRAYA KOEINGIL

Family : Rutaceae

English/Trade name : Curry leaf plant

Vernacular names : H. Kathuim, mithaneeru, kurrapatta, grandhela, bar sanga; Kan. Karibevu; Mal. Kariveppilu; Tam. Karivempu, Karuveppilu; Kattu veppilu, Tel. Karepaku, Konda karivepaku.

Description : A handsome, aromatic, more or less decidous shrub or a small tree, upto 6 m. in height and 15-40 cm in diameter, bark dark brown or almost black, leaves imparipinnate, leaflets 9-25, ovate, lanceolate or somewhat rhomboid, irregularly crenate-dentate, acuminate, obtuse or acute base usually oblique, dotted, strongly aromatic, flowers in terminal corymbose cymes, white fragrant, berries subglobose, ellipsoid, purplish black when ripe, 2-seeded.

Distribution : Found almost throughout India and Andaman Islands upto an altitude of 1,500 m. It is commonly found in forests often as gregarious undergrowth.

Propagation : Natural regeneration by seeds.

Parts used for consumption : The leaves of the plant are extensively employed as flavouring in curries and chutneys.

Season of availability : Throughout the year.

Growth flowering : The plants remain leafless for a short time in later part of winter and flowers appear in February–March along with new leaves. The fruits ripen in June (Bose et al., 1998; Trees of the World).

Medicinal value : The leaves, root and bark are considered tonic, stomachic and carminative. Leaves are used internally in dysentery and diarrhoea, and also for checking vomiting. They are applied externally to bruises and eruptions. The juice of root is taken to relieve pain associated with kidney (WI Vol. VI, 1962, 446, CSIR).

Estimated
Carotene value (mg/100 g)

Total carotenoids	:	10.24
Beta carotene	:	2.45
Retinol equivalents	:	0.41.

Murraya koeingil

OXALIS CORNICULATA Linn

Family : Oxalidaceae

English/Trade name : Indian Sorrel

Vernacular names : H. Amrulsak, Cukatripati; Kan. Hulichikkai. Pullampurachi; Mal. Puliyaral, Puliyarila; San. Amlika, Cangeri; Tam. Puliyarai; Tel. Pulichintakura, Amboti kura, Pilliadugula kura.

Description : A diffuse annual or perennial procembent or more or less erect creeping acid herb, 6-25 cm in height, leaves palmately 3 foliate, long, stalked, leaflets obcordate, entire, cuneate at the base; flowers yellow, axillary or subumbellate; fruits loculicidal cylindrical capsules, seeds numerous, dark brown, transversely striate.

Distribution : Throughout India, upto 3000 m, found commonly in cultivated and fallow lands, garden and waste lands particularly in moist and shady localities.

Propagation : By seeds.

Parts used for consumption : The leaves of the plant are pleasantly acidic and freshing, and are eaten both raw as a salad, and used as a pot herb, they are also used for making sandwiches, chutneys and pickles. Leaves are good sources of vitamin C and carotene. The leaves and stems contain tartaric and citric acids, stems also contain malic acid.

Season of availability : Almost throughout the year, mostly during July to December.

Medicinal value : The plant possess astringent, vermifuge, emmenagogue and antiseptic properties. Fresh juice of the plant cures dyspepsia, piles. anaemia, and tympanitis. The leaves of the plant are considered cooling, refrigerant, stomachic, anti-scorbutic and appetizing. They are used in fever, dysentery, scurvy and biliousness and for removing worms, warts. and other excrescenes of the skin. An infusion of leaves is used to remove opacities of the cornea, it is dropped into sore eyes for itching lids. It is used externally to remove warts and fibres over the cornea. Famous as a cure for scurvy (WI VII 1966 CSIR).

Estimated
Carotene value (mg/100 g)

Total carotenoids	:	25.81
Beta carotene	:	6.83
Retinol equivalents	:	1.14.

Oxalis corniculata

PHYLLANTHUS MADERASPATENSIS Linn

Family : Euphorbiaceae

English/Trade name : —

Vernacular names : H. Kanocha, bazarmani; Tam. Nela Nelli; Tel. Nalla usrike, chintalakura.

Description : An erect or decumbent herb or sometimes an under shrub, 30—90 cm high. Leaves ovate or obovate-cuneate, flowers in axillary clusters; capsules depressed-globose, 3-lobed or shallowly 6-lobed, seeds triangular, grey, muriculate, prettily marked with dark brown lies.

Distribution : Occurs throughout the drier parts of India.

Propagation : By seeds.

Parts used for consumption : Leaves of the plant are used as a vegetable.

Season of availability : July to November.

Medicinal value : An infusion of the leaves is used in headache. The seeds possess laxative, carminative and diuretic properties (WI Vol. VIII, 1974, 35 CSIR).

Estimated
Carotene value (mg/100 g)

Total carotenoids	:	19.45
Beta carotene	:	3.52
Retinol equivalents	:	0.59.

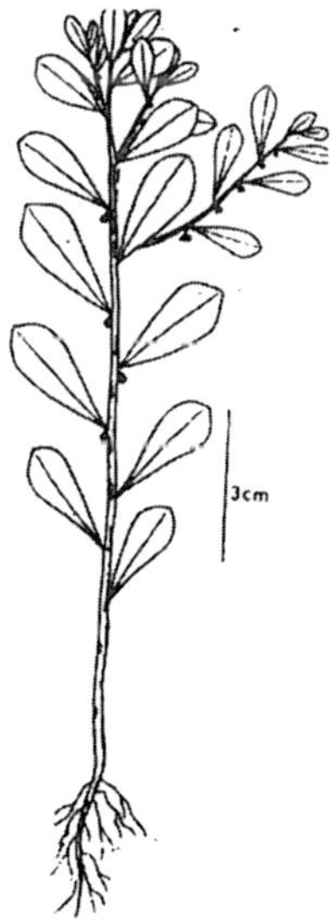

Phyllanthus maderaspatensis linn

PHYSALIS MINIMA Linn

Family : Solanaceae

English/Trade name : Sun berry/country goose berry chin mitti.

Vernacular names : H. Bandha pariya, Tulatipati, Papotan; Kan. Gudde hannu; Mal. Nottanotiyan; Tam. Tottakkali, Manathakkali. Tel. Kuppante, Budama, Budda, Budama, Sillerukura.

Description : A herbaceous annual 15—30 cm in height, leaves simple, alternate, ovate, shallowly toothed or lobed, more or less-pubescent; flowers yellow, solitary, nodding, fruits green, many seeded round berry, enclosed in enlarged calyx which is 5—10 ribbed. Seeds many, discoid, orange yellow.

Distribution : Throughout India, upto 2,300 m as a weed on cultivated land.

Propagation : Common in moist shady area as a weed.

Parts used for consumption : Leaves and whole plant used as a vegetable.

Season of availability : August to December.

Medicinal value : The plant is bitter, sweet, cooling diuretic, laxative, expectorant, appetising and tonic. It is useful in vitiated conditions of pitta, burning, sensation, strangury, splenomegaly, ascites, gastropathy. Colic, ulcers, cough, bronchitis, pruritus and erysipelas. (IMP. (OL) Vol. 4, 1995, 266-267).

Estimated
Carotene value (mg/100 g)

Total carotenoids	:	22.94
Beta carotene	:	7.79
Retinol equivalents	:	1.30.

Physalis minima

PORTULACA OLERACEAE Linn

Family : Portulacaceae

English/Trade name : Common purstane

Vernacular names : H. Badinoni, Baralaniya, Khursa; Kan. Budagora; Mal. Koluppa, Koluppaccira, Kariccira; San. Ghotika; Tam. Karikkirai, Paruppukirai; Tel. Pedda-pavilakura, pappu kura.

Description : A succulent prostrate or erect herbaceous annual with green or purple stems, swollen at the nodes, quite glabrous; leaves simple, fleshy variable, oblong-ovate, spathulate, linear with cuneate sessile base, 6—25 mm long; flowers bright yellow, in sessile, terminal or axillary clusters, fruits ovoid, circumscissile capsules, seeds numerous, black, concentrically striate and granulate.

Distribution : Throughout India as a weed upto 1,500 m, also cultivated.

Propagation : Natural regeneration by seeds.

Parts used for consumption : The leaves and young shoots are used as vegetable; young shoots also makes excellent salad. Fleshy stems are pickled, they are also dried and preserved for use in times of scarcity.

Season of availability : July to November.

Medicinal value : The stem and leaves are sour, bitter, salty, thermogenic, stomachic, alexeteric, antibacterial, antiscorbatic, subdorific, aperient, alterant, diuretic, vulnerary and tonic. They are useful in gastropathy, tumours, inflammation, nephropathy, cystalgia, cystitits, splenopathy, haemorrhoids, jaundice, diabetes, scalds and burns, dipsia, cephalalgia, otalgia, odontalgia, scurvy, burning sensation, dysentery, vomiting, skin diseases, cardio vascular diseases, dysuria, haematuria, gonorrhoea and ulcerative stomatitis. The seeds are cooling, diuretic and antidysenteric, and are useful in burns and scalds, strangury and dysentery.

In Jamaica it is employed as a cooling and moistening herb in 'burning fevers'. Bruised, it is applied to the temples to allay "excessive heat" and pain, and the juice is "of use in spitting of blood".

In North America, it has been considered a cooling diuretic, seeds as anthelmintic.

In Indo-China, the juice of fresh leaves is applied to abscesses, and used as a collyrium, a decoction is given in dysentery.

In Nigeria, the leaves are used as a local application to swelling (IMP (OL) – Vol. IV, 1995 – 345 & IMP (KKR & BBD) – Vol. I, 1988 – 242).

Estimated

Carotene value (mg/100 g)

Total carotenoids	:	6.69
Beta carotene	:	0.40
Retinol equivalents	:	0.07.

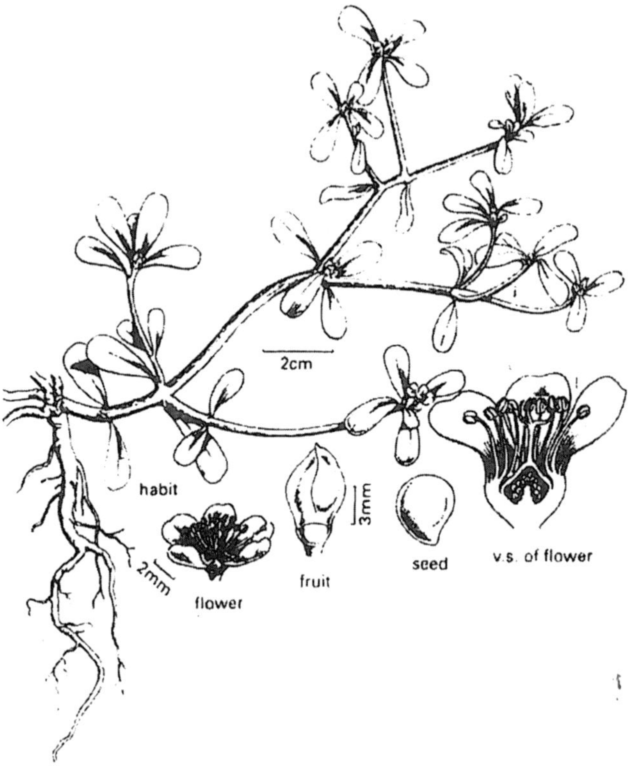

Portulaca oleraceae linn

PREMNA LATIFOLIA Roxb

Family : Verbenaceae

English/Trade name : Dusky leaved fire brandeak.

Vernacular names : H. Agnium, Bakar, Bakarcha, Tumari; Tam. Erumaimunnai, Munnai, Pasumunnai; Tel. Nelli, Pedda nellakura, Peddanelli kura, Doddanelli kura.

Description : A low bushy tree with trunk upto 1.2 m girth, or shrubby with usually ovate, sometimes elliptic, leaves 5—17 cm long entire, pubescent beneath or both sides where young and often permanently pubescent on the nerves beneath. Panicles 3 chotomous 5-12.5 cm diam. hairy pubescent with short oblong or lauceolate bracts, or upper bracts very small linear. Calyx pubescent or stingose, 5 toothed, not ors scarcely 2 lipped. Corolla distinctly 2 lipped 4-5 mm (including the lobes) long, upperlip oblong rounded entire or emerginate lower longer with three spreading obtuse or rounded lobes. Drupes 6 mm depressed globose, seated on the saucer-shaped or patelliform, subentire calyx.

Distribution : Bengal, N. Circars and Carnatic to Tinnevelly, near the coast in dry forest areas.

Propagation : Natural regeneration by seeds.

Parts used for consumption : Leaves.

Season of availability : Throughout year.

Medicinal value : The leaves are diuretic, and are given internally and applied externally in dropsy. An infusion of 10 drachms of the leaves and 2 drachms of coriander in ten ounces of boiling water has been used with advantage in acute dropsy.

The milk of the bark is applied to boils (IMP (KKR & BBD) III, 1988, pp. 1929-1930).

Estimated
Carotene value (mg/100 g)

		Doddanellikura (Kurnool + Prakasam) district)	Nellikura (Visakhapatnam) district)
Total carotenoids	:	18.40	23.07
Beta carotene	:	3.00	5.70
Retinol equivalents	:	0.50	0.95

PTERIDIUM AQUILINUM

Family : Polypodiaceae

English/Trade name : —

Vernacular names : Mal. Tavi; Tam. Parnai; Tel. Konkadi kura.

Description : A tufted fast growing fern, with a stout, creeping, rhizome, producing numerous fronds, fronds mostly tripinnate, the uppermost pinnae simple, usually 0.6 to 1.8 m long and 30—90 cm broad, but may grow upto 3.6 m in length.

Distribution : The fern is found on exposed grasslands and in the hills throughout India, at altitudes of 600—3600 mts.

Propagation : It can be propagated through division of rhizomes or from spores.

Parts used for consumption : The tender fronds are mucilaginous. They are used as a vegetable, also employed in soups. The fronds contain 0.98 mg/100g of B carotene. Free amino acids present in good amounts in the fronds are valine, tyrosine, alanine, leucine, aspartic acid, glutamic acid and aspargine. The fern on dry basis contain iodine, 900 ug/kg. In times of scarcity, the rhizomes are boiled or roasted and eaten or are ground into powder used for making bread (WI Vol. VIII, 1969).

Season of availability : July to December.

Medicinal value : The rhizomes are astringent and are useful in diarrhoea and inflammation of the gastric and intestinal mucous membranes. Boiled in oil or hogs fat, they are made into ointment of wounds. The juice of the plant is active against Gram positive bacteria (WI Vol. VIII, 1969 CSIR).

Estimated

Carotene value (mg/100 g)

Total carotenoids	:	21.78
Beta carotene	:	2.42
Retinol equivalents	:	0.40.

PYGMAEOPREMNA HERBACEA NOLDEUKA
(P. herbacea Roxb. Syn.)

Family : Verbanaceae

English/Trade name : —

Vernacular names : H. Bharang; Tam. Buma, Samba, Sirutekku; Kan. Nai thega; Tel. Neala Neareadu, adavinelli kura, Gandu Bharangi, Ghanta bharani kura.

Description : A small herb or sometimes an under-shrub, arising from a perennial root stock, leaves in a rosette, closely appressed to the ground or in 2 or 3 pairs. Flowers greenish yellow, in small corymbs, drupes globose, black.

Distribution : Commonly throughout the subtropical Himalayas from Kumaun eastward to Bhutan and in Assam, extending southwards through West Bengal-Bihar and Orissa into the Deccan peninsula.

Propagation : Natural regeneration by seeds.

Parts used for consumption : Leaves.

Season of availability : May to July.

Medicinal value : Fresh root stocks and roots along with ginger are given in Asthma, rheumatism and dropsy. The rootstocks are used to cure toothache. They are reported to contain an acid resin and traces of an alkaloid. The leaves are prescribed in fevers, cough and rheumatism and their poultices are applied to boils. The ripe fruit is reported to be eaten (WI, VIII, 1969, 239, CSIR).

Estimated
Carotene value (mg/100 g)

Total carotenoids	:	7.49
Beta carotene	:	3.24
Retinol equivalents	:	0.54.

RIVEA HYPOCRATERIFORMIS

Family : Convulvulaceae

English/Trade name : Midnopore creeper

Vernacular names : San. Aparajita, Ajantir, Ajar, Jerna, Jimadaru, Sankamapatra, Jains Muchutti, Musuttai, Tel. Bodditega, Beddikura.

Description : Climbing, stems stout, terete, finely pubsecent (especially when young) with white appeared hairs. Leaves 3.8—10 cm long usually broader than long, orbicular or reinform, obtuse, often opiculate, base cordate, petioles 2.5—7.5 cm long, densely silky. Peduncles stout stiff articulated to the peduncle. Sepals 1.6-2.0 cm long ovate, lauceolate, acute or subacute, fleshy, silky, persistent corella at first white afterwards becoming creamy coloured during yellow, sweetly fragrant, tube 3.8—5.0 subglobose, less than 2.5-dia nucronate by the style base glabrous polished, brown.

Distribution : Ronkau, Deccan, Karnatic, Ceylon.

Propagation : Natural regeneration by seeds.

Season of availability : June to February.

Parts used for consumption : Leaves and young shoots.

Medicinal value : The plant is acrid, pungent sweetish, oleageous, cooling, tonic, causes, kapha, cures, vata, billousness, diseases of the heart, bronchitis, effects of fatigue. On the konkan, the juice enters into the composition of ointment for phthiriasis and preparation applied to piles (IMP (KKR & BBD) Vol. III, 1988, 1706).

Estimated
Carotene value (mg/100 g)

Total carotenoids	:	23.55
Beta carotene	:	8.57
Retinol equivalents	:	1.43.

SOLANUM NIGRUM

Family : Solanaceae

English/Trade name : Black night shade

Vernacular names : H. Mokai; San. Kakamchi; Tam. Munatakali; Tel. Kachchi Pundu, Kachi, Kamanchi, Gaju kura.

Description : A variable annual; stem erect, glabrous or more or less pubescent, much divaricately branched. Leaves numerous, 2.5-9 by 2.5 cm, ovate-lanceolate, subacute or acuminate, glabrous, thin, entire, sinuate toothed, tapering into the petiole; flowers small, in extra-axillary subumbellate 3-8 flowered cymes, peduncles 6—20 mm long, slender; Berry 6 mm diameter, globose, usually purplish black, but sometimes red or yellow, smooth, shining. Seeds discoid, 1.5 mm. diam., minutely pitted, yellow.

Habitat : Throughout India, Ceylon–All temperate and tropical regions of the world.

Propagation : Natural regeneration by seeds.

Parts used for consumption : Leaves used as a vegetable.

Season of availability : July to November.

Medicinal value : The berries are oleaginous, bitter, pungent, heating; laxative, alternative, aphrodisiac, tonic, diuretic; improve appetite and taste; useful in diseases of the heart and the eye, in pains, piles, inflammation, leucoderma, itch, worms in the ear, dysentery, hi-cough, vomiting, asthma, bronchitis, fever, urinary discharges; improve the voice; favour conception and facilitate delivery; useful in erysipelas and rat-bite. The root bark is laxative; useful in diseases of the ear, the eye, and the nose; good for ulcers on the neck, burning of the throat, inflammation of the liver, chronic fever, griping; leaves used for headache and diseases of nose; fruit useful in thirst due to fever and in inflammation, seeds laxative, useful in giddiness, gonorrhoea, thirst and inflammation.

In Bengal, the berries are employed in fever, diarrhoea, eye diseases, etc.

In Bombay, the juice is given in treatment of chronic enlargement of liver, and is considered a valuable alternative.

In North-Western provinces, the juice is used in blood-spilling, piles, dysentery, etc. (Imp (KKR) Vol. III, 1988, 1748).

Estimated

Carotene value (mg/100 g)

Total carotenoids	:	35.25
Beta carotene	:	14.05
Retinol equivalents	:	2.34.

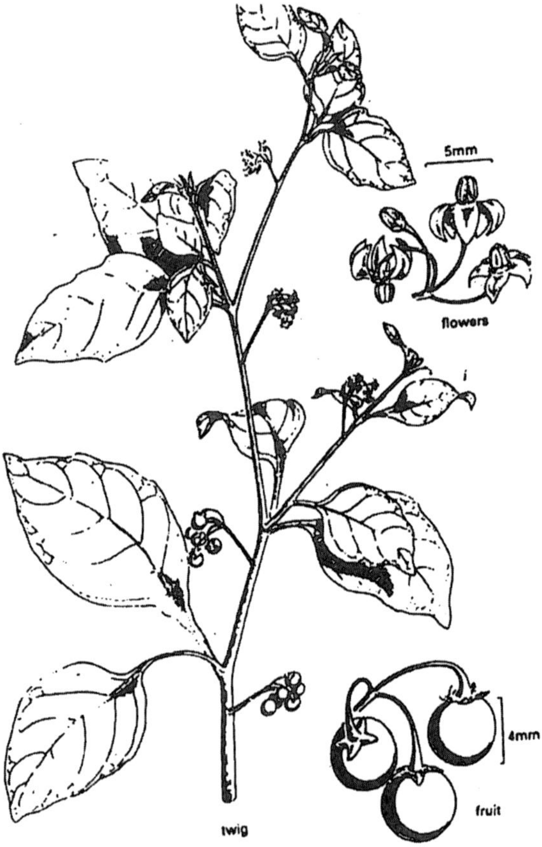

Solanum nigrum

T. PORTULACIFOLIUM/T. CUNEIFOLIUM, ORYGIA PORTULA CIFOLIA/TALINUM INDICUM/PORTULACA CUNEIFOLIUM

Family : Portulacaceae

English/Trade name : Thota pavali

Vernacular names : Telugu : Sima bachchali, Tella bachchali

Description : A perennial, suffrutescent, shrubby plant branches pink in the basal portion; leaves 8.0 cm × 3.4 cm alternate, cuneiform obovate, uppermost mucronate; flowers purple in a terminal raceme or a raceme of dichasial cymes; capsules tri-ridged 5-7 mm long; seeds black, shining, subreniform.

Distribution : Distributed from Rajasthan southwards into the Peninsular region, also recorded from Nepal. The plant has been introduced into the Indian gardens for its profuse flowering and foliage.

Availability : Throughout the year.

Parts used for consumption : Like spinach, it is used as vegetable.

Medicinal value : It is also said to be used as aphrodisiac (WI, X, 1976, 113, CSIR).

Estimated

Carotene value (mg/100 g)

Total carotenoids	:	11.59
Beta carotene	:	3.99
Retinol equivalents	:	0.66.

TRIANTHEMA PORTULACASTRUM

Family : Aizoaceae

English/Trade name : Horse-purslane

Vernacular names : H. Svet sabuni; Lal-sabuni, santhis; San. Shvetapunarnava; Tam. Shaaranaj; Kan : Muchchugoni, Pasalaesoppu; Mal : Pasalikeera; Tel : Ambalimadu/Ambatimadu.

Description : A prostrate, globrous, succulent annual, stems often tinged purplish, leaves broadly obovate, unequally paired, flowers pink or sometimes white, solitary, capsules 5 mm × 3 mm, transversely breaking into an upper coriaceous lid containing one seed and a lower membranous cup with 3-5 seeds, seeds dull black.

Two forms are reported to occur in this species a red coloured form, in which the stem, leaf margin and flowers are red and a green coloured form, which has a green stem and white flowers.

Distribution : Throughout India as a weed in cultivated and waste lands.

Propagation : Natural regeneration by seeds.

Parts used for consumption : The leaves and stems are eaten as vegetable.

Season of availability : July to December.

Medicinal value : The leaves are diuretic and used in oedema and dropsy and in ascites. A decoction of the herb is used as a vermifuge and is useful in rheumatism. It is also an antiolote to alcoholic poison (WI, IX, 1972, 281).

Seeds with bitter sharp taste, cooling tonic, carminative, aphrodiasiac, cure diseases due to kapha and vata, intestinal complaints, stomatatis, good in diseases of the heart, allay thirst and check vomiting.

In Bombay the seeds are rubbed to a paste with milk and used to cure itch.

In Manila they are given for urinary calculus.

In America they are considered a specific antidote for the venom of the rattle snake and in the West Indies they are given in the cure of snake bites being both internally and externally.

In Guinea the seeds are considered stomachic and tonic.

In Brazil the herb is used as a fermentation and an enema. (IMP (KKR & BBD), 1988, I, 331, 332).

Estimated

Carotene value (mg/100 g)

Total carotenoids	:	17.61
Beta carotene	:	6.41
Retinol equivalents	:	1.07.

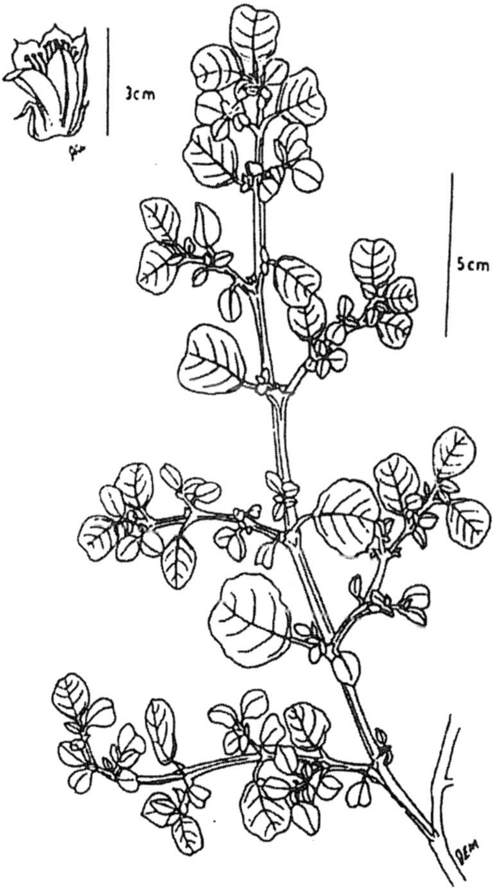

Trianthema portulacastrum

COCCINIA INDICA

Family : Cucurbitaceae

English/Trade name : Kovai fruit, Iny gourd

Vernacular names : San. Bimba, H. Kunduri; Kan. tondekai; Tam. Kovaikai; Tel. Dondakai, Kaidonda, Kakidonda, Aradonda.

Description : A climbing or prostrate perennial herb, with long tuberous roots and ovoid or elliptic fruits 1-2 in long and 1/2 in diam. The fruits are smooth and bright green with white stripes when immature, becoming bright scarlet when ripe.

Distribution : Growing wild throughout India and Ceylon-Malaya, Tropical Africa.

Propagation : The plant is propagated by its tuberous roots or by stem cuttings. On well-drained, well prepared, deep, friable, loamy red soil and under irrigated conditions, it grows well.

Season of availability : Fruits from April to September giving heavy yields.

Parts used for consumption : Fruits.

Medicinal value : Various preparations of roots, stems and leaves have been mentioned in indegenous systems of medicine as being efficacious in the treatment of skin diseases, bronchial catersh, bronchitis and diabetes (WI II, 1950, 257, CSIR).

The fruit is aphrodisiac, allays thirst, useful in billiousness and diseases of the blood (Yunani).

In the Konkan, the root pounded with the juice of the leaves is applied as a lepam to the whole body to induce perspiration in fever. The green fruit is chewed to cure sores on the tongue.

The bark of the root, dried and reduced to powder is said to act as a good cathastic in a dose of 30 grains.

The leaves are applied externally in eruptions of the skin, and the plant internally in gonorrhoea (Balfour).

The plant has the reputation in Bengal of having remarkable effect in reducing the amount of sugar in the urine of patients suffering from diabetes-mellitus. The fresh juice extracted from the roots and leaves, either by itself or incombination with certain metallic preparations, is given in the treatment of diabetes.

The fruit (Sushruta, Bapat) and the leaves (Roberts) are prescribed in the treatment of snake-bite. The fruit is also recommended for scorpion sting (Sushruta) (IMP (KKR & BBD) II, 1988, 1151—1153).

Estimated

Carotene value (ug/100g)

Total carotenoids	:	1958.15
Beta carotene	:	129.37
Retinol equivalents	:	21.56.

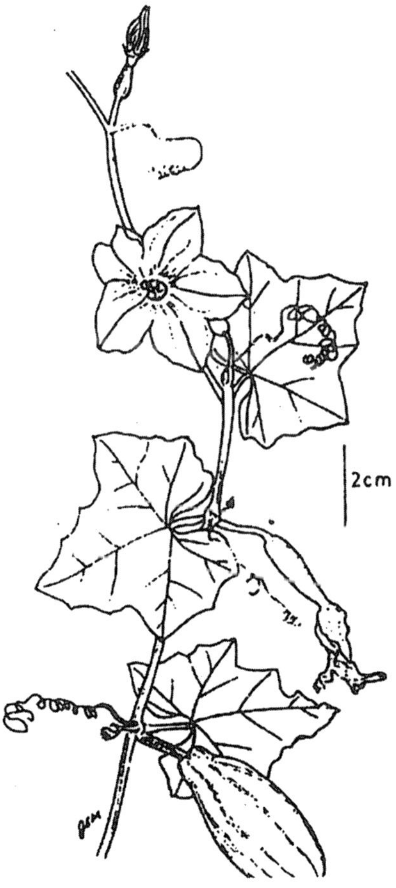

Coccinia indica

TRICHOSANTHUS DIOICA Roxb. Hort

Family : Cucurbitaceae

English/Trade name : —

Vernacular names : Hindi : Palval, Parvar; San. Meki, Parvagi, Parvara, Patola, Rajpatola, Vrittabija; Tam. Kombuppu dalai; Tel. Kommupotla.

Description : Stems slender, extensively climbing more or less scabious and woolly, tendrils 2-4 fid. Leaves 7.5 by 5 cm, ovate-oblong, cordate, acute, sinuate, dentate, not lobed, rigid rough on both surfaces, petiole 2 cm. Flowers dioecious. Male flowers not racemed, woolly outside. Calyx tube 4.5 cm, narrow, teeth linear erect. Anthers free, fruit 5.9 cm oblong or nearly special acute, smooth, orange-red when ripe. Seeds 1/2 ellipsoid, compressed, corrugated on the margin.

Distribution : Throughout the plains of N. India extending to Assam and East Bengal.

Propagation : By seeds.

Parts used for consumption : Fruits.

Season of availability : April to September.

Medicinal value : The plants cures bronchitis. The root is cathartic. The leaves are antipyretic, anthelmintic, aphrodisiac, cure biliousness, bronchitis. The fruit is sweet, oleaginous, stomachic, cardiotonic, fattening, appetiser, digestible, anthelmintic, cures tridosh, cough blood diseases (Ayurveda).

The plant alterative, tonic, useful in heat troubles, obstinate fevers, boils—The root is cathartic—the leaves are anthelmintic, cure boils, biliousness. The flower is tonic and sprodisiac. The ripe fruit is sour, sweet, tonic, aphrodisiac, expectorant, removes blood impurities (Yunani).

In Gujarat, the fruit is used as a remedy for spermatorrhoea.

The fresh juice of the unripe fruit is often used as a cooling and laxative adjunct to some alternative medicines. In billious fever a decoction of patola leaves and coriander in equal parts, is given as a febrifuge and laxative.

The root is a hydragogue cathartic. It has also been described as a febrifuge and laxative.

The fruit in combination with other drugs is prescribed in snake bite (Sushruta, Vaidyavinoda) and scorpion sting (Charaka sushruta) IMP (KKR & BBD) Vol. II, 1988, 1110).

Estimated

Carotene value (µg/100 g)

Total carotenoids	:	295.41
Beta carotene	:	122.87
Retinol equivalents	:	20.48.

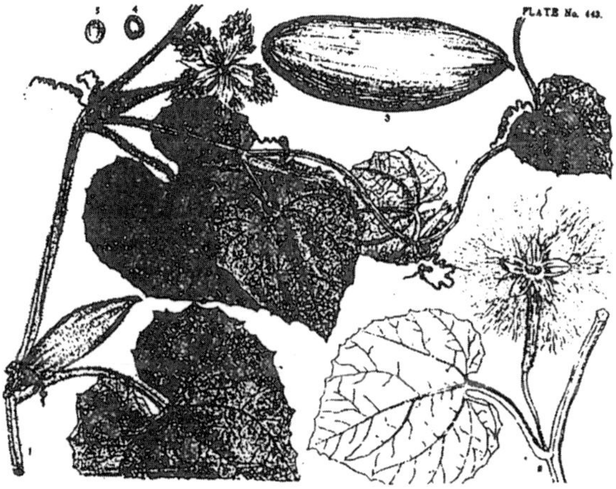

Trichosanthus dioica roxb. hort

Amorphophallus paeoniifolius var. campanulatus

AMORPHOPHALLUS PAEONIIFOLIUS
(Var. Companulatus Decne)

Family : Araceae

English/Trade name : Elephant foot yam

Vernacular names : H. Surau, Jamikand; San. Suranah; Kan. Suvarnagadda; Tam. Karunaikilanku; Tel. Kandagadda, Chandagadda.

Description : A stout herbaceous plant with underground hemispherical depressed dark brown corn, leaves compound, large solitary, petioles, stout, mottled 60-90 cm long, leaflets 5-12.5 cm long of variable width, obovate or oblong, acute, strongly and many nerved, male and female inflorescences contiguous, neuters absent, appendage of spadix sub-globose or amorphous, equalling or longer than the fertile region, spathe companulate, pointed, strongly, closely veined, greenish, pink externally, base within purple margins recurved, unolulate and cripsed male inflorescence subturbinate, female 7.5 cm or more long, fruits obovoid 2-3 seeded red berries.

Distribution : Throughout India, cultivated.

Propagation : Tuberous roots or by stem cuttings.

Season of availability : Throughout the year.

Parts used for consumption : Corns.

Medicinal value : The corns are acrid, astringent thermogenic, irritant, anodyne, anti-inflammatory, antihaemorrhoidal, haemostatic, expectorant, carminative, digestive, appetiser, stomachic, antehelmintic, liver tonic, aphrodisiac, emmenagogue, rejuvenating and tonic. They are useful in vitiated conditions of vata and kapha, arthralgia, elephantiasis, tumours, inflammations, haemorrhoids, haemorrhages, vomiting, cough, bronchitis, asthma, anorexia, dyspepsia, flatulence, colic, constipation helminthiasis, hepatopathy, splenopathy, amenorrhoea, dysmenorrhoea, seminal weakness, fatigue, anaemia and general debility.

The roots are opthalmic and emmenagogue, and are useful in ophthalmia, amenorrhoea and boils (IMP (OL) I, 1995, 132).

Estimated

Carotene value (ug/100 g)

Total carotenoids	:	230.43
Beta carotene	:	140.78
Retinol equivalents	:	23.46.

DIOSCOREA BULBIFERA

(D. Crispata Roxb.)

Family : Dioscoreaceae

English/Trade name : Potato yam, otaheite–potato

Vernacular names : H. Ratalu, Suaralu, Pitaalu; Kan. Heggenasu; Tam. Kodikilangu, Pennukilangu; Tel. Chedupaddu dumpa, malaka kaya pendalamu.

Description : A large unarmed climber with stems twining to the left. Leaves alternate, simple, broadly ovate cordate. Bulbils abundant and of different sizes and shapes, in certain cuttings, the tuber is suppressed in favour of rather large bulbils, which contain all the reserve food. Skin purplish black or earth coloured. usually coated with abundant small feeding roots.

Distribution : The species is a native of the tropics of the old world and occurs in rain forests, extending from the west coast of Africa to the farthest islands in the pacific. It is common throughout India ascending upto 6000 ft. in the Himalayas.

Propagation : By tuberous roots or by stem cuttings.

Season of availability : Throughout year.

Parts used for consumption : Tubers.

Medicinal value : Dried and powdered tubers are used as an application for ulcers. They are also used in piles, dysentery and syphilis. Bulbils of wild species are used as an application for sores (WI, Vol. III, 1952, 72, CSIR).

Estimated
Carotene value (ug/100 g)

Total carotenoids	:	50.01
Beta carotene	:	Traces
Retinol equivalents	:	Traces

Dioscorea bulbifera

DIOSCOREA PENTAPHYLLA

Family : Dioscoreaceae

English/Trade name : Prickly yam, mouse root.

Vernacular names : H. Bhusa, Gazaria, Kanta alu; Tam. Kattukkillangu; Kan: Nuraigenusu; Tel. Dukapendalam, pandi dumpa.

Description : A tall slender, prickly climber with stems twining to the left. Leaves alternate, 3-5 foliate. Bulbils globose or cylindrical, usually plentiful. Tubers almost invariably single, texture and shape variable, skin brown, yellow or purplish flesh, firm in ovoid tubers covered with bristly roots and soft in elongated tubers with few roots, pale cream or lemon yellow with purple flecks.

Distribution : Native of tropical Asia extending eastwards to the remotest islands of the pacific. It occurs throughout India ascending to 5500 ft, in the Himalayas and in Andaman Islands.

Propagation : By tuberous roots or by stem cuttings.

Parts used for consumption : Leaves, flowers and tubers.

Season of availability : Throughout year.

Medicinal value : Tubers are used to disperse swellings and as tonic (WII, III, 1952, CSIR).

Estimated
Carotene value (ug/100 g)

Total carotenoids	:	10.03
Beta carotene	:	traces
Retinol equivalents	:	traces

Dioscorea pentaaphylla

DIOSCOREA PUBER

(D. Anguina Roxb)

Family : Dioscoreaceae

English/Trade name : Greater yam, Asiatic yam

Vernacular names : H. Kasaalu; San : Ajukam; Tam : Peruvu valli kilanku; Kan. Tengugenasu, Heggenasu; Tel. Thega dumpa, Pendalamu.

Description : A large unarmed climber twining to the right. Leaves alternate or opposite. Bulbils as large in size as a man's first. Tubers 1 or 2, descending deep into the soil with tawmy-orange skin, sparingly beset with small rooflets fresh, lemon yellow.

Distribution : This plant occurs in the wet regions of Himalayas at altitudes of 3000-5000 ft, from central Nepal eastwards to northern Bengal, Assam and Chittagong. It is found also in the areas extending southwards from Indore to North Circars and in Travancore.

Propagation : By tuberous roots or by stem cuttings.

Season of availability : Throughout the year.

Parts used for consumption : Tubers.

Medicinal value : The tubers considered anthelmintic and useful in leprosy, piles and gonorrhoea (WI, III, 71). The tubers are sweet, cooling, aphordisiac tonic diuretic and are useful in vitiated conditions of pitta (IMP (OL), 1995, II, 334).

Estimated

Carotene value (ug/100 g)

Total carotenoids	:	10.04
Beta carotene	:	Traces
Retinol equivalents	:	Traces

MANIHOT ESCULENTA CRANTZ

Family : Euphorbiaceae

English/Trade name : Cassava, Manioc, Tapioca

Vernacular names : H. Sakkarkand; San. Daru kandah, Kalpakandah; Kan. Maraganasu; Tam. Maravallikkilanku; Tel. Karrapendalamu.

Description : A shrub 2—5 m. in height with stems and branches of varying colour, marked by leaf scars and cluster of tuberous roots, leaves palmate, palegreen, 5-9 lobed, lobes lauceolate, acuminate, entire, flowers yellow or greenish white, unisexual in terminal, cymes, fruits. Capsules containing 3 seeds.

Distribution : Cultivated widely in Kerala and Tamil Nadu.

Propagation : Tuberous roots or by stem cuttings.

Parts used for consumption : Tuberous roots.

Season of availability : Throughout year.

Medicinal value : The tuberous roots are sweet, appetiser, aperient, vulnerary, nourishing and tonic. They are useful in anorexia, dyspepsia, constipation, wounds, foul ulcers and general debility (IMP (OL) 3, 1995, 391).

Estimated

Carotene value (ug/100 g)

Total carotenoids	:	30.88
Beta carotene	:	Traces
Retinol equivalents	:	Traces

Manihot esculenta crantz

ALANGIUM SALVIFOLIA

Family : Alangiaceae

English/Trade name : Stone Mango, Hill racktree, Ancole fruit.

Vernacular names : H. Akola, Ankera, Dhera; Tel. Uduga ooduga. Ankolamu, urgu, Nalladugu; Tam. Alagi, Alingi, Nettilangi Azhinsal. Acchanchedi; Kan. Kallu-maanu.

Description : A small deciduous tree, shrub or straggler, leaves alternate, usually unequal at the base; flowers white or yellowish-white. fragrant, in axillary fascicles; fruits 1-2 seeded berries crowned by the calyx lobes, yellowish or red when ripe.

Distribution : Found in the drier parts of India and Ceylon and growing vigorously in the forests of South India and Burma (WI, I, 1948, 42).

Propagation : Natural regeneration by seeds.

Parts used for consumption : Fruits and roots.

Season of availability : May to July.

Medicinal value : The root bark is anti-helmintic and purgative. It is useful in fevers and skin diseases and is generally administered in the form of powder. Bark powder of the plant increases the peristalitic movements of the intestines. Fruits are sweet cooling and purgative and are useful in treating burning sensation and haemorrhages (IMP (OL), I, 1995, 77).

Estimated Carotene value (ug/100 g)

Total carotenoids	:	Traces
Beta carotene	:	Traces
Retinol equivalents	:	Traces

Udikipandu/ooduga pandu

ANACARDIUM OCCIDENTALE

Family : Anacardiaceae

English/Trade name : Cashewnut tree

Vernacular names : H. Kaju, Tam. Mindiri, Kan. Geru bija; Tel. Jeedimamidi, Munthamamidi.

Description : A small semi olecioluous tree. Leaves 4 to 6 in long by 2 to 3 in wide, leathery obovate, or elliptic, rounded at the tip and narrowed into the base (cuniate). Flowers in panicles, at the ends of the branches, small. Petals 5, bent backwards, linear-lanceolate. Sepals 5. Fruit a kidney shaped nut borne on the enlarged colourful peduncle. Peduncle some-what broadly conical, 2 to 3 in. by $1^1/_2$ to 2 in. broad.

Distribution : A native of tropical America, much cultivated in India, especially along the coast.

Propagation : It is best propagated by sowing.

Parts used for consumption : Fruits and nuts, roots, bark and leaves.

Season of availability : December to February.

Medicinal value : The roots are considered purgative. The bark has alterative properties and is used along with the inflorescence for the treatment of snake bite. The bark and leaves are useful in adontalgia and ulitis. The gum from the bark is recommended in leprosy, ringworm, corns, and obstinate ulcers. Fruits are acrid, sweet, thermogenic, aphrodisiac, trichogenous and anthelmintic, and are useful in vitiated conditions of vata and kapha, skin diseases, dysentery, haemorrhoids and anorexia. They are used for preventing hair loss and to increase the growth of hair. The kernels constitute a highly nutritious and concentrated food. A delicious drink is also derived from the spongy thalamus. (IMP (OL) I, 1995, 137).

Estimated
Carotene value (ug/100 g)

Total carotenoids	:	72.48
Beta carotene	:	Traces
Retinol equivalents	:	Traces.

Anacardium occidentale

ANNONA RETICULATA

Family : Annonaceae

English/Trade name : Bullocks heart, West Indian custard apple.

Vernacular names : H. Ramphal, Kan. Raamaphala; Mal. Manilantham; Tam. Aninuna, Manilvatta; Tel. Ramaphalamu.

Description : A small deciduous semideciduous tree, 20-25 mt high, leaves 10-20 cm long, glabrous, flowers yellowish green, fruit 7-5-8.5 cm diameters.

Distribution : This tropical America tree was introduced into India long ago and cultivated in many parts of India, now naturalised in different parts of peninsular and Eastern India.

Propagation : By seeds.

Parts used for consumption : Ripe fruits are largely eaten. The white pulp has the consistency of tallow. It has glucose 12.5 per cent and protein 2 per cent.

Season of availability : November to March.

Medicinal value : The fruit is astringent, sweet, useful in blood complaints. It alleviates biliousness and thirst and aggrevates vata and kapha (Ayurveda). The bark is a powerful astringent, and is used as a tonic by the Malays.

In Brazil, the leaves are used as a naturant.

In West Indies and in central and South America, the fruit is much used as an antidysenteric and an antihelmintic (IMP (KKR & BBD) I, 1988, 68).

Estimated
Carotene value (ug/100 g)

Total carotenoids	:	15.21
Beta carotene	:	Traces
Retinol equivalents	:	Traces

Annona reticulata

ARTOCARPUS INTEGRIFOLIA

Family : Moraceae

English/Trade name : Jack fruit

Vernacular names : H. Kathal; Sans & Tel. Panasa; Tam. Pilapalam; Kan. Halasu; Mal. Chakka.

Description : A large tropical fruit-tree with a dense crown reaching a height of 50' or more. The straight, cylindrical stem is covered with rough bark which exudes milky latex. The fruits are borne on the trunk and on the main branches. They are oval or oblong, 1-2' in length and 6-12" in diameter, and sometimes weigh as much as 60 lb. The skin, which is studded with short spikes, is "pale green when immature, becoming greenish-yellow to brownish, when ripe". The fruit contains a large number of seeds, each enclosed in a yellowish juicy sheath, with strong flavour. There are two common varieties : Kapa and barka. The former has a sweet, fleshy and crisp pericarp, and the latter, which is considered inferior, has a thin mucilaginous and sour pericarp.

Distribution : The plant is indigenous to India. It is grown plentifully throughout the warmer parts of the country, especially in Bengal, Bihar and the Deccan. It is also grown in Ceylon, Burma, Malaya and Brazil and has been introduced into many other tropical countries.

Propagation : Propagated by seeds, therefore, sown in site during the rainy season.

Parts used for consumption : Unripe jack fruit and seeds are used as a vegetable or made into pickles, while the ripe one is eaten fresh or preserved in syrup.

Season of availability : May to July.

Medicinal value : A crystalline steroketone, artostenone, $C_{30}H_{56}O$, M.P. 109°C, has been isolated from the dried latex. This has been converted to artosterone, a compound with highly androgenic properties.

The roots are credited with antidiarrhoeal property. The leaves are useful in fever, boils, wounds, skin diseases and vitiated conditions of pitta and vata. The unripe fruits are acrid, astringent, carminative and tonic. They are useful in vitiated conditions of kapha, dyspepsia and debility. The ripe fruits are sweet, cooling, oleagenous, laxative, aphrodisiac and tonic, and are useful in vitiated conditions of vata, and pitta, and ulcers. The seeds are sweet, diuretic, aphrodisiac and constipating. The wood is a nervine sedative and is useful in convulsions. The latex is useful in dysopia, ophthalmitis and pharyngitis (IMP (OL) I; 1995, 208).

Estimated

Carotene value (μg/100g)

Total carotenoids	:	38.92
Beta carotene	:	4.97
Retinol equivalents	:	0.828

Artocarpus integrifolia

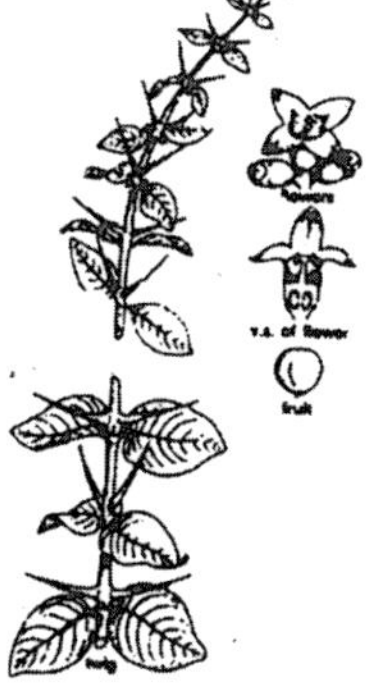

Canthium parviflorum

CANTHIUM PARVIFLORUM Lam

Family : Rubiaceae

English/Trade name : Carray cheddie.

Vernacular names : H. Kirma, Kadbar, Kan. Kakegida, Karai, Therane, Achchumullu; Mal. Cerukara, Kantankara, Karamullu, Kara, San. Gangeruki, Chayatinisah, Tam. Karaicceti, Theranai karai, Karaychedi, Nalakarai, Mullukarai, Sengarai; Tel. Chinna balusu, balusu, *Nakiri Pandlu.*

Description : A rigid thorny subscandent shrub with 2.5-5 cm. long, straight spines spreading branches; leaves usually crowded on shortened lateral shoots 1.5-2.5 cm long, simple, small, ovate, orbicular or obovate, opposite with interpetiolar stipules and axillary spines; flowers yellowish white, 4-merous, small in axillary cymas corolla tube short, fruits oblong–ellipsoid or compressed drupes, yellow when ripe.

Distribution : Throughout India in scrub forests and dry plains.

Propagation : Natural regeneration by seeds and stem cuttings.

Parts used for consumption : Leaves are used as vegetable. The fruits of the plant are also edible.

Season of availability : Throughout the year.

Medicinal value : The roots and leaves are astringent, sweet, thermogenic, diuretic, febrifuge constipating, anthelmintic and tonic. They are useful in vitiated conditions of kapha, diarrhoea, strangury, fever. Leu corrhoea, intestinal worms and general debility.

Estimated

Carotene value (mg/100 g)

		Edible portion	Rind portion
Total carotenoids	:	9.51	9.37
Beta carotene	:	6.10	6.80
Retinol equivalents	:	1.02	1.13

CARICA PAPAYA

Family : Caricaceae

English/Trade name : Papaw, Papaya

Vernacular names : H. papaya, papai, papiya, papita; Kan. Pappaya, Pharangi, Mal. Omakai; San. Brahmairandah; Tam. Papali; Tel. Boppasa, Paringi, Boppaipandu.

Description : A herbaceous tree, growing to a height of 10-15 flowers, bearing a crown of large deeply lobed leaves giving a palm like appearance. It is normally dioecious, but occasionally monoecious, plants bearing hermaphrodite flowers have also been recorded. The fruits are borne near the top of trunk closely packed at the bases of leaves. They vary greatly in number, size and shape depending on the variety, soil, season, climate and cultural practices. They may be spherical or cylindrical in shape and weigh upto 20 lb.

Distribution : It is grown practically all over the tropical and subtropical countries of the world, particularly India, Ceylone, Hawaii, Philippines, South Africa and Australia.

Propagation : By seeds.

Parts used for consumption : Unripe fruits used as a vegetable. Mature ones are eaten and also employed in the preparation of candies, marmalades, and soft drinks. It is source of vitamins and papain.

Season of availability : Throughout the year.

Medicinal value : The fruits are bitter, acrid, thermogenic, anodyne, aphrodisiac, stomachic, appetiser, digestive, carminative, anthelmintic, styptic, anti inflammatory, antifungal, demulcent and diuretic. They are useful in vitiated conditions of vata, cough, bronchitis, stomachalgia, dyspepsia, anorexia, intestinal worms, haemoptysis, haemorrhoids, inflammations, splenomegaly, ringworm, skin diseases, psoriasis, urinary calculus and injures of the urinary tract. The latext is anthelmintic, anodyne, laxative, digestive, emmenagogue, galactogogue, depurative, sudorific, febrifuge and tonic. It is useful in round worm infestation, stomachalgia, dyspepsia, constipation, amenorrhoea, dysmenorrhoea, agalactia, skin diseases, leprosy, haemorrhoids, fever, strangury and general debility (WI, II, 1950).

Seeds : The seeds of papaya are used for extraction of oil, as a source of protein and in medicine to quench first and as a vermifuge.

Leaves : Papaya leaves are used as poultice for nervous pains and in the treatment of elephantoid growth. They have been used by African natives for washing clothes, specially linen and soiled ones, as a substitute for soap.

Bark : Stem bark is quite fibrous and thus can be used for making ropes. The Africans and West Indians have been using papaya bark to make ropes since ages. Roots of papaya have medicinal properties. It is said to cure yaws, piles and act as a generative tonic.

Papaya is a rich source of several types of natural compounds like papain, carpaine, pectin and other volatile compounds (NIN, 1997).

Estimated

Carotene value (ug/100 g)

Total carotenoids	:	3110.14
Beta carotene	:	360.59
Retinol equivalents	:	60.09.

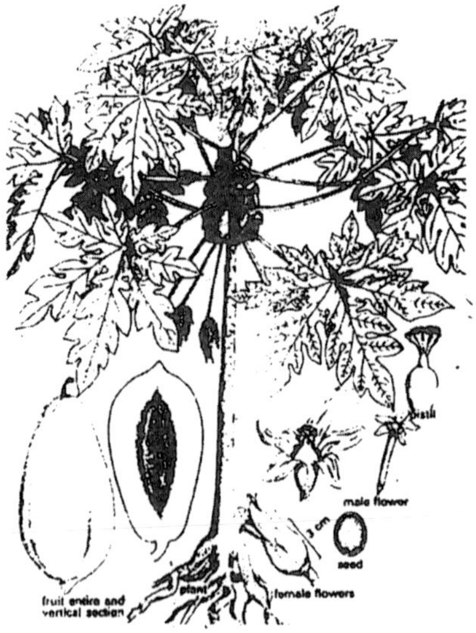

Carica papaya

CORDIA MYXA Linn.

Family : Boraginaceae

English/Trade name : Sebesten plum, Bhokar

Vernacular names : H. Lasura, Lasora; San. Slesmatakah; Kan. Cikkacalli, Doducallu; Tam. Naruvili; Tel. Cinnanakkeru, Bankapandu.

Description : A medium sized tree with a short crooked trunk, leaves simple, entire or slightly dentate, elliptic – lanceolate to broad – ovate with a rounded or cordate base; flowers white, small in lax terminal or axillary cymes, fruits drupes, yellowish brown, pink or nearly black when ripe with a viscid sweetish transparent pulp surrounding a central stony part.

Distribution : Throughout India in the warmer regions, Burma and Ceylon. It also occur in Egypt, Cochin-China and tropical Australia.

Season of availability : April—July.

Propagation : Natural regeneration by seeds. Growth is rapid.

Parts used for consumption : Fruits.

Medicinal value : The bark is bitter, astringent, acrid after digestion, constipating, anthelmintic, cooling and depurative and is useful in dyspepsia, fever, diarrhoea, burning sensation, vitiated conditions of kapha and pitta, helminthiasis, leprosy and skin diseases. The leaves are aphrodisiac, and are useful in gonorrhoea, and ophthalmodynia. The fruits are sweet, cooling, emollient, anthelminthic, purgative, vulnerary, diuretic, expectorant, aphrodisiac, depurative and febrifuge and are useful in vitiated conditions of vata and pitta, ulcers, leprosy, skin diseases, hyperdypsia, burning sensation, bronchitis, dry cough, pectoral diseases, strangury, urethralgia urethritis, chronic fever, arthralalgia, pharyngopathy, splenopathy and ring worm (IMP (OL) II, 1995, 180).

Estimated
Carotene value (ug/100 g)

Total carotenoids	:	21.78
Beta carotene	:	9.31
Retinol equivalents	:	1.55.

Cordia myxa

CORDIA OBLIQUA Willd

Family : Boraginaceae

English/Trade name : Sebesten plum.

Vernacular names : H. Bhairala, Bhokar, Chotalasore, Gondi; Kan. Challangayi, Challe, Chikkachalle; Tam. Naruvili, Selu, Vallagu, Violi, Viri; Tel. Banka nakkera, Nakkera, Nakkeri, Banka neredu.

Description : A medium sized tree, branchlets glabrous, wood soft, light grey, no heart wood. Leaves entire or slightly dentate, glabrous but more or less rough when full grown, variable in shape, from elliptic, lanceolate to broad ovate, often with a rounded or cordate base, basal nerves 3, rarely 5, blade 3-6, petioles 2.5-5 cm. long. Flowers small in large lax terminal axillary pedunculate almost glabrous. Cymes peduncles 2.5-5 cm. buds nearly globose. Drupe 1.3-2.5 cm. long, when ripe yellowish brown, pink or nearly black, shining but minutely rugose, endocarp rugose, very hard in a sweetish viscid almost transparent pulp.

Distribution : Widely spread over nearly the whole of the warmer parts of India and Ceylone, Malacca-Indo-China, Hainau, Formosa, Java, Philippines, New Genia, tropical Australia.

Propagation : Natural regeneration by seeds.

Parts used for consumption : Fruits.

Season of availability : May to July.

Medicinal value : The fruit is sweetish, slightly cooling, anthelmintic, bechic used as a expectorant, and astringent, valuable in all diseases of the lungs, used as a substitute for C. wallichii (Ayurveda).

The fruit is sweet, pectoral, diuretic, anthelmintic purgative, expectorant, maturant, vulnerary, useful in dry cough, diseases of the chest and urethra in biliousness and chronic fever, lessens thirst and the scalding of urine, causes suppuration, removes bad tumours, pains in the joints, burning of the throat, good in diseases of the spleen (Yunani).

The juice of the bark, along with coconut oil, is given in colic pains. The bark and also unripe fruit are used as a mild tonic.

The kernels are a good remedy in ring worm. The leaves are useful as an application to ulcers and in headache.

The santals use a powder of the bark as an external application in prurigo.

The Javanese use the bark in fevers (IMP (KKR & BBD) III, 1988, 1675-1676).

Estimated

Carotene value (ug/100 g)

Total carotenoids	:	180.69
Beta carotene	:	Traces
Retinol equivalents	:	Traces.

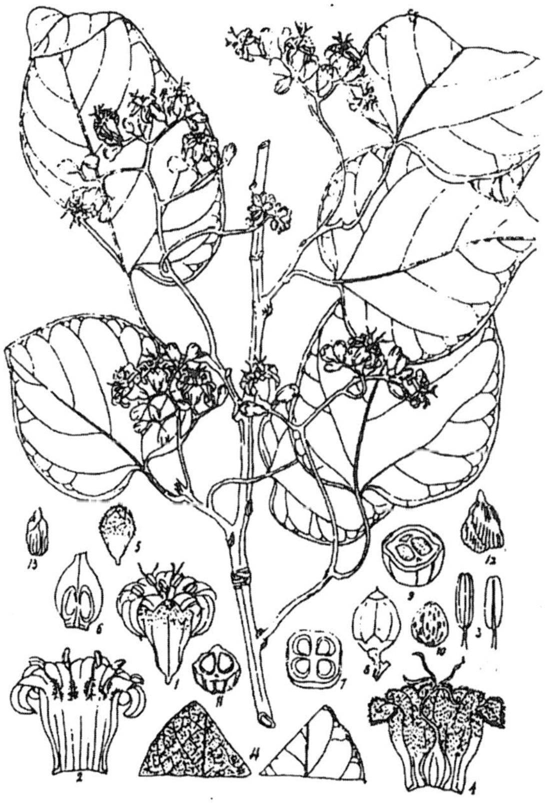

Cordia obliqua willd

DIOSPHROS MELANOXYLON Roxb

Family : Ebenaceae

English/Trade name : Coromandal ebony, Persimmon.

Vernacular names : H. Tendu; Kan. Balai, Tupra, Abanasi, Mal. Kari; San. Dirghapatraka; Tam. Beedi Elai, Tummi, Thumbi, Karun-Thumbi; Tel. Thillagada, Beedipandu, Tumiki pandu, Tunikipandu

Description : A large or moderate-sized deciduous tree. Bark greyish black, cleft into small rectangular plates, showing the black inner bark in the clefts; young parts and inflorescence densely velvety with golden or rust-coloured tomentum leaves sometimes alternate, mostly opposite, oblong or oval, acute or obtuse or sometimes, cordate at the base, tomentore on both sides while young, densely velvety beneath, less so or blabresant above when old, 3-07 in long by $1^1/_2$-3 in broad, flowers 4-6 merous; fruit edible globose or ovoid, 1-$1^1/_4$ in diameter, yellow when ripe, supported by the thickly coriaceous calyx, the segments with more or less recurved edges; seeds 4-8, compressed oblong.

Distribution : Occurs in dry mixed deciduous forests of Bihar, Orissa, Andhra Pradesh, Madhya Pradesh, Maharashtra.

Propagation : The seed of the species germinates readily under natural condition naturally propagated by raising seedlings in narrow baskets and transplanting them intact with the basket. It is also possible to raise this species by budding, grafting and root cutting.

Parts used for consumption : The fruit is largely eaten and also dried, mixed with flour and made into cakes.

Season of availability : February to April.

Medicinal value : The bark is astringent, acrid, cooling, anti inflammatory, constipating, depurative and febrifuge, and is useful in vitiated conditions of pitta, burning sensation, inflammations, diarrhoea, dysentery, leprosy, skin diseases, pruritus, dyspepsia, haemorrhages, burns, diabetes, fever, spermatorrhoea and vaginal disorders. The leaves are diuretic, carminative, laxative, opthalmic and styptic and are useful in strangury, dyspepsia, flatulence, scotoma, nyctalopia, opthalmia, epistaxis, haemoptysis, burns, tubercular glands, scabies and wounds. The flowers are diuretic and aphrodisiac and are useful in leucorrhoea, urethrorrhea, splenomegaly, nyctalopia, anaemia and scabies. The fruits are bitter, acrid, cooking digestive, carminative and oleaginous, and are useful in aphthae, pharyngodynia and viticated conditions of pitta and vata (WI III 1952).

Estimated

Carotene value (ug/100 g)

		Edible fresh fruit (without rind)	Tummik fruit rind portion (fresh)	Rind (oven dried)
Total carotenoids	:	104.24	3676.29	7141.10
Beta carotene	:	Traces	793.80	2170.03
Retinol equivalents	:	Traces	132.30	361.67

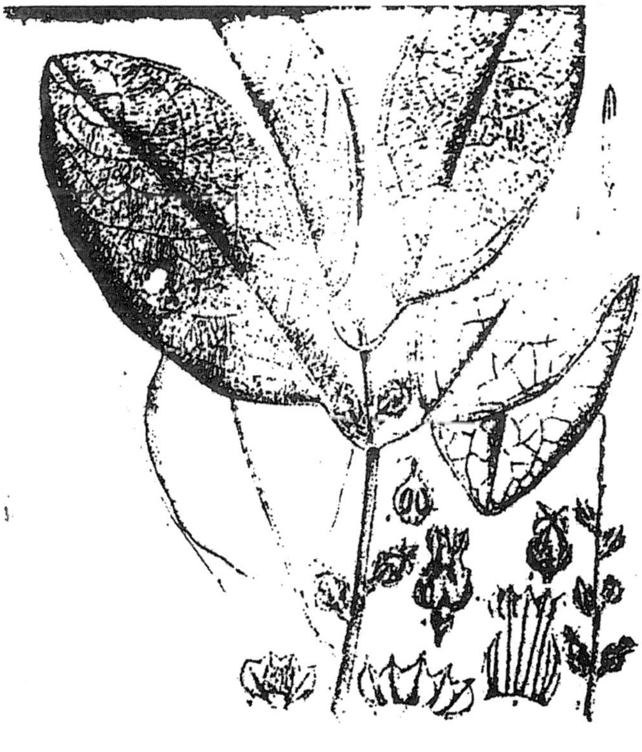

Diosphros melanoxylon roxb

EUGENIA JAMBOLANA

Family : Mystaceae

English/Trade name : Black plum, Java Plum

Vernacular names : H. Jaman, Jam; Tam. Neredom, neval, Sambal; Kan. Nerale; Mal. Noval perinnaral; Oriya : Jamo; Tel. Neredu pandu.

Description : A large evergreen tree with a dense shady crown of shining dark green foliage, often reaching 80 ft. or more. Leaves leathery $2^1/_2$ to 7 in. long by 1 to 1/2 in. wide, very variable in shape from broadly ovate to elliptical, or lance shaped, tip blunt, acute or acuminate base narrowed into the petiole, petiole 1/2 to 1 in long. Flowers small, crowded in short race, creamy white, fragrant, peduncles arising below the leaves (rarely in the axils of the leaves). Fruit egg shaped or elliptic, crowned with the remains of the calyx, turning deep purple when ripe.

Distribution : Common throughout India, Ceylon, Burma, Malaya, Australia.

Propagation : Propagated by seed.

Parts used for consumption : Fruits.

Season of availability : May to July.

Medicinal value : The juice of unripe fruits is used for preparing vinegar. The vinegar is considered to be stomachic, arminative and diuretic. Extracts of the bark, stems, leaves, buds and flowers posses moderate antibiotic activity. The bark is astringent, and is used in the preparation of gargles and mouth washes. A decoction of the bark and also powdered seeds are useful in diarrhoea and dysentery. Extracts of the bark and seeds, and also leaves are used in the treatment of diabetes. The fruits have also been used in the treatment of diabetes (Trees of India, 1985, 27).

Estimated
Carotene value (μg/100 g)

Total carotenoids	:	107.77
Beta carotene	:	Traces
Retinol equivalents	:	Traces

Eugenia jambolana

FEROXIA ELEPHANTUM

Family : Rutaceae

English/Trade name : Curd fruit, Elephant apple, Monkey fruit, Wood apple

Vernacular names : H. Bilin, Kait, Katbel, Kavitha, Kobitha; San. Akshasasya, Bhukapittha, Chirpaki, Dadhiphala, Gandhaphala, Kapipriya, Phala sugandha; Tam. Kabittam, Karuvila, Kuttvila, Narivila, Pitavila, Suvarasam; Tel. Kapitthamu, Puspaphalam, Velaga.

Description : A moderate sized tree with straight sharp strong spines 1.2—3.7 cm long. Leaves smelling of aniseed, alternate imparipinnate, petiole and rhachis flat often narrowly winged. Leaflets 3—9, opposite 2.5—5 by 1.2—2.5 cum cuneate or obovate, tip often erenulate. Flowers small, numerous, dull red, in lateral or terminal pubescent panicles, male and female flowers often in the same panicle. Calyx small, 5-6 lobed, lobes triangular. Petals 5-6, free, elliptic-oblong, 5 mm. long, spreading or deflexed. Stamens 10-12, 1-seriate, filaments equal, subulate, denselv hairy at the base with in, anthers large, linear oblong a very glabrous sessile. Fruit 5-6.3 cum diam. globose hard, pericarp woody, rough, grey-coloured. Seeds embedded in an edible pulp.

Distribution : Indigenous in South India, Ceylon, Java cultivated in many parts of India.

Propagation : By seeds.

Parts used for consumption : Fruits.

Season of availability : May to September.

Medicinal value : The fruit is sour, sweet, acrid, with flavour and taste, difficult to digest, refrigerant, aphrodisiac, alexipharmic, cures cough, dysentery, heart diseases, vomiting, removes biliousness, vata tridosha and blood impurities, fatigue thirst, hiccough, good for throat, asthma, constipation, tumours, ophthalmia, leucorrhoea, the juice put in the ear cures earache. The unriped fruit is alexipharmic, astringent to the bowels, removes itching of the body increases vata, pitta and kapha. The seeds cure heart diseases, headache an antiodote to poisons. The oil is acrid, astringent, alexiteric, stops hiccough and vomiting cures rat bite and all poisonings destroys biliousness. The flowers are an antidote to poisons. The leaves are good for vomiting, hiccough, and dysentery (Ayurveda).

The fruit is aromatic and used as a stomachic and stimulant in diseases of children.

The pulp, applied externally, is a remedy for the bites of venomous insects (IMP (KKR & BBD) I, 1988, 496-498).

Estimated

Carotene value (µg/100 g)

Total carotenoids	:	300.04
Beta carotene	:	150.29
Retinol equivalents	:	25.05.

Feroxia elephantum

FICUS GLOMERATA Coxb

Family : Moraceae

English/Trade name : Cluster fig. Gular fig. country fig. Gum fig. insect fig.

Vernacular names : H. Gular, Cemar; Tam., Kan., Mal. Athi; Tel. Atti, bodda, paidi, udumbaramu.

Description : A moderate sized to large spreading tree with ovate, ovate-lanceolate or elliptic, dark green leaves, fruits red when ripe, 1-2 inches in diameter, sub-globose or pyriform, borne in large clusters on short leaf less branches emerging from the trunk and the main branches.

Distribution : The tree is found throughout the greater part of India in moist localities, e.g., along banks of streams and sides of ravines. It is found also on rocky slopes sometimes gregariously. It is often cultivated around villages for its edible fruits.

Parts used for consumption : Fruits when fully ripe have a pleasant odour, resembling that of cider apples. Often they are full of maggots of the fertilising wasp and unfit for eating. They may be dehydrated, ground into flour and taken with milk and sugar, or used for preparing cold jelly. The powder from the roasted food forms a valuable breakfast food.

Propagation : By seeds.

Season of availability : March to July.

Medicinal value : The fruits are astringent, stomachic and carminative. The bark is astringent, and a decoction of it is used as a wash for wounds. The root is reported to be useful in dysentery. The leaves ground to powder, and mixed with honey are given in bilious affections. The milky juice is administered in piles and diarrhoea (WI Vol. IV, 1956, 36 CSIR).

Estimated

Carotene value (μg/100 g)

Total carotenoids	:	15.76
Beta carotene	:	Traces
Retinol equivalents	:	Traces

Ficus glomerata

MANGIFERA INDICA

Family : Anacardiaceae

English/Trade name : Mango tree, spring tree, cupids favourite, cuckoo's joy.

Vernacular names : H. Am, Amo; San. Amra, Chuta; Tel. Mamidi, Mavi; Tam. Manga, Mau; Kan. Mavu.

Description : A large spreading evergreen tree with dark green leathery foliage. Leaves crowded at the ends of the branches, 5 to 1 cm. long by 1 to 3 in. wide, oblong or lanceolate, tip acute or ocuminate, base narrowed into the petiole. Flowers in large bunches at the ends of the branches small disagreeable in odour. Fruit a drupe, large fleshy, obliquely, peas-shaped or somewhat compressed.

Distribution : Common throughout the greater part of India, Burma and Ceylon, both in the wild and cultivated state.

Propagation : Propagated by seed and by grafts. The seedlings should be transplanted during the rains.

Parts used for consumption : Fruits both riped and unriped. Tender mango leaves are consumed as vegetable in Java and Philippines. The kernals are used as human food in certain parts of India in times of scarcity.

Season of availability : April to July.

Medicinal value : Extracts of leaves, bark, stem and unripe mangoes are reported to possess to a limited extent antibacterial properties against some micro-organisms. The roots and bark are astringent, acrid, refrigerant, styptic, anti-syphilitic, vulnerary, antiemetic, antiinflammatory and constipating. They are useful in vitiated conditions of pitta, metrorrhagia, colonorrhagia, preumorrhagia, leucorrhoea, syphilis, wounds, ulcers, vomiting, uteritis, diarrhoea, dysentery, diphtheria and rheumatism.

The leaves are astringent, refrigerant, styptic, vulnerary and constipating. They are useful in vitiating conditions of kapha and pitta hiccough, hyperdipsia, burning sensation, haemorrhages, haemoptysis, haemorrhoids, wounds, ulcers, diarrhoea, dysentery, pharyngopathy and stomatopathy. The ash of the burnt leaves are useful in burns and scabies.

Dried mango flowers are astringent. They are said to be used in the treatment of diarrhoeas, chronic dysentery and some conditions of the bladder. Tender mango leaves known as mango tops are consumed as a vegetable in Java and Philippines. They are good sources of vitamic C. Manure mango leaves are also used as fodder for cattle in times of scarcity.

The flowers are astringent, refrigerent, stypic vulnerary, constipating and haematinic. They are useful in vitiated conditions of pitta, haemorrrhages, haemoptysis, wounds, ulcers, anorexia, dyspepsia (IMP (OL) III (380).

Mango bark contains about 16 to 20 per cent tannin and many be used for training process. The bark yields a colouring matter which is used in drying cottons to a beautiful rose pink (NIN 1980).

Estimated

Carotene value (μg/100 g)

		Mango (Adavi)	Mango (Chitti)
Total carotenoids	:	760.12	930.86
Beta carotene	:	210.82	270.12
Retinol equivalents	:	35.14	45.02

Mangifera indica

MANILKARA HEXANDRA (Roxb.) DUBARD
SYN. MINUSOPS HEXANDRA Roxb

Family : Sapotaceae

English/Trade name : Obtuse leaved mimusops

Vernacular names : H. Khirni; Mar. Ranjana, rayan, raini; Kan. Hale Hannu, Bakula; Mal. Palamunpala, Palamunnippala, Pala; Tam. Ulakkaippalai, Palla, Palai; San. Rajadanah; Tel. Manjipala, Pala, Patla, Pola, Kirni.

Description : A small to medium sized glabrous evergreen tree, 15–18 m in height with smooth grey, bark and conical hard degenerate branchlets; leaves simple, alternate, elliptic-obovate or oblong, coriaceous, rounded or emarginate at the apex, glabrous on both sides, main nerves 12–20 pairs; flowers white or pale yellow, axillary, solitary or in fascicles; fruits one seeded reddish yellow berries, ovoid or ellipsoid, seeds ovoid, reddish brown with shining testa.

Distribution : Throughout India, in evergreen forests, also cultivated.

Season of availability : The tree flowers from November-January and the fruits ripen from April-July.

Propagation : Natural regeneration by seeds and also the tree may be artificially propagated by seed during rains.

Parts used for consumption : Fruit. Ripe fruits of the tree are eaten fresh or dried.

Medicinal value : The bark is astringent, sweet, refrigerant, aphrodisiac, alaxipharmic, stomachic and anthelmintic. It is useful in ulorrhagia, ulitis, odontopathy, fever, flatulence, colic, dyspepsia, helminthiasis, hyperdipsia, burning sensation and vitiated conditions of pitta. It retards the fermentation process in toddy.

The fruits are milky, sweet, sour, cooling, aphrodisiac, appetiser, emollient and tonic. They are useful in consumption, hallucinations, loss of consciousness, anorexia, dypsia, bronchitis, urethrorrhea, leprosy and vitiated conditions of pitta. The seeds are useful in ulcers and the opacity of the cornea (Imp (OL) IV 1995).

Estimated

Carotene value (μg/100 g)

Total carotenoids	:	550.13
Beta carotene	:	440.02
Retinol equivalents	:	73.34.

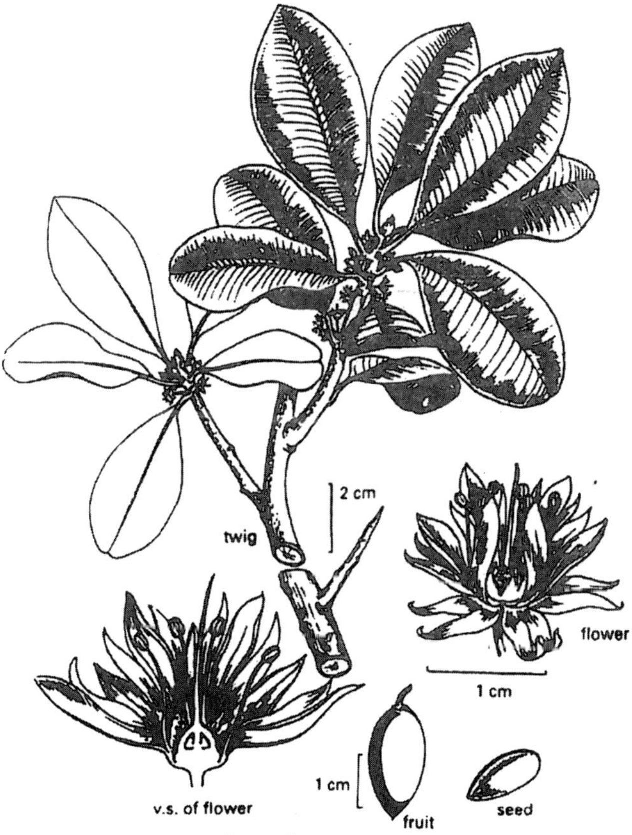

Manilkara hexandra

MURRAYA PANICULATA

Family : Rutaceae

English/Trade name : China box, orange Jessamine

Vernacular names : Hindi. Marchula, Bilgar, Kamini, Bisar; Kan. Angara-Kina, Angara Kunagida; Tam. Kattu-karuveppilai; Tel. Golimi, Naga Golugu, Gana Renu, Nara Gonji.

Description : A landsome evergreen shrub or small tree, with spreading crown and short often crooked trunk. Bark pale yellowish brown, rather corky, fragrant, leaves imparipinnate, leaflets 3-9, ovate or elliptic–lanceolate or rhomboid, gland-dotted, flowers in corymbose cymes, white fragrant, berries oblong or ovoid red or deep orange when riped, 1-2 seeded.

Distribu'.on : Found almost throughout India and the Andaman Islands upto an altitude of 1500 m.

Propagation : By seeds, cuttings or layering.

Parts used for consumption : Fruits.

Season of availability :

Growth and Flowering : It is a slow growing plant and bears clusters of flowers in flushes during summer in rains (Bose *et al.*, 1998; Trees of the World).

Medicinal value : The leaves are stimulant or astringent. They are reported to be used for diarrhoea and dysentery in Philippines. Powdered leaves are applied to cuts. Leaves and root bark are sometimes used against rheumatism, cough and hysteria. Twigs are used for cleaning teeth (WI, VI, 1962).

Estimated
Carotene value (μg/100g)

Total carotenoids	:	1.51
Beta carotene	:	Traces
Retinol equivalents	:	Traces

PHOENIX HUMILIS

Family : Palmae-Bold

English/Trade name : Dwarf date palm, Hilldate palm.

Vernacular names : H. Khajuri, Tel. Kondaita, Chittita, Tam. Inj. Kan. Sun ichil.

Description : A handsome palm, upto 3 m. in height sometimes with bulbiferous or short tufted stems, leaves sub-glacous, pinnae scattered, interruptedly fascicled, fruiting spadix, slender, spreading, fruit oblong C-1.25 cm long, pericarp thin.

Distribution : Found almost throughout India, chiefly in hilly districts upto an altitude of C. 2000 m.

Propagation : Natural regeneration by seeds.

Parts used for consumption : Fruits and the pith from the top of the stem is eaten.

Seasons of availability : May to July.

Medicinal value : The fresh juice is cooling and laxative. The gum is used in diarrhoea, and in genito-urinary diseases (IMP (KKR & BBD IV, 1987, 2566).

Estimated
Carotene value (μg/100g)

Total carotenoids	:	98.03
Beta carotene	:	Traces
Retinol equivalents	:	Traces

PHOENIX SYLVESTRIS

Family : Palmae

English/Trade name : Date-sugar palm, Indian wine palm, sugar palm, wild date palm.

Vernacular names : H. Kejur, Khaji, Khajur, Khajuri salma, Sendhi, Thakil, San. Bhymi kharjurika, Duraroha; Tam. Ichambauai, Inju, Karavam; Tel. Ita, Peddayita.

Description : A very graceful palm. 9–15 m high. Trunk rough from the persistent bases of the leaf stalks. Crown hemispherical, very large and thick leaves 3-4.5 m. long, greyish green, quite glabrous pinnate, pinnules very numerous, densely fascicled 15–45 by 2-2.5 cm. long, subulately occuminated, almost spinous pointed. Spadix 60–90 cm long, erect, peduncle highly compressed flowers 6–8 mm. long, very numerous, angular oblique. Calyx cup shaped with 3 short-rounded teeth. Fruit scattered on long pendulous similarly coloured spikes 2.5-3.2 cm. long, oblong-ellipsoid. Orange yellow with a terminal stigma, surrounded at the base by perianth. Seed 17 mm long, rounded at the ends.

Distribution : Tolerably common throughout India, wild or more often cultivated.

Propagation : Naturally regenerated by seeds.

Parts used for consumption : Fruits.

Season of availability : May to July.

Medicinal value : The fruit is sweet, cooling, oleaginous, cardiotonic, fattening, constipating aphrodisiac, good in heart complaints, abdominal complaints, fevers, vomiting, wandering of the mind, loss of consciousness (Ayurveda). The juice obtained from the tree is considered a cooling beverage. The central tender part is used in gonorrhoea and gleet. The root is used in toothache.

A paste, formed of the kernels with the root of Achyranthes aspera is eaten with beetel leaves as a remedy for ague (IMP (KKR & BBD) IV, 1988, 2563–65).

Estimated

Carotene value (μg/100 g)

Total carotenoids	:	380.86
Beta carotene	:	110.33
Retinol equivalents	:	18.39.

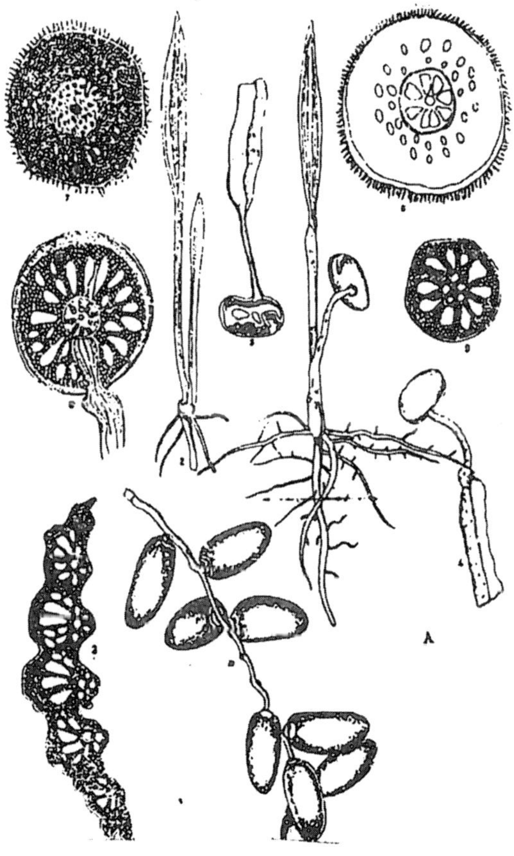

Phoenix sylvestris

PHYLLANTHUS EMBLICA Linn.

Family : Euphorbiaceae

English/Trade name : Indian gooseberry

Vernacular names : H. Amlika, Amalak, Amivala; Kan. Nellika; Mal. Nellimaran, Nellikka; San. Amalaki, Dhatri; Tan. Nelli; Tel. Usirikaya, Amalakamu.

Description : A small to medium sized deciduous tree, 8–18 m in height with thin light grey bark exfoliating in small thin irregular flakes; backs simple, very many, subserrile, closely set along the branchlets, distinchous, light green having the appearance of pinnate leaves; flowers greenish yellow, in axillary fasicles, unisexual, males numerous on short slender pedicels, females few, subserrile, ovary 3-called, fruits globose, fleshy, pale yellow, with six obscure vertical furrous enclosing 6 trigonous seeds in 2-seeded 3 crustaceous cocci.

Distribution :

Parts used for consumption : Fruits are used for pickling or preserved in sugar.

Propagation : Propagated by seeds.

Season of availability : October to January.

Medicinal use : The seeds are given internally as a cooling remedy in bilioces infections and nausea, and in infusion make. Good drink in fevers. They are also used in diabetes. Infusion of the leaves is applied to the sore eyes. Bark of the root mixed with honey is applied to aphthous inflammations of the mouth. The bark of the tree is used in diarrhoea. The young leaves mixed with sour milk are given by the natives in dysentery.

The flowers are employed for their supposed refrigerant and aperient qualities (WI, VIII, 1969, CSIR).

Estimated
Carotene value (μg/100 g)

Total carotenoids	:	31.82
Beta carotene	:	Traces
Retinol equivalents	:	Traces

Phyllanthus emblica

POLYALTHIA CERASOIDES

(Guatheria Cerasoides)

Family : Annonaceae

English/Trade name : —

Vernacular names : H. Kudumi, Kan. Nettalingamara, Sannahesara, Tam. Nakulsi, mullili, Tel. Gutti, chilkadudduga, Chilukadudduru.

Description : Trees about 10 m tall branches toecrete, Wrinkled young branchlets, pubescent, leaves 14 × 5.5 cm. elliptic acuminata; rounded at base, chartaceous, pilose below, flowers pedunculate, petals ovate-oblong dirty green, fruit red, fleshy, globose oblong, carpels 1 cm. long.

Distribution : Plant occurs in dryhills, monsoon and deciduous forests and sometimes evergreen forests, but nowhere common. Distributed in Bihar, Orissa and in Assam.

Propagation : Natural and cultivated by root suckers.

Growth and flowering : The tree is deciduous in winter for a short period. Flowers are produced from February to May followed by fruiting in cluster (Bose *et al.*, 1998; Trees of India).

Season of availability : May to July.

Parts used for consumption : Fruits

Medical Value : —

Estimated Carotene value (μg/100g)

Total carotenoids	:	1320.00
Beta carotene	:	490.00
Retinol equivalents	:	81.67.

Polyalthia cerasoides

SEMECARPUS ANACARDIUM

Family : Anacardiaceae

English/Trade name : Marking nut

Vernacular names : H. Bhela, Belatak, Bilaram; Mal. Chera, Cherkkuru; Tam. Kalaga, Pallam, Pallikkai, Vingi Virasagi; Tel. Bhallataki, Bhallatamu, Nalla Jeedi, Tummada mamidi.

Description : A moderate sized tree. Leaves 18-60 by 10-30 cm, obovate-oblong, rounded at the apex, coriaceous, glabrous above, ashy grey or buff and more or less pubescent beneath and with cartilaginous margins, base rounded, cordate or cuneate, sometimes shortly auricled, main nerves 15–25 pairs making a large angle with the costa, sometimes nearly horizontal, prominent or both surfaces; flowers greenish white, subsessile, fascicled in pubescent panicles which are equal to or shorter than the leaves, the female panicles shorter than the male, fruit, drupe, 2.5 cm. long, obliquely ovoid or oblong, smooth and shining, black when ripe, seated on a fleshy receptacle or hypocarp about 2 cm. long, smooth and yellow when ripe.

Distribution : Sub-Himalayan tract from the Base eastwards, ascending in the outer hills upto 3,500 ft., Assam, Khasia Hills, Chittagong, Central India and the Western Peninsula.

Propagation : Propagated by seeds.

Parts used for consumption : Fleshy orange pulp of the fruit eaten when ripe, significantly astringent, kernels edible.

Season of availability : December to February.

Medicinal value : The fruit is acrid, hot, sweetish; digestible, aphrodisiac, anthelminthic; stays looseness of bowels; removes "vate", "kapha", ascites, skin diseases, piles, dysentery, tumours, fevers, loss of appetite, urinary discharges; heals ulcers; strengthens the teeth; useful in insanity, asthma; the rind of the fruit is swelt, oleogenous, digestible, acrid, sharp; stomachic, anthelmintic, laxative; cures bronchitis, leprosy, ulcers, ascites, piles, dysentery, tumours, inflammations, fevers; causes ulceration.

In Goa, the nut is used internally in asthma after having been steeped in buttermilk and is also given as vermifuge.

In Madagascar the fruit is considered caustic and vesicant, and used in scrofula, venereal diseases, ainhum, rheumatism, leprosy and herpes.

Estimated

Carotene value (µg/100 g)

Total carotenoids	:	850.80
Beta carotene	:	20.00
Retinol equivalents	:	3.33.

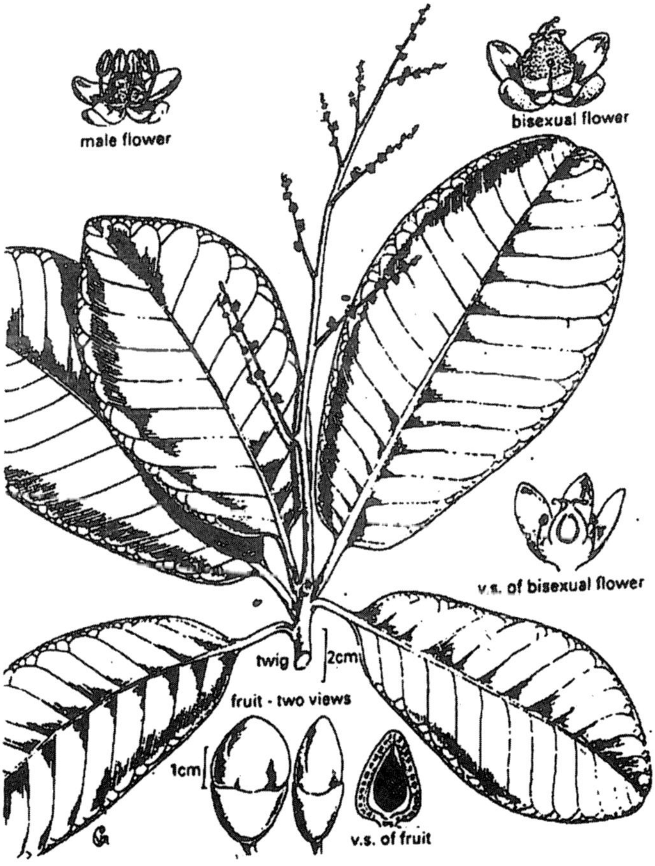

Semecarpus anacardium

ZIZYPHUS JUJUBA (Lam.)

Family : Rhamnaceae

English/Trade name : Jujube tree, Chinese data.

Vernacular names : Hindi. Ber; Kan. Yelachi; Mal. Reygoo; Tam. Elantha pazham; Tel. Regupandu.

Description : Small tree, 16 feet, stipulary prickles short, in pairs or solitary, often wanting, especially on the young branches; leaves elliptical or oblong, sometimes coarsely toothed at the apex, serrulated, acutish or obtuse or slightly cordate at the base, upper side glabrous, underside as well as young branches and petioles covered with dense tawney tomentum; cymes serrile, or very shortly peduncled; ovary 2-celled; styles 2, united to the middle, drupe spherical, yellow when ripe; nut ragore, 2-celled; flowers greenish yellow.

Distribution : Throughout India ascending to 5000 ft. The ber thrives in the drier parts of the country. It is also found in Afghanistan, Ceylon, China, Australia and Africa.

Propagation : Propagated by seed.

Parts used for consumption : The fruit is eatable. It is sweet and mealy.

Season of availability : November to January.

Medicinal value : The root is bitter and cooling, cures Kapha, biliousness, headache. The bark cures, boils, good in dysentery and diarrhoea. The leaves are bitter and cooling, cure kapha, biliousness, diarrhoea antipyretic, reduce obesity. The riped fruit is cooling, indigestible, ephordisiac, tonic, laxative, invigorating, remove biliousness, burning sensation, thirst, vomiting, good in constipation and blood diseases. The dried fruit is a laxative and appetiser removes impurities from the blood allays thirst (Ayurveda, Yunani).

The fruit is said to be mucilagious, pectoral and styptic. The berries are considered to purify the blood and assist digestion.

The young leaves pounded with those of ficus glomerata and applied to scorpion stings in konkan. In Combodia, the bark is used as a astringent in gingivitis and dysentery. The leaves are used in conjunctivitis, and are prescribed in antifebrile baths and lotions.

In the moluccas the bark is employed as a remedy for diarrhoea (IMP (KKR & BBD) I 1988, 589-590).

Estimated

Carotene value (µg/100 g)

Total carotenoids	:	27.91
Beta carotene	:	Traces
Retinol equivalents	:	Traces

Zyzyphus jujuba

BAMBUSA ARUNDINACEA (RET) WILLD

Family : Bambusaceae

English/Trade name : Thorny bamboo

Vernacular names : Hindi. Bams, Kantabams, Sani Vamsaha Venuh; Tam. Mulmunkil; Kan. Bedru; Tel. Veduru.

Description : A tall thorny bamboo upto 30 m in height with many stems, tufted on stone root stock, nodes prominent, the lowest rooting, internodes upto 45 cm long, stem sheath coriaceous, orange yellow straked glabrous or puberulous beneath, base rounded, celiate tip stiff, mid rib narrow, leaf sheaths with a short brisky ouricle, lingule short, spikelets glabrous, yellow or yellowish green, in very long penicles, often occupying the whole stem, floral glumes 3–7 in number, the upper most 1–3 male or neuter lodicules 3, hyaline 1–3 nerved, ciliate, fruits oblong grains, beaked by the style base, grooved on one side.

Distribution : Throughout India, in areas upto 2100 m elevation.

Propagation : Natural regeneration by seeds.

Parts used for consumption : Sprouts, and grains.

Season of availability : July to December.

Medicinal value : The roots are sweet, astringent cooling, taxative, depurative, diuretic and tonic. The leaves are sweet, astringent, cooling, emmenagoguepe, opthalmic, vulunery, constipatory and febrifuge. The sprouts are aerial better laxative, thermogenic, autoinflammatory, digestive carminative, anthelminitic and diuretic. They are useful in inflammations, ulcers and wounds, dyspepsia, nausea, intestinal worms, flatulence and strangery. The grains are useful in viliated conditions of kapha, gonorrhea, intestinal worms and general debility.

The bamboo mamma is the silicious secretion found in the internodes of the stems of various species of bamboo. It occurs in fragments or masses and in translucent or transparent and of bluish white colour. It is useful in viliated conditions of Pitta and Kapha, vomiting, diarrhoea, hyperdypsia, burning sensation, leprosy, jaundice, cardiac diseases, fever, opthalmia and general debility (IMP (OL) 1, 245-46, 1995).

Estimated

Carotene value (μg/100 g)

Total carotenoids	:	Traces
Beta carotene	:	Traces
Retinol equivalents	:	Traces

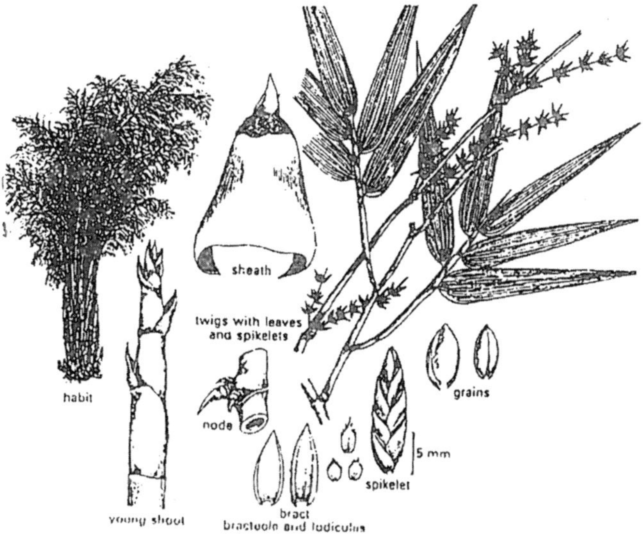

Babbusa arundinacea

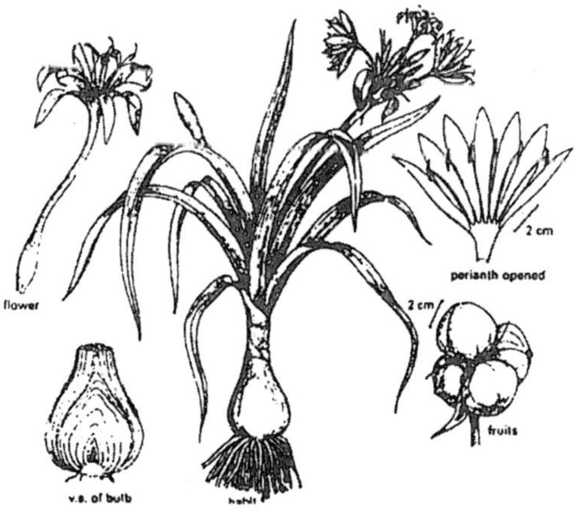

Crinum asiaticum

CRINUM ASIATICUM Linn

Family : Amaryllidaceae

English/Trade name : Poison bulb

Vernacular names : Hindi : Cintar, Nagadamani, Pindar, Sukhdarshan, Kanwal
Mal : Pulattali
Mar : Nagdavana
San : Nagadamani, Nagapatra
Tam : Visamumgil
Tel : Chengalva, Kesar chettu, Vishamungali

Description : A bulbous herb with leaves upto 6 ft. long, bulb 5–10 cm in diameter, narrowed into a neck and clothed with old leaf sheaths; leaves linear–Lanceolate, shortly acuminate, 50–75 cm long, flat, narrow with a sheathing base; flowers white, fragrant at night, in umbels; fruits sub-globose, capsules bursting irregularly, beaked by the fleshy base of the perianth, 1-2 seeded.

Distribution : Throughout India along river beds also in forests.

Parts used : Bulb

Season of availability : July–December.

Medicinal value : The bulbs are bitter, acrid, thermogenic, expectorant, vulnerary, laxative, carminative, anthelmintic, aphrodisiac, diuretic, diaphoretic, nauseant, emetic, antiflammatory, antipyretic and tonic and are useful in vitiated conditions of pitta and kapha cough, bronchitis, tumours, wounds, dyspepsia, flatulence, helminthiasis, strangury, unethrorrhea, gonorrhoea, inflammations, splenopathy, odontalgia, intermittent, fever, nyctolopia, dysopia and general debility.

The root contains the alkaloid, narcissine (iycorine). A minor alkaloid, crinamine, has been isolated from crinum asiaticum var. Japonicum. Narcissine is relatively non-toxic to mammals (IMP (OL) II 1995, 209).

Carotene value : Not estimated.

MADHUCA LONGIFOLIA

Family : Sapotaceae

English/Trade name : South Indian Mahua

Vernacular names : Hindi. Mahua, mohva; Kan. Erappe; Mal. Ilippa, Irippa; San. Madhukah; Tam. Iluppai; Tel. Ippa.

Description : A large evergreen tree with a dense spreading crown with dark grey or brownish scaly bark leaves thin, clustered near the ends of branches upto 18 cm long, 4 cm broad with slender petioles and 12–15 pairs of main nerves, flowers pale yellow and fleshy appearing in dense clusters near the ends of branches, corolla tubular, fleshy. Pale yellow, aromatic and caducous; fruits ovoid berries yellow when ripe.

Sap wood is pale yellowish brown to brownish white and heartwood reddish brown.

Distribution : In the forests of Karnataka and Kerala at low elevations.

Parts used for consumption : Flowers, fruits and oil from seeds.

Season of availability : May to June.

Propagation : Natural reproduction takes place by seeds which germinate early in the rainy season, soon after falling. For germination to take place the seeds should become covered with earth or debris. Natural seedlings are thus found chiefly in small hollows into which earth is washed at commencement of rains.

Artificial propagation may be done by direct sowing or by transplanting nursery raised seedlings. Fresh seeds should be sown about July-August and covered with earth. Direct sowing in lines or patches is preferred to transplanting which is troublesome as the seedlings develop long and delicate tap roots. For transplanting, seeds should be either sown direct in deep pots or basket or seedlings transplanted into them from the nursery during the first rainy season a few weeks after germination. They are planted in the forest early in the second rainy season (WI, VI, 1962).

Medicinal value : The bark is sweet, bitter, astringent and emollient and is good for inflammations, sprains and pruritis. The heart-wood is recommened for epilepsy and alleviates vata and pitta. Flowers are stimulant, diuretic, sweet, refrigerant and anthelmintic, and are useful in stangury, verminosis, haemoptysis and hepatopathy and gastropathy especially in children. The fruits are sweet, refrigerant, aphrodisiac and tonic. They are useful in dipsia, bronchitis, consumption. The oil obtained from the seed-mahua oil is emollient and laxative and in useful in dermatopathy, rheumatism, cephalagia and haemorrhoids (Imp (OL), III, 1994, 362).

Estimated

Carotene value (μg/100 g)

Total carotenoids	:	1955.04
Beta carotene	:	2.15
Retinol equivalents	:	0.36.

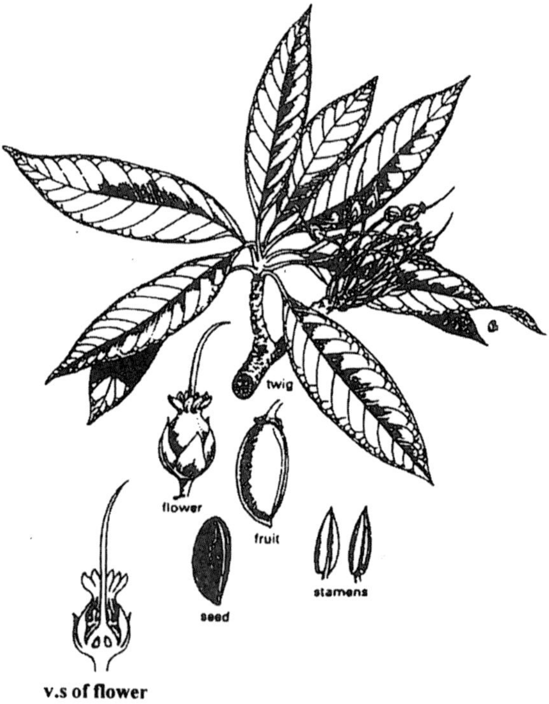

Madhuca longifolia

CHAPTER 9

AN OVERVIEW OF CAROTENOIDS IN HUMAN NUTRITION

The carotenoids are an electric array of compounds which currently consume both scientific and popular interest because of their functional roles which include antioxidant activity, modulation of detoxifying enzymes, enhancing the immune system, upregulating cell-to-cell communication, including cellular apoptosis and regulating gene expression.

Carotenoids represent a group of aliphatic or aliphatic—alicyclic fat soluble yellow to red coloured compounds which are synthesized de novo in plants. They occur in the green chloroplasts present in the parenchyma of the leaves, yellow and orange coloured fruits and vegetables and hence contribute considerably to the pigmentation in the plant kingdom. The intensity and hues of food colours depend on which carotenoids are present, their concentration and their physical state.

Carotenoids are hydrophobic, lipophilic substances and are virtually insoluble in water. They dissolve in fat solvents such as acetone, alcohol, ethyl ether, tetrahydrofuran and chloroform. Carotenes are readily soluble in petroleum ether and hexane. Xanthophylls dissolve best in methanol and ethanol. In plants and animals, carotenoids occur as crystals or amorphous solids in solution in lipid media, in colloidal dispersion or combined with protein in an aqueous phase. Aside from permitting access to aqueous environments, the association of carotenoids with protein stabilizes the pigment and changes its colour Table 1.

TABLE 1

Stability of Selected Nutrients in Food

Nutrient	*Solubility*	*Effect of pH*			*Effect of environment*		
		Acid	*Base*	*Neutral*	*Air/O_2*	*Light*	*Heat*
Vitamin A	Fat soluble	U	S	S	U	U	U
Carotene	Fat soluble	U	S	S	U	U	U
Ascorbate	Water soluble	S	U	U	U	U	U
Tocopherols	Fat soluble	S	S	S	U	U	U
Minerals	Water soluble in some forms	S	S	S	S	S	S

S : Stable (not easily destroyed); U : Unstable (easily destroyed). Data adopted from Gregory 1996.

These are generalisations and do not take into account the stability of all forms of the micronutrient (Gregory, 1996).

Our primary food sources for naturally occurring forms are plant materials. There are over 600 identified carotenoids and only about 50 of these have vitamin A activity. From a nutritional stand point, five carotenoids are of most importance for humans. These are carotene, beta carotene, leutin, beta cryptoxanthin and lycopene. (Mangets et al 1993)

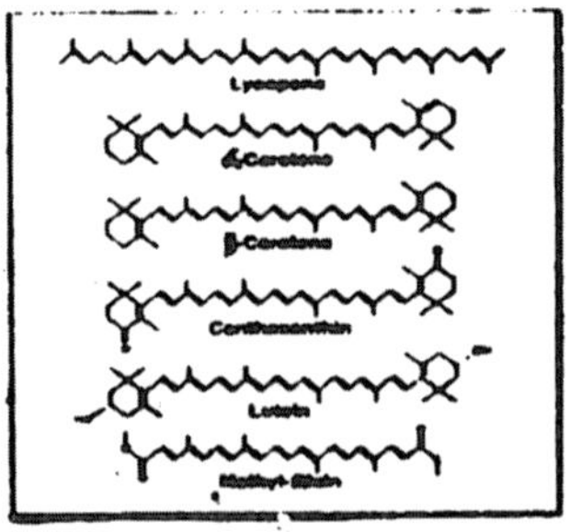

Fig. 1. Principal carotenoids.

TABLE 2

Dietary Carotenoids in Human Serum and Milk

all-trans (E)-Carotenoids	*cis (Z)*-Carotenoids	*Chemical Class*
1. α-Carotene 2. β-Carotene 3. γ-Carotene 4. Lycopene 5. Neurosporene 6. ζ-Carotene 7. Phytofluene 8. Phytoene	14. *9-cis*-b-Carotene 15. *13-cis*-β-Carotene 16. *cis*-Lycopenes 17. *cis*-Phytofluenes	Hydrocarbons (Carotenes)
9. α-Cryptoxanthin 10. β-Cryptoxanthin	18. *cis*-β-Cryptoxanthin	Monohydroxy-carotenoids
11. Lutein 12. Zeaxanthin 13. Lactucaxanthin	19. *13, 13'-cis*-Lutein 20. *9-cis*-Lutein 21. *9'-cis*-Lutein 22. *13-cis*-Lutein + *13'-cis*-Lutein 23. *9-cis*-Zeaxanthin 24. *13-cis*-Zeaxanthin 25. *15-cis*-Zeaxanthin	Dihydroxy-carotenoids

Ref.: Britton & Young (1993)

Carotenoids can exist in all trans-and cis isomeric forms Table 2 of which the former can be converted to the latter by exposure to light, heat or chemical reaction. Carotenoids possessing biologic activity of vitamin A are called provitamin A carotenoids.

Carotenoids are a family of compounds abundantly found in fruits. vegetables and green plants.

Among various carotenoids, beta carotene is the most abundant in plant foods, and has maximum vitamin A activity. Other carotenoids like alpha, gamma and cryptoxanthin have about 50 per cent activity as compared to beta carotene Table 3.

TABLE 3
Relative activity of carotenoids

Carotenoids	*Colour*	*Relative activity per cent*
Beta carotene	Orange	100
α- carotene	Light yellow	50-54
γ- carotene	Red-orange	42-50
Lycopene	Red	Inactive
Cryptoxanthine	Orange	50-60

Ref.: Narasinga Rao (1991).

For dietary carotenoid mixtures, it is generally acknowledged that, in terms of vitamin A activity, 6 ug of beta carotene or 12 ug of mixed dietary carotenoids are converted to 1 ug of retinol (WHO, 1982).

Vitamin A provided in the diet as preformed vitamin A from foods of animal origin such as liver, egg yolk, milk and milk products, meat. fish etc. possess the highest vitamin A activity and is used directly in the body.

On the other hand, provitamin A compounds like beta carotene and other carotenes have to be converted into retinol in the body before they can function as vitamin A. Although theoretically one molecule of beta carotene should yield two molecules of retinol, under physiological conditions, the conversion efficiency is only 50 per cent i.e., 1 ug beta carotene yielding only about 0.5 ug of retinol. Other carotenes α-γ and Beta-carotene derivatives are converted into vitamin A with much less efficiency Table 3. The provitamin A activity of carotene containing plant foods (fruits and vegetables) will depend upon the proportion of these carotenes present in the carotenoid pigments of these foods.

On a world wide basis, about 60 per cent of dietary vitamin A is estimated to come from provitamin A whereas in developing countries the figure raises as high as 82 per cent. Provitamin A also has an advantage of being converted to vitamin A only when needed by the body thus avoiding potential toxicity from an overdose of vitamin A.

Green leafy vegetables (GLVs) have the highest content (80 per cent) of beta carotene of total carotenes while other vegetables and fruits have beta carotene distributed to about 15 to 85 per cent of total carotene Table 4.

TABLE 4
Distribution of carotenes in foods

Source	*Per cent distribution*	
	Beta carotene	*Other carotenes*
GLVs	80	20
Amaranth	96	4
Deep yellow vegetables and fruits	85	15
Carrots	69	31
Mango	55	45
Papaya	15	85
Tomato	55	45
Spirulina	60	40
Red palm oil	65	35

Ref.: Narasinga Rao (1991).

India is fortunately blessed with a wide range of inexpensive foods rich in provitamin A carotenoids and is the second largest producer of vegetables and the third largest producer of fruits in the world. It produces 24 million tons of fruits, and 44 million tons of vegetables. India's share in the world production is about 7.5 per cent for fruits and 10 per cent for vegetables.

Currently, it is estimated that GLVs are grown in 1.1 lakh hectares with a production of about 7.3 lakh tonnes. This constitutes about 2.6 per cent of the land area covered and 1.5 per cent of the total vegetables produced in the countory. The per capita availability of beta carotene in terms of retinol equivalents is 400 ug per day, which is much below the per capita requirements of vitamin A. Relative to their availability and potential nutrient contribution, GLVs are under utilized. The intake of vitamin A may be limited by seasonal availability as well as the socio-cultural influences. Another reason also may be that community is neither aware of the sequelae of vitamin A deficiency nor of the dietary means to protect themselves against it. Several carotene rich foods are avoided due to false beliefs.

Apart from few common perennial and seasonally available GLVs, large number of less known GLVs which are region specific are consumed in rural areas which are to be identified botanically and are not accounted for in their dietaries.

Lycopene is one over 600 carotenoids that occur in plants. The best source of lycopene are tomatoes, and tomato products, water melon, pink guava, papaya, water melon, pink grape fruit and apricots, tomato products such as sauces and paste. The high temperature used in processing renders lycopene more absorbable by the intestine.

Absorption and Biological role of Carotenoids

Carotenoids interact with fat and possibly fiber, which is important from a health perspective. The food matrix, fat content and dietary fiber affect intestinal absorption (Rock and Swendseid, 1992); Klein and Kurilich, 2000).

Absorption of carotenoids ranges from 10 to 30 per cent, with the majority ingested being excreted into the feces. The absorption pathway is similar to that of dietary fat, and indeed, the amount of fat consumed profoundly influences the absorption rate, as it does for other lipid soluble nutrients. Studies comparing carotenoid absorption rate with a 40 per cent fat diet to 20 per cent, a common level for health conscious people, showed a significant reduction in absorption.

Carotenoid levels in plasma and human tissues are directly a reflection of dietary intake. Other factors can affect absorption including fiber, and particularly pectin, which significantly lowers the rate.

Once inside the intestinal cell, carotenoids can either be converted to vitamin A or be taken up by chylomicrons which transport them in the blood stream via the lymph system to the liver. From the liver, carotenoids reenter circulation carried by lipoproteins, in similar proportions as cholesterol among the various fractions. Plasma carotenoid levels are lowered by smoking, increasing body weight, and alcohol consumption although the alpha-tocopherol beta carotene cancer preventive study (ATBC) showed that smokers who drank heavily had higher plasma carotenoid levels.

Many tissues convert carotenoids first to retinal, then to retinol, including liver intestinal mucosal cells, adipose, lung and kidney.

Researchers theorize that carotenoids may be converted to other compounds similar to retinoids which are possibly involved in various cellular processes including growth. Carotenoid concentration in various body tissues varies, as does the predominant type of carotenoids, but the major site is adipose tissue. Interestingly, concentrations of the carotenoid isomeric forms vary in plasma compared to peripheral tissues, trans-beta carotene is the predominant isomeric form in blood.

The importance of carotenoids in foods goes beyond the role as natural pigment.

Originally known only for serving as vitamin A precursors, subsequent and ongoing research of carotenoids has demonstrated other biologic and pharmacologic activity. It is the effect indepndent of vitamin A activity which hold current scientific interest. Chief among these is the carotenoids potent antioxidant activity, specifically quenching singlet oxygen in biological systems. They trap peroxyl radicles, highly reactive oxygen species, which arise from normal body metabolism and environmental exposure to cigarette smoke, air pollutants, radiation, certain drugs and environmental toxins. Both species may react with DNA, protein or lipids and impair their physiological function. It is believed that these processes are the initial events in the pathogenesis of diseases such as cancer, cardiovascular disease and age related degeneration.

Beta carotene has been shown to rapidly quench singlet oxygen, but its role as a radical scavenger has not been fully established. Carotenoids vary as to their antioxidant abilities, with lycopene significantly outpacing both beta carotene and leutin. This is widely assumed to be the sole mechanism for their potential role in coronary vascular disease (CVD) and cancer prevention. However, in the case of cancer, in vitro studies suggest that in addition to antioxidant activity, carotenoids exert an inhibitory effect on cell proliferation and differentiation as with the retinoids, an important step in carcinogenesis. In addition, research as demonstrated other biologic activities of the carotenoids which include immunodilutory effects, modification of cytochrome P-450 detoxifying enzyme system.

Preventive Role of Carotenoids

Carotenoids derived from plant foods are the chief sources of vitamin A in the diet of many population groups in many developing countries and are thus important for the prophylactic treatment of xerophthalmia.

Riding in the crest of the scientific and public interest in the prevention of chronic disease, the carotenoids, and in particular, beta carotene were hailed as key antioxidant nutrients in the quest for finding the protective factor in fruits and vegetables. As with vitamin C, studies of carotenoids in CVD prevention have been conflicting. The carotenoids represent an enigmatic class of compounds and research continues into their biologic activities, which are varied, and potential in preventing host of chronic diseases, as enumerated below (BASF, 1997).

An epidemiological evidence for a protective effect of beta carotene is convincing. In a study of middle aged men, beta carotene intake was inversely correlated with CVD mortality with 21 per cent fewer deaths among men in the highest tertile. In vitro studies supported the link by demonstrating that beta carotene and other antioxidants could effectively inhibit the oxidation of LDL. But recent controlled trials have failed to substantiate beta carotene as a protective agent against CVD.

An important epidemiologic study in the early 90's assessed adipose tissue concentrations of carotenoids and fatty acids in subjects from 9 European countries to determine if carotenoids lowered risk for myocardial infraction (MI). They found a strong inverse correlation between beta carotene concentrations and risk for MI.

In a cohort study, the prospective basal study, plasma from 2,974 subjects was evaluated for carotene level. The study indicated the lower plasma carotene concentrations in the subjects died of ischemic heart disease and stroke, compared to controls, for a relative risk of 53 per cent greater in those subjects in the lowest quartile.

A 13-year study with type IIA hyperlipedemia, the lipid research clinics coronary primary prevention trial (LRC-CPPT), higher carotenoid concentrations correlated with lowered risk for CVD events.

In addition to CVD events, a 1-year study demonstrated that plasma beta carotene concentrations were inversely correlated to intimal thickening, which is known to be indicative of CVD risk, while epidemiology still suggests a protective effect, the results of large intervention trials have not been consistent. Large randomised trials of long duration are needed to provide definitive evidence as it may be possible that the effects of preventive factors may take longer time periods to become evident. Another difficulty with human studies is the variation in absorption, in particular of beta carotene, which can vary from 5 to 50 per cent. This could potentially influence the dose required from one individual to another for effectiveness.

Another study supporting beta carotenes role in immunity and cancer prevention conducted in England revealed that subjects who received the beta carotene supplement had significant increase in plasma levels of beta carotene and in the MHC 11 proteins, compounds which sit on the surface of monocytes and facilitate the destruction of cancer cells. In addition, beta carotene supplementation increased the level of tumor necrosis factor and which seeks out cancer cells and helps kill them. The beneficial effects persisted for several weeks after the subjects stopped taking the beta carotene. These findings suggest that moderate increases in intake of beta carotene can enhance immune responses linked to cancer prevention.

Lycopene lead other carotenoids in antioxidant function and may affect the immune system, which is also important in cancer development. Carotenoids may inhibit cell proliferation and differentiation key steps in carcinogenesis.

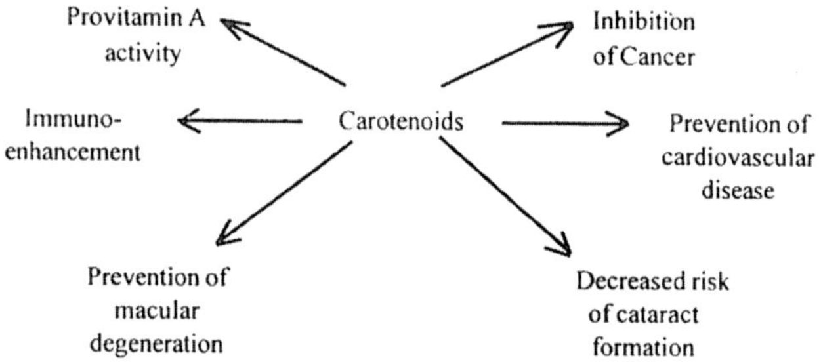

Fig. 2. Health promoting functions or actions attributed to carotenoids.

Source: Delia B. Rodriguez–Amaya (1997).

Carotenoids have also been linked with enhancement of the immune system and decreased risk of degenerative diseases such as cancer, cardiovascular disease, age-related macular degeneration and cataract formation Fig. 2. These biological effects are independent of the provitamin A activity and have attributed to an antioxidant property of carotenoids, through deactivation of free radicals Fig. 3.

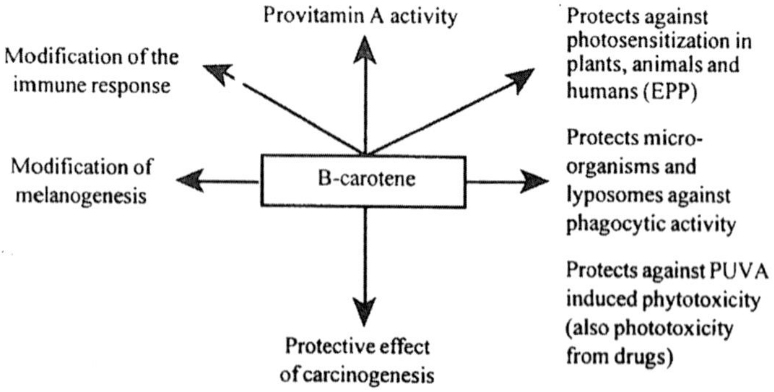

Fig. 3. Selected Biological Properties of B-carotene.

Source: Khinsky et al (1989).

The first and foremost important functions of provitamin A carotenoids in humans is for its conversion to retinol and prevention of many diseases more particularly xerophthalmia, nightblindness and keratomalacia.

Human Requirements of Vitamin A/Beta-carotene

Human requirement of vitamin A has been determined through long term depletion and repletion and radio labelled retinol turnover studies in human volunteers. Based on these studies the human requirement of vitamin A (retinol) has been defined at two levels, a minimal or basal level of intake of vitamin A to fulfil it's function and prevent deficiency symptoms and a safe level to permit addition, adequate liver storage of retindl. The requirement and RDA of vitamin A for Indians at different ages in terms of both retino! and Beta carotene is given in Table 5.

TABLE 5
Retional and B-carotene Requirements and Recommended Dietary Allowance (RDA) for Indians (ug/day)

	Age	*Basal requirement*		*Safe requirement*		*RDA ICMR, 1990*	
Group	*Years*	*Retinol*	*B-carotene*	*Retinol*	*B-carotene*	*Retinol*	*B-carotene*
Infants	0-1	181	724	351	1404	350	1200
Children	1-6	202	808	403	1612	400	1600
	6-10	253	1012	405	1620		
	10-12	291	1164	490	1960		
	12-15	351	1404	540	2160		
	15-18 M	336	1344	512	2048	600	2400
	15-18 F	299	1196	456	1824		
Adults	18 + M	288	1142	550	2200		
	F	240	960	465	1860		
Per capita requirement		269	1075	489	1965	573	2291

Ref: ICMR, 1992

Source: Gopalan C., Rama Sastry B.V. and Balasubramanian S.C., revised and updated by Narsinga Rao B.S., Deosthale Y.G. and Pant K.C. (1992) Nutritive value of Indian foods, National Institute of Nutrition, Indian Council of Medical Research, Hyderabad, A.P. India.

Vitamin A requirement of Indians have been defined in terms of B-carotene equivalents by assuming that on an average, only 50 per cent of carotenes in vegetables and fruits are bioavailable and 1 mg of absorbed β-carotene yields 0.5 ug of retinol in the body. The net retinol equivalents of 1 ug of dietary beta-carotene is thus 0.25 ug.

Traditional AOAC calorimetric procedures for carotenoid analysis are known to lack specificity and accuracy. Newer HPLC methods provide the investigator with a more precise, reproducible and rapid tool for carotenoid quantification in foods and tissues. It creates fewer artifacts.

Much progress has been made to the development of methodology for quantifying individual carotenoids in foods. Estimation of carotenoids by the High Pressure Liquid Chromatography (HPLC) is now accepted as the standard method. Although HPLC analysis is relatively new, it is considered to be rapid, reproducible, accurate and creates fewer artifacts.

Food Diversification Programmes

Since inadequate intake of vitamin A is the main cause of vitamin A deficiency, the solution lies in providing adequate amounts of the vitamin to population at risk. Inspite of the high dose vitamin A supplementation programmes in operation in countries such as Bangladesh and India, Vitamin A deficiency remains a public health problem.

Vitamin A in foods consists of provitamin A and preformed vitamin A. Foods containing preformed vitamin A such as liver, milk, butter, ghee, etc., are expensive and beyond the regular reach of the poor, but alternative, less expensive sources of provitamin A are easily available. However, seasonal variability and cultural beliefs seem to be the blocking factors in their use.

FAO/WHO recommendations to alleviate the problem include identification of newer rich source of beta carotene, increase in production of less expensive perennial carotene rich foods and the use of techniques in breeding, selection, and genetic engineering so as to improve carotene content and its bioavailability.

World Wide Food Sources of Provitamin A

Surveys done in different countries show that in terms of the provitamin A content, the most important food sources are dark green leafy vegetables, red palmoil, palm fruits, carrot, orange, sweet potatoes, mature squashes, pumpkin and some other yellow/orange tropical fruits. Table 6.

Data on the provitamin A content of foods are still not considered ideal. The discrepancy of results often exceeds expected natural variation, indicating that analytical errors are still prevalent and colloborative inter laboratory studies to validate methods and evaluate laboratory performance are urgently needed. Nonetheless, important food sources of pro-vitamin A around the world can now be pinpointed.

Heat Processing and Stability of Carotenoids

The stability of nutrients in foods varies considerably based on their chemical form, solubility, and susceptibility to environmental conditions.

Vitamin A and carotene are fat soluble and are unstable in acid medium but stable in base and neutral conditions. They are unstable to air, O_2, light and heat. Carotenoids are fat soluble, so they are relatively unaffected by an aqueous environment. Generally thermal processing results in an increase in available carotene.

Important Food Sources of Provitamins A (Data from Different Countries)

Leafy Vegetables

In surveys done in different countries (Table 6), dark green, leafy vegetables figure as the most common rich sources of provitamin A. Relatively easy to produce, and available practically all year round, they are inexpensive, accessible sources of provitamin A for most of the developing world. In these vegetables, β-carotene is essentially the sole contributor to vitamin A activity, with α-carotene and α-or β-crytoxanthin being reported only occasionally and at very low levels. However, the β-carotene content of leafy vegetables varies markedly.

TABLE 6
Important Provitamin A Sources in Different Countries[a]

Country/Reference	*Food*	*Common name*	*Scientific name*	*β-carotene content (μg/g edible portion)*
INDIA				
Begum and Pereira 1977	Leafy vegetables	Nerringi keerai	*Tribulus terrestris*	74±9
		Kuppai keerai	*Amaranthus viridis*	72±28
		Manathakkali keerai	*Solanum nigrum*	70±37
		Agathi keerai	*Sesbania grandiflora*	66±22
		Pacharisi keerai	*Euphorbia hirta*	62±6
		Puliara keerai	*Oxalis corniculata*	60±22
		Mullu keerai	*Amaranthus spinosus*	57±28
		Kasini keerai	*Raphanus sp*	56±12
		Sirukeerai	*Amaranthus polygonoides*	53±14
		Poonanganni keerai	*Alternanthera sessilis*	52±5
		Muringa keerai	*Moringa oleifera*	52±22
		Seemai Poonanganni	*Alternanthera sp*	46±8
		Chakravathy keerai	*Amaranthus sp*	39±3
		Nadirsan keerai	*Portulaca wightiana*	36±10
		Modakathan keerai	*Cardiospermum helicacabum*	35±7
		Knol khol keerai	*Brassica oleracea* var. *caulorapa*	35±7
		Arai keerai	*Amaranthus tristis*	34±10
		Panna keerai	*Celosia sp*	34±10
		Pulichai keerai	*Hibiscus cannabinus*	34±20
		Thandu keerai	*Amaranthus gangeticus*	32±11
		Molai keerai	*Amaranthus sp*	31±9

Country/Reference	*Food*	*Common name*	*Scientific name*	*β-carotene content (μg/g edible portion)*
		Uttareni	*Achyranthes aspera*	43±7
		Tummikura	*Leucas aspera*	41±9
		Chitramulan	*Plumbago zeylanica*	39±11
Bhaskarachary et al. 1995; Reddy et al. 1995	Non-leafy vegetables	Carrot	*Daucus carota*	65±15
Bhaskarachary et al. 1995; Reddy et al. 1995	Fruit	Indian dates	*Phoenix sp*	30±3
THAILAND				
Speek et al. 1988	Leaf vegetables	Common fennel	*Eryngium foetidum*	44
		Bitter melon leaves	*Momordica charantia*	34
Wasantwisut et al. 1995	Leaf vegetables	Garlic leaves	*Allium sativum*	50
		Ivy gourd	*Coccinia arandis L. Voist*	32-41
		Lead tree leaves	*Leucaena glauca*	31-33
		Amaranth	*Amaranthus viridis*	15-39
		Chinese swamp cabbage	*Ipomoea reptans*	12-42
MALAYSIA				
Tee and Lim 1991	Leafy vegetables	Daun turi	*Sesbania grandiflora*	136
		Cekur manis	*Sauropus androgynus*	133

Country/Reference	*Food*	*Common name*	*Scientific name*	*β-carotene content (μg/g edible portion)*
Bhaskarachary et al. 1995; Reddy et al. 1995	Common leafy vegetables	Drumstick	*Moringa oleifera*	197±55
		Agathi	*Sesbania grandiflora*	154±69
		Methi	*Trigonella foenum graecum*	92±15
		Amaranth	*Amaranthus gangeticus*	86±28
		Curry leaf	*Murraya koenigii*	71±24
		Gogu	*Hibiscus sabdariffa*	58±28
		Chammakura	*Colocasia antiquoram*	55±19
		Onion leaf	*Allium cepa*	49±2
		Koyyalakura	*Sueda monoica*	48±6
		Coriander	*Coriandum sativum*	48±2
		Pudina (mint)	*Menta arvensis*	43±20
		Palak	*Spinacea oleracea*	32±12
		Ceylon bacchali	*Talinum triangular*	30±6
Bhaskarachary et al. 1995; Reddy et al. 1995	Less familiar leafy vegetables	Botla benda	*Abutilon indicum*	126±15
		Chennangiaku	*Cassia sp*	119±22
		Yerramolakakaura	*Amaranthus sp*	119±15
		Mulla thotakura	*Amaranthus spinosus*	109±12
		Tulasi	*Ocimum sanctum*	82±11
		Chirrakura	not cited	71±11
		Harichandamkura	not cited	75±14
		Betel leaf	*Piper beetle*	59±10
		Ponnagantikura	*Alternanthera sessilis*	57±16

Country/Reference	*Food*	*Common name*	*Scientific name*	*β-carotene content (μg/g edible portion)*
		Tanki	*Neptunia oleracea*	114
		Curry leaves	*Murray koenigii*	93
		Drumstick leaves	*Moringa oleifera*	75
		Ranti	*Solanum nigrum*	70
		Wolfberry leaves	*Lycium chinese*	59
		Tapioca shoots	*Manihot utilissima*	57
		Spinach, red	*Amaranthus gangeticus*	51
		Mint leaves	*Mentha arvensis*	48
		Chinese kale	*Brassica alboglabra*	41
		Pegaga gajah	*Hydrocotyle javanica*	38
		Ceylon spinach	*Basella rubra*	35
		Chinese chives	*Allium odorum*	35
		Salted vegetable	—	34
		Spinach	*Amaranthus viridis*	32
		Coriander leaves	*Coriandrum sativum*	32
		Cemperai	*Champereia griffithii*	32
		Daun mengkudu	*Morinda citrifolia*	31
		Chinese cabbage	*Brassica chinensis*	30
Tee and Lim 1991	Non-leafy vegetables	Carrot	*Daucus carota*	68[b]
Choo 1994	Oil	Red palm oil Tenera	*Elaeis guineensis*	377[c]

Country/Reference	Food	Common name	Scientific name	β-carotene content (μg/g edible portion)
BANGLADESH				
Rahman et al. 1990, 1995	Leafy vegetables	Pat sak	*Chorchorus capsularis*	100±11
		Motor sak	*Pisum sativus*	89±9
		Sharisha sak	*Brassica campestris*	88±7
		Kalmi sak	*Ipomoea reptans*	83±4
		Helencha sak	*Enhydra fluctans*	82±3
		Kachu sak	*Colocasia antiquoram*	80±10
		Lal sak	*Amaranthus gangeticus*	80±9
		Lau sak	*Lagenaria vulgaris*	66±3
		Palang sak	*Spinacea oleracea*	64±10
		Mula sak	*Raphanus sativus*	63±6
		Thankuni sak	*Centella asiatica*	61±1
		Pui sak	*Basella alba*	56±7
		Nunia sak	*Portulaca oleracea*	54±3
Rahman et al. 1990, 1995	Flower	Sharisha phool	*Brassica campestris*	160±10
TAIWAN				
Chen et al. 1993	Leafy vegetables	Basil	not cited	105±28
		Green onion fragrant	not cited	92±9
		Kale	*Brassica oleracea* var. *acephala*	70±11
Chen et al. 1993	Non-leafy vegetable	Carrot	*Daucus carota*	54±6[b]

Country/Reference	Food	Common name	Scientific name	β-carotene content (μg/g edible portion)
NEPAL				
Vaidya 1995	Common leafy vegetables	Garden cress	*Lepidium sativum*	58
		Spinach	*Spinacea oleracea*	30
Vaidya 1995	Leafy portion of other vegetable	Carrot leaves	*Daucus carota*	42
Vaidya 1995	Traditional/wild leaves	Pahadi pig weed	*Amaranthus blitum*	92
		Pig weed	*Amaranthus viridis*	75
		Edible fern	*Dryopteris cochleate*	44
		Mint	*Mentha aquatica*	37
		Prostrate yarba-detegra	*Eclipta prostrate*	36
		Lamb's quarter	*Chenopodium albus*	33
		Amaranth	*Amaranthus leucocarpus*	33
Vaidya 1995	Non-leafy vegetable	Carrot	*Daucus carota*	43
JAPAN				
Izaki et al. 1986	Vegetables	Perilla green leaves	Not cited	187
		Komatsuna	*Brassica campestris*	63
		Celery leaves	*Apium graveolens*	61
		Parsley	*Petroselineum hortense*	58
		Collard	*Brassica oleracea var. acephala*	54
		Ashitaba	*Angelica keiskei*	51

Country/Reference	Food	Common name	Scientific name	β-carotene content (μg/g edible portion)
		Mitsuba	*Cryptotaenia japonica*	48
		Turnip leaves	*Brassica rapa*	46
		Hatakena	*Brassica campestris var. oleifera*	46
		Chinese chive	*Allium odorum*	46
		Spinach	*Spinacea oleracea*	44
		Carrot Kintoki	*Daucus carota*	43
		Sugukina	*Brassica rapa var. neo suguki*	41
		Shungiku	*Chrysanthemum coronarium*	41
		Water dropwort	*Oenanthe javanica*	40
		Malabar spinach	*Basella alba*	39
		V:tamin-na	*Brassica campestris var. narinosa*	37
		Hiroshimana	*Brassica campestris var. pekinensis*	36
		Broad-leaved mustard	*Brassica juncea*	35
		Water cress	*Nastrutium officinale*	31
		Leaf mustard	*Brassica juncea*	31
		Hamaboufuu	*Glehnia littoralis*	30
Kon 1989	Green vegetables	Chingentsuai leaves	*Brassica campestris var. chinensis*	91
		Komatsuna leaves	*Brassica campestris*	86
		Perilla, leaves	Not cited	72
		Spinach leaves	*Spinacea oleracea*	66
		Leaf-blade, green	Not cited	52
		Spinach, whole	*Spinacea oleracea*	35
		Komatsuna, whole	*Brassica campestris*	33

Country/Reference	Food	Common name	Scientific name	β-carotene content (μg/g edible portion)
FINLAND				
Heinonen et al. 1989	Leafy vegetables	Parsley	*Petroselinum hortense*	56
		Dill	*Anethum graveolens*	45
		Spinach	*Spinacea oleracea*	33
Heinonen et al. 1989	Non-leafy vegetable	Carrot	*Daucus carota*	76[b]
TANZANIA				
Pepping et al. 1988	Leafy vegetables	"Kayeba" leaves	not cited	45
		Dried cowpea leaves	*Vigna spp*	23-57
		Dried pumpkin leaves	*Cucurbita moschata*	90-102
Pepping et al. 1988	Oil	Red palm oil	*Elaeis guineensis*	93-330[c]
UNITED STATES				
Khachik et al. 1986; Bureau and Bushway 1986; Bushway 1986; Bushway and Wilson 1982; Bushway et al. 1986; Quackenbush 1987	Leafy vegetables	Kale	*Brassica oleracea var. acephala*	82-146
		Spinach	*Spinacea oleracea*	43-82
		Beet greens	*Beta vulgaris*	19-50
		Swiss chard	*Beta vulgaris*	21-46

Country/Reference	Food	Common name	Scientific name	β-carotene content (μg/g edible portion)
Bureau and Bushway 1986; Bushway 1986; Bushway and Wilson 1982; Bushway et al. 1986; Quackenbush 1987; Khachik and Beecher 1987	Non-leafy vegetables	Carrot	*Daucus carota*	36-182[b]
		Sweet potato	*Ipomoea batatas*	50-160
		Squash	*Cucurbita maxima*	24-84
		Pumpkin	*Cucurbita moschata*	80[d]
Bureau and Bushway 1986; Bushway 1986; Bushway and Wilson 1982; Bushway et al. 1986; Quackenbush 1987; Khachik and Beecher 1989	Fruit	Cantaloupe	*Cucumis melo*	16-216
BRAZIL				
Southeastern Region				
Ramos and Rodriguez-Amaya 1987; Minazzi-Rodrigues and Penteado 1989; Godoy and Rodriguez-Amaya 1996	Commercial leafy vegetables	Mustard leaves	*Brassica juncea*	60±15
		Parsley	*Petroselinum hortense*	50±15
		Coriander leaves	*Coriandrum sativum*	47±5
		Cress	*Nastrutium officinale*	42±10
		Kale	*Brassica oleracea* var. *acephala*	35±13
		Roquette	*Eruca sativa*	35±13
		Common chicory	*Chicorium intybus*	34±10

Country/Reference	*Food*	*Common name*	*Scientifi c name*	*β-carotene content (μg/g edible portion)*
Minazzi-Rodrigues and Penteado 1989; Mercadente and Rodriguez-Amaya 1990	Native or uncultivated leafy vegetables	Caruru	*Amaranthus viridis*	110±6
		Mentruz	*Lepidium pseudodidymum*	85±19
		Taioba	*Xanthosoma spp*	67±21
		Serralha	*Sonchus oleraceus*	63±14
		Beldroega	*Portulaca oleracea*	30±8
Godoy and Rodriguez-Amaya 1996; Arima and Rodriguez-Amaya 1988; Almeida and Penteado 1987; Godoy and Rodriguez-Amaya 1993	Non-leafy vegetables	Pumpkin Menina Verde	*Cucurbita moschata*	39±12[d]
		Carrot	*Daucus carota*	34±15[b]
Northern Region				
Penteado et al. 1986	Leafy vegetables	Quiabo	*Hibiscus esculentus*	116
		Macaxeira	*Manihot esculenta*	129
		Vinagreira branca	*Hibiscus sabdariffa*	86
		Vinagreira roxa	*Hibiscus acetosela*	78
		Indian spinach	*Amaranthus sp.*	63
		Taioba	*Colocasia esculenta*	57

Country/Reference	Food	Common name	Scientifi c name	β-carotene content (μg/g edible portion)
		Bertalha	*Basella rubra*	55
		Mentruz	*Chenopodium ambrosioides*	55
		Tomato	*Lycopersicum esculentum*	55
		Chinese kale	*Brassica chinensis*	49
		Orelha de macaco	*Alternanthera sp.*	46
		African spinach	*Amaranthus sp.*	39
		Jambu branco	*Spilanthes acmella*	39
Rodriguez-Amaya et al. 1995a	Fruit	Tucuma	*Astrocaryun vulgaris*	107±31
Northeastern Region				
Arima and Rodriguez-Amaya 1990	Non-leafy vegetable	Pumpkin Baianinha	*Cucurbita moschata*	235[d]
Godoy and Rodriguez-Amaya 1994	Fruit	Buriti	*Mauritia vinifera*	360±32[c]
Trujillo-Quijano et al. 1990	Oil	Red palm oil Tenera	*Elaeis guineensis*	363[c]
Centralwestern Region				
Hiani and Penteado 1989b	Fruit	Bocaiuva	*Acrocomia makayayba*	55

Country/Reference	Food	Common name	Scientific name	β-carotene content (μg/g edible portion)
EGYPT				
Abdel-Kader 1991	Leafy vegetables	Spinach	*Spinacea oleracea*	53
Abdel-Kader 1991	Roots crops	Carrot	*Daucus carota*	63[b]
		Sweet potato	*Ipomoea batatas*	64

[a] Only foods with β-carotene content equal to or higher than 30 μg/g are included.

[b] Carrots from Malaysia, Taiwan, Finland, United States, Brazil, and Egypt also had 34, 28±3, 5.3, 20-106, 22±10, and 34 μg/g α-carotene, respectively.

[c] Red palm oil from Malaysia, Tanzania, and Brazil also contained 237, 58-144, and 164 μg/g *trans* α-carotene, respectively, and small amounts of *cis*-isomers of α- and β-carotene.

[d] The U.S. pumpkin and the Brazilian pumpkins Menina Verde and Baianinha also had 55, 23, and 47 μg/g α-carotene, respectively.

[e] Buriti also contained 80±9 μg/g α-carotene and 37±4 μg/g γ-carotene.

Source: Delia. B, Rodriguez-Amaya (1997) Carotenoid and food preparation: The retention of provitamin A, Carotenoids in prepared, processed and stored foods, John Snow Inc./omni project.

TABLE 7

Retention of β-carotene During Home Processing in Different Countries

Country/Reference	*Calculation of Retention*	*Cooking conditions*	*Food product*	*Retention of β-carotene (%)*
U.S.A.				
Dietz et al. 1988	Retention calculated according to Murphy et al. (1975)	**Water blanching:** 10 g sample cooked in 100 ml boiling water 30 minutes	Winged beans	119
			Lettuce	47
			Carrot	60[a]
			Spinach	112
		Steam blanching: 10 g sample steamed in household steamer 30 minutes at 100°C.	Winged beans	83
			Lettuce	104
			Carrot	90[a]
			Spinach	132
PAKISTAN				
Nagra and Khan 1988	Retention calculated on the basis of original weight of uncooked vegetable.	**Cooking:** 5 g cut sample cooked in distilled water 60 minutes (simulating traditional method)	Bitter gourd	78
			Brinjal	62
			Cabbage	56
			Colocasia	67
			Carrot (red part)	41
			Carrot (white part)	67
			Cauliflower	67
			Colbash	66
			Gand godhi	50
			Green turnip	67
			Lady's finger	50

Country/Reference	Calculation of Retention	Cooking conditions	Food product	Retention of β-carotene (%)
			Large chillies	76
			Peas	61
			Spinach	75
			Squash	50
			Vegetable sponge	90
			Yellow turnip	81
THAILAND				
Speek et al. 1988	Retention calculated as percentage of fresh	**Cooking:** 20 g sample submerged for 2-8 minutes in boiling tap water.	Bitter melon leaves	89
			Coriander	85
			Sweet basil	68
			Celery	84
			Vine spinach	89
			Lettuce, unheaded	77
			Hairy basil	76
			Cha-om	69
			Swamp cabbage	50
		Sautéing: 20 g sample cut into pieces, fried 3-5 minutes in 5 ml pre-heated oil at 200°C, 3 ml water added during frying	Chinese swamp cabbage	76
			Chinese cabbage	84
			Chinese kale	24
			Chinese chive	19
			Cabbage	57
			Sugar peas	92

Country/Reference	*Calculation of Retention*	*Cooking conditions*	*Food product*	*Retention of β-carotene (%)*
		Fermenting: 20 g sample crushed, salt and supernatant of already fermented vegetable were added, fermentation allowed for 1.5 days	Chinese chive	95
			Whole onion plant	78
			Pickled leaf mustard	67
			Eggplant, round shape	22
		Sun-drying: leaves were exposed to direct sunlight for 2 days	Neem tree	53
			Neem tree, duplicate	56
			Amarnath	50
			Sweet basil	39
Wasantwisut et al. 1995	Retention based on β-carotene content per fresh and cooked weight	**Blanching:** 98°C, 5 minutes	Swamp cabbage	89
			Chinese cabbage	93
			Bai kaprao	95
		Boiling: 97°C, 5 minutes	Water mimosa	96
		2 minutes	Bai kaprao	80
		Stir-frying: 178°C, 3.5 minutes	Swamp cabbage	82
		2 minutes	Water mimosa	58
		3 minutes	Bai kaprao	72
INDIA				
Padmavati et al. 1992	Calculation of retention based on weight of raw vegetable	Processing conditions not specified		
		Minimum processing (Salads)	Tomato salad (pieces)	94
			Carrot salad (pieces)	91
			Carrot salad (grated)	89
			Tomato raita	81

Country/Reference	*Calculation of Retention*	*Cooking conditions*	*Food product*	*Retention of β-carotene (%)*
		Short time cooking-chopping, sautéing	Carrot bhaji	82
			Methi chanadal bhaji	71
			Palak bhaji	71
			Palak paneer	70
			Mayalu bhaji	67
			Aloo methi	56
			Aloo palak	50
			Yellow pumpkin bhaji	39
			Amaranth curry	34
			Colocasia patal bhaji	36
			Methi dal	34
		Chopping + steaming + shallow frying	Coriander vadi	92
			Methi muthia	56
			Colocasia patra	38
		Chopping + deep-frying	Mayalu pakoda	39
			Palak bhaji	28
			Palak pakoda	26
			Coriander vadi (deep-fried)	29
			Methi muthia (deep-fried)	26
			Patra (deep-fried)	15
		Chopping and roasting	Methi thepla	90
		Maceration/grinding	Coriander chutney (blender)	87
			Curry leaves chutney	81

Country/Reference	Calculation of Retention	Cooking conditions	Food product	Retention of β-carotene (%)
			Mint ratia	81
			Gongura chutney	74
			Mint chutney (stone grinder)	67
			Mint + coriander chutney (stone grinder)	60
		Prolonged cooking + grating/grinding	Pumpkin halwa	31
			Cream of carrot soup	30
			Palak soup	21
			Carrot halwa	20
			Tomato chutney	19
Reddy et al. 1995	Basis of retention calculation not specified	Processing conditions not specified		
		Cutting/sautéing	Amaranth dhal (with tamarind)	71
			Palak dhal (with tomato)	77
		Grinding	Coriander chutney	76
			Curry leaf powder	76
		Grating/prolonged heating	Carrot halwa	48
			Pumpkin halwa	10
		Cooking without lid	Amaranth	17
			Koyyalkura	36
			Bacchali	52
			Palak	46
			Sweet potato	21

Country/Reference	Calculation of Retention	Cooking conditions	Food product	Retention of β-carotene (%)
			Carrot	67
			Pumpkin	39
			Tomato	100
		Cooking with lid	Amaranth	31
			Koyyalkura	45
			Bacchali	62
			Palak	49
			Sweet potato	43
			Carrot	65
			Pumpkin	36
			Tomato	100
		Steaming	Amaranth	17
			Koyyalkura	60
			Bacchali	63
			Palak	70
			Sweet potato	36
			Carrot	72
			Pumpkin	36
			Tomato	100
		Sautéing	Amaranth	60
			Koyyalkura	62
			Bacchali	75

Country/Reference	Calculation of Retention	Cooking conditions	Food product	Retention of β-carotene (%)
			Palak	71
			Sweet potato	46
			Carrot	74
			Pumpkin	53
			Tomato	100
BANGLADESH				
Rahman et al. 1990	Retention based on β-carotene content per fresh and cooked weight.	**Method I:** leafy vegetable chopped, washed, heated 7-9 minutes in water adhering to leaves, then transferred to another pot in which salt, onion, garlic, and chillies had been fried in oil. The mixture fried for 4-6 minutes	Lal sak	69
			Mula sak	60
			Palang sak	57
			Pui sak	67
		Method II: chopped and washed vegetables, with some amount of salt, oil, and condiments as Method I, boiled for 8-10 min with pot lid on.	Lal sak	88
			Mula sak	86
			Palang sak	89
			Motor sak	89
BRAZIL				
Rodriguez-Amaya et al. 1995b	Retention calculated according to Murphy et al. (1975).	**Boiling:** cut vegetable cooked 5 minutes in boiling water.	Broccoli	84
			Okra	68
			Spinach	77
		Boiling: cut vegetable cooked 10 minutes in boiling water.	Carrot Nantes	91[b]
			Carrot Imperador	94[b]
			Green beans	82
			Indian eggplant	82

Country/Reference	Calculation of Retention	Cooking conditions[a]	Food product	Retention of β-carotene (%)
		Boiling: cut vegetable cooked 15 minutes in boiling water.	Squash	90[b]
		Sautéing: cut vegetable stir-fried 10 minutes in small amount of oil.	Green beans	63
			Squash	83
Almeida and Penteado 1987	Basis of retention calculation not specified.	**Boiling:** conditions not specified	Carrot	86[c]
Almeida-Muradin and Penteado 1992	Calculation of retention based on weight of raw root.	**Boiling:** Sweet potatoes peeled and cut into small pieces and cooked 10 minutes in boiling water (98°C).	Sweet potato	
			Acadian	96
			Centennial	87
			Heart Gold	94
			Vineland Bush	82

[a] Boiling and steaming resulted in 64 and 139 percent retention, respectively, of α-carotene.

[b] α-carotene of Nantes carrots, Imperador carrots and squash was retained 90, 92 and 90 percent, respectively, on boiling,. In the sautéed squash, 80 percent of α-carotene and 78 percent of α-cryptoxanthin were retained.

[c] α-carotene was retained 88 per cent.

Source: Delia. B, Rodriguez-Amaya (1997) Carotenoid and food preparation: The retention of provitamin A, Carotenoids in prepared, processed and stored foods, John Snow Inc./omni project.

Once processed, frozen or canned fruits and vegetables retain the level for prolonged periods. If the presence of oxygen affects a minonutrient, it is likely to be a good antioxidant. If light and heat affect it as well, processing conditions of high heat in the presence of light could be deleterious, on the other hand, absence of oxygen, as in canning, will help stabilize these nutrients, and the environment (water or fat) will also influence retention.

It is possible that carotenes from some vegetable sources are resistant to complete extraction while in the raw state. Carotenoids in the bound form with proteins have important functions in photosynthetic processes, some heat treatments such as steaming may help to release these bound carotenoids and cause them to be more readily extracted.

Some types of processing will reduce the antioxidant potential of fruits and vegetables. For example, dehydration whether by sun or artificial heat sources, will affect not only ascorbate, but also tocopherols and carotenoids as a result of exposure to ultraviolet light, air and heat.

Processing methods, such as dehydration, blanching and canning are thought to result either in loss of carotenoids, or their isomerization from trans to cis isomers. Carotenoids are much more stable than ascorbic acid but present a unique challenge in accurate measurement. Early studies of carotene content in fruits and vegetables used assays that measured total carotenes. With the advent of HPLC, methods were developed that can seperate not only the α-and beta-carotenes but also the cis and trans forms. Thus large discrepancies in carotenoid content in vegetables among studies can be attributed to measurement variability and variation in the original material.

Another unique characteristic of carotene is that they can be bound in carotenoproteins or may be associated with the plant matrix. Following heating, the carotenes are released, resulting in apparent increases in carotene content after cooking or thermal processing. This can be viewed as an artifact of the assay procedure, because the carotenes are more easily extracted when they are not bound. Almost uniformely, we find, for example, that cooked carrots or pumpkin (curcubita pepo) have more measureable carotene than the non-cooked food. One of the challenges in nutrition is to establish whether the protein bound carotenes are as bioavailable as those that have been released. Evidence suggests that they are not, and that release of carotenoids, such as lycopene in tomatoes, is needed, for their effective utilization. Heating tomato juice or steaming spinach (spinacia oleracea), for example, increases the amount of carotenoids extracted. Studies of the effects of cooking or thermal processing show little effect on B-carotene retention. Table 7.

The trans form of Beta carotene is dominant in plant foods, but some studies show that thermal processing converts the all-trans forms to cis forms. Many of the cis-isomers are found in human tissues so transformation of trans to cis takes place in the body, as well as during processing. Isomerization of trans B-carotene can also be induced by exposure to light, acid, processing and chemicals such as hypochlorite resulting in loss of activity.

Because of discrepancies in the results obtained and the different behaviour of carotenoids in different foods, specific recommendations cannot be given in relation to the optimum conditions for home preparation/processing and storage for given foods. However, general guidelines can be made such as keeping processing/heating time and temperature to a minimum, avoiding cutting into small pieces or macertation, reducing the time lag between cutting/chopping and processing; washing before cutting, cooking with the pot lid on and keeping storage time to a minimum. In general, provitamin A losses increases from microwaving, steaming, boiling, sauteing, deep frying and prolonged cooking. Combinations of several preparation/processing methods, baking, halwa making and pickling result in substantial losses of provitamin A (Madhava *et al.*, 1994).

Storage and Stability of Carotenoids

Retention of carotenoids during storage of processed foods is favoured by low storage, temperature, protection from light, exclusion of oxygen by vaccum or hot-filling, modified atmosphere, packaging or oxygen impermeable packaging, and the presence of a natural or added antioxidant. In general, salt treatment and sulfiting also increase retention. Provitamen A in canned or bottled products are generally well retained for atleast a year.

Carotenoids in dehydrated products are more likely to undergo degradation during storage because the greater surface area and porosity increase their exposure to oxygen and light. Blanched products generally resist carotenoids decomposition during storage better than unblanched foods.

Drying is the cheapest and most accessible means of food preservation in developing countries, but considerable losses of provitamins A occur. Drying with a solar dryer and protecting the food from direct sunlight minimize destruction of the provitamins, Blanching to inactivate degradive enzymes also reduces losses during drying and storage. Table 20-21.

Bioavailability of Carotenoids in Foods

Bioavailability or the body's ability to use certain micronutrients like vitamin A, can be influenced by many factors such as the presence of other nutrients in the diet which might inhibit or facilitate vitamin A absorption and use. Absence of fat in the diet and cultural practices which prevent consumption of carotene rich foods, cooking, preservation methods which require prolonged heating of the foods and prolonged storage may affect vitamin A activity.

There is a perception that carotenoids are destroyed by the heat process involved in cooking of vegetables. Infact, carotenoid loss is minimal with moderate cooking and in many cases, carotenoids become more bioavailable after cooking probably because heat processing liberates them from cell matrices. Steaming, micro wave cooking and/or boiling had no effect on beta carotene and leutin (Cis and trans concentration). The widely held belief that fresh produce is nutritionally superior to commercially processed produce is not valid with regard to carotenoids. Bioavailability of carotenoids is reported to be enhanced as a result of commercial food processing (Rock *et al.*, 1995).

However, conflicting results were found in past studies. Insufficient and uncorrelated data do not allow an appraisal of the effect of processing and storage on the bioavailability of provitamin A in foods at this time. It is especially important to pursue investigation of the bioavailability of beta carotene in dark green leafy vegetables because they are the most widely available and affordable sources of provitamin A world wide.

SUGGESTIONS FOR FUTURE LINES OF RESEARCH

— The vast potential of forests as a repository of a variety of vitamin A rich foods is not yet fully realized.

— Edible forest foods from other tribal zones of South India rich in vitamin A need to be further explored.

— Forest foods attributed to have medicinal value and used in the native treatment of eye diseases by the tribals need to be further explored.

— The study focuses the need for promotion and popularisation of the identified vitamin A rich plant species as a practical solution to the public health problem of vitamin A deficiency.

— Forest foods with high vitamin A activity needs special promotional attention.

— Further investigations on the bioavailability of the carotene from the vitamin A rich forest foods needs attention.

— Intervention strategies should be worked out by Health and Nutrition professionals, policy planners and programme managers combinedly for promotion of diversified protective foods which are uncommon/ unconventional.

— The specific nutrient rich uncommon forest GLV's may be used for genetic manipulation for the benefit of mankind.

— Preserving the practice of consumption of the forest foods in younger generation from tribal areas through nutrition education needs attention.

— Cultivation of the forest GLV's should be taken up in Ashram school (residential schools for tribals) to encourage consumption of their traditional foods rich in vitamin A.

— Motivating farm/home cultivation of vitamin A rich forest GLV's in tribal, non-tribal areas goes a long way in popularisation of the same.

— Products with cooking water retained had maximum β-carotene. GLV cooked in acid media (tamarind) showed maximum loss of carotene. Frying in oil causes oxidation and loss of β-carotene. Cooking GLVs in dhal and less exposure to heat as in chutney proved to be beneficial in minimising losses of β-carotene.

— The tribals were found to have distinct attitudes and beliefs towards foods and they follow certain native treatment for eye related diseases.

SUMMARY AND CONCLUSIONS

— The study made possible to unravel various edible forest plant species rich in Vitamin A. The findings are of immense practical value to Botanists/Agriculturists, Horticulturists/Agronomy/Social forestry/ Agroforestry/Health and Nutritional personnel and policy makers and common man.

— The hill tribes possess abundant traditional knowledge about various forest species and techniques of utilisation of some of the species which ensures their regeneration.

— 104 edible forest foods containing of 70 GLVs, 23 fruits, 3 other vegetables, 5 roots and tubers and 3 miscellaneous foods collected from selected forest areas in eastern ghats of Andhra Pradesh were analysed for total carotene content.

— Among the 70 GLVs analysed, 36 were found to have high vitamin A activity (0.87–2.34 mg per cent) and 30 with moderate vitamin A activity (0.36–0.8 mg per cent) and 4 GLVs had the least vitamin A activity.

— Other vegetables, roots and tubers analysed were found to have no significant vitamin A activity.

— Among the fruits, canthium parviflorum had high vitamin A activity (1.02 mg per cent). The inedible orange colour fresh rind portion of the fruit analysed found to have the highest β-carotene content (6.10 mg per cent).

— Another fruit Diosphros melanoxylon, the edible pulp portion of fruit containd no β-carotene. However, rind (fresh) had good amount of β-carotene (0.79 mg per cent) and the dried rind had high amounts of β-carotene (2.17 mg per cent).

Boiling is the common cooking practice of tribals. Vegetables are boiled in large amount of water with/without draining (depending on the vegetable). The effect of boiling on retention of β-carotene (pro-vitamin A) content showed wide variation of 6 to 97 per cent.

— By selective cultivation of perennial/seasonal GLV's the supply of vitamin A can be maintained through out the year.

— New methods and recipes that have potential to be accepted into practices by non-tribal members need to be worked out.

— Value added products with unconventional foods which have potential for market need to be explored.

— The utilisation aspect of inedible but vitamin A rich portions of the fruits need to be further explored.

APPENDICES

Appendix I

List of Edible Forest Foods Collected from Tribal Areas of Andhra Pradesh, South India

Vizianagaram district (Local Name)	Visakapatnam district	East Godavari district	Kurnool and Prakasam districts
GLVs			
Silleru kura	Konkadi kura	Pedda Pindi kura	Beddi kura
Chenchel kura	Tenteb kura	Puvvutota kura	Dela kura
Ambali madukura	Gummadi chiguru	Garam masalaaku	Pedda makula kura
Peddatantem kura	Teddu kamma kura	Konda karivepaku	Devadari kura
White kura	Rasi saru kura	Chamakura	Desara kura
Nelli kura	Sashap kura	Amsu kura	Dodda nelli kura
Gurum kura	Mandi kura	Tella bacchali	Chikkakura
Adavigummadi kura	Saru kura	Pappu kura	Perugutota kura
Elukachevula kura	Godrung kura	Gongura/Janapa kura	Mellikura
Bodantan kura	Chirumirapa kayakura	Sikaya chiguru	Pendli Beddi kura
Pindi kura	Mullu kura	Pilliadugula kura	Kolem kura
Pedda Tummi kura	Godrung kura	Ambatimadu kura	
Venneduru kura	Podi kura	Gummadi kura	**Other Vegetables**
Pulleru kura	Doruga/Venneduru kura	Ponnaganti kura	
Chinna Tummi kura		Gaju kura	Adavi potla kaya
Gummadiaaku	**Roots and Tubers**	Adavikanda kura	Aradonda kaya
Simmadri kura		Chintala kura	
Nagali sare kura	Chedu dumpa	Tellatota kura	**Roots and Tubers**
Chitti kura		Yerra bacchali	
Dukkina kura	Pandi dumpa	Garisa kura	Chanda Gadda
Balusu kura	Thega dumpa	Vuri kanda	
Munagaaku		Daggula kura	
Cheepuru kura		Chappi kura	
Nela benda			
Korla kura			
Gantabharani kura			
Isukarasi kura			
Ghantikamma kura			
Chilaka pabanna kura			
Chinna tentem kura			

Vizianagaram district (Local Name)	Visakapatnam district	East Godavari district	Kurnool and Prakasam districts
Roots and other vegetables			**Fruits**
Teepi Gummadi			Pala pandu
Karra pendalam			Banka pandu
			Banka neredu pandu
			Chilukadudduru pandu
			Elakkaya
Fruits			Nakri pandu
			Chitimiti pandu
Papaya pandu			
Chitti mamidi pandu			
Adavi mamidi pandu			
Pedda Etha pandu			
Chitti Etha pandu			
Nalla jeedi pandu			
Parasa pandu			
Nerudu pandu			
Tummik pandu			
Jeedimamidi pandu			
Regu pandu			
Bodda pandu			
Rama phalam			
Golimi pandu			
Usiri kayalu			
Udiki pandu			
Others			
Ippa flowers			
Ippa fruits and seeds/nut			
Ippa oil			
Veduru kommulu			
mango sheet (dried)			

Appendix II

An interview schedule for collection of information on food consumption, storage practices, morbidity, attitudes and knowledge pertaining to Eye Diseases of Tribals of Five Districts of South India

I. General Information

District :

Mandal :

Village :

Name of the Respondent :

Age :

Tribe :

Occupation :

(a) Major :

(b) Subsidiary :

II. Family Particulars

S. No.	*Name*	*Age*	*Sex*	*Relation to Respondent*	*Clinical symptoms of any disease (Observations)*

III. What foods you collect from forest ?

Food Items	*Months available*	*Quantity brought at a time*	*How often collected*	*Do you store foods YES/NO*

IV. Storage practices (pertaining to vitamin A rich foods)

Do you store any fruits, vegetables and tubers? YES/NO

S. No.	*Food stores*	*Form stored*	*Period stored*	*Place of storage*	*Method of storage (pre treatment)*

V. Do you feel any foods is good/bad for the general health of eyes YES/NO

If Yes

S. No.	*Foods good for eyes*	*Reasons*	*Foods bad for eyes*	*Reasons*

VI. Do you recommend/avoid any foods in eye-diseases

If Yes YES/NO

S. No.	*Eye problem*	*Food recommended*	*Reasons*	*Foods avoided*	*Reasons*

VII. Do you recommend/avoid any foods in any physiological state?

S. No.	**Physiological State*	*Food preferred*	*Reasons*	*Foods avoided*	*Reasons*

*1. Pregnancy

2. Lactation

3. Children below 6 years

4. Old age

5. Diseases

Fever

Gastric problems

Respiratory problems

Skin problems

Eye problems

VIII. Do you attribute any medicinal value to any plants especially for the health of the eye or for curing eye diseases, YES/NO

S. No.	*Name of the Plant*	*Part Used*	*Method of Usage*	*Treatment Duration*	*Where Treated*				
					PHC	*Local*	*Own*	*Other*	*Effective or not*

IX. Do you suffer from other diseases ? Yes/No

If yes,

S. No.	Health Problem	Reason for Occurrence	Duration Suffered	Seasonal Reoccurrence	Where Treated				Duration	Result
					PHC	Local	Own	Other		

Appendix III

Methodology for Estimation of Carotene Content in Forest Foods using HPLC

Forest foods comprising of GLVs, fruits, roots and tubers were obtained from the forests with the assistance of tribals in the quantity of 1-2 kg. Prior to analysis, the foods were cleaned under running water and excess water is wiped off by pressing gently between tissue paper. Edible portion was used for estimation of carotene content. Moisture content of the samples was estimated using AOAC (1984).

The foods were sealed in polythene bags and carried to the laboratory in an ice box and stored at—20°C till the time of analysis. However, care was taken to analysis the foods within 24 hours of their collection.

Preparation of Glass Powder

One hundred grams of neutral glass (Borosil) was made to fine powder by grinding it in the glass pestle and mortar. The glass powder was thoroughly washed with deionised water and dried in an oven at 100°C. The powder was stored in air-tight container till use.

Chemicals and Solvents

Acetonitrile, methanol and dichloromethane (HPLC grade) solvents (Qualigens, Glaxo, India). Acetone, petroleum ether (60-80°C), hexane, potassium hydroxide and anhydrous sodium sulphate were of analytical reagent grade.

Extraction of total Carotenoids from Good Stuff

The widely quoted methodologies for carotene extractions, speek *et al.* (1986) and Zakaria *et al.* (1979), Bhaskarchary (1996) were standardised. Ultimately, Zakaria *et al.* (1979) method of extraction was used with modification for total carotenoid quantitation.

A representative sample of leaf, fruit, tuber or any other vegetable (fresh or dried), 5 to 25 g was taken into a glass pestle and mortar. Samples were ground in presence of fine glass powder (5-10 g) to a fine paste by adding with 5-25 ml of acetone. The ground sample paste was then transferred quantitatively to a conical flask by adding 30 ml of acetone. The contents were stirred on a magnetic stirrer for 10 minutes and filtered through a sintered glass funnel. The residue was then extracted with a 40 ml mixture of acetone and hexane (3:5 v/v) and stirred on a magnetic stirrer for 15 minutes. The extract was passed through a sintered glass funnel and the residue was reextracted twice with 25 ml hexane and stireed for 30 minutes each time. The pooled extract was then transferred into a separating funnel. The extract was washed with enough water (200 ml water) three times to remove traces of acetone. Non-removal of acetone causes aldol condensation under alkaline conditions. The purified hexane layer was dried by passing through anhydrous sodium sulphate column to remove the traces of water.

Saponification

The hexane extract was evaporated to dryness under a stream of nitrogen and the residue was dissolved in 5-10 ml of 15 per cent KOH in methanol (W/V) and was saponified overnight at room temperature in dark. The contents were then transferred into a separating funnel, by adding 10 ml of petroleum ether and 10 ml of water. The aqueous phase was reextracted, each time with 25 ml of petroleum ether till there was no colour observed in the extract. The pooled petroleum ether extract was washed free of alkali with 100 ml water and then passed through anhydrous sodium sulphate and made up to a known volume with petroleum ether.

Quantitation of Total Carotenoids

Total carotenoid content of the extract was determined by measuring the absorbance at 450 nm in a spectrophotometer (Shimadzu). The extinction coefficient of B-carotene (E_{1cm} 1 per cent at 450 in petroleum ether is 2500) was used for calculating the concentration, and the results were expressed as mg/100 g.

Total carotenoid content of the extract

$$= \frac{\text{Optical density of the extract}}{\text{B-carotene extinction coefficient}} \times \text{volume}$$

Qualitative and Quantitative Analysis of Carotenoids by HPLC

The most frequently used nonaqueous reversed-phase HPLC methods for carotene separation in vegetables were that of Zakaria *et. al.* (1979) and Nelis and Deleenheer (1983). Both the methods were standardised and ultimately Nelis and Deleenheer (1983) method was used with modification (Baskarchary, 1996).

HPLC System

The chromatographic system consisted of Shimadzu, model LC6A equipped with system controller, SCL6A, available wavelength detector SPD-6AV (ultraviolet and visible range) and an integrator C-R3A chromatopack.

Columns

Reversed-phase analytical column Zorbax, C_{18}, Du Pont; a stainless steel column, 25 cm long with 4.6 mm internal diameter and 5 um particle size was used for chromatographic separations. The stationary phase is consisted of octa decylsilane, which serves as non-polar base for chromatography. The guard column which protects analytical column was connected between injecting loop and main column.

Mobile phase: Mobile phase consisting of polar solvents acetonitrile, dichloromethane and methanol was used for HPLC analysis.

Standards: Chrystalline B-carotene (C-0126), –Carotene (C-0251), Lutein (X-6250) and Lycopene (L-9879) were purchased from Sigma, USA. The other carotenoid standards, zeaxanthine, B-cryptoxanthin, and –carotene were generous gifts from Hoffman-La-Roche, Basal, Switzerland.

Spectral Analysis of Carotenoids

Sample and standard carotenoids like α, β, γ-carotenes, lycopene, lutein, zeaxanthin and B-cryptoxanthin were scanned for the spectra on Shimadzu spectrophotometer. Each carotenoid was dissolved in petroleum ether (1-2 ug/ml W/v) and scanned from 300 to 500 nm at a speed of 50 nm/minute. The extinction co-efficients E_{1cm} 1% used were 2500 at 450 nm for B-carotene, 2710 at 444 nm for –carotene, 2720 at 461 nm for –carotene, 2386 at 452 nm for B-cryptoxanthin; 3470 at 474 nm for lycopene; 2550 at 445 nm for lutein and 2480 at 452 for zeaxanthin in petroleum ether.

Syringe: HPLC syringe of 25 ul volume capacity (Hamilton 710) was used for injecting the sample and standards.

Chromatographic Separation

All solvents were filtered through 0.45 um hydrophobic membrane filters and the sample extracts were filtered through 0.22 um membrane filters (Millipore). Prior to the analysis, analytical column was thoroughly washed with methanol. The column temperature was maintained at 25°C throughout the analysis period. The isocratic solvent system consisting of acetonitrile, dichloromethane and methanol in the ratio of 70:20:10 (v/v) was used as a mobile phase. Mobile phase was mixed thoroughly and degassed on line while pumping through a single pump. The flow rate of this mobile phase was maintained at 2 ml per minute throughout the analysis time. The detector wavelength was set at 450 nm and the sensitivity was adjusted to 0.01 absorption units full scale on the dual channel Shimadzu CR-3A integrator. The rheodine system, consists of an injecting loop with a capacity of 20 ul volume. By injecting more than loop volume (25 ul) (it will accept exactly 20 ul) of sample extract on to the HPLC column, separation of carotenoids was accomplished with mobile phase and stationary phase interaction. External standards α–carotene, β-carotene, γ–carotene, B-cryptoxanthin, lutein, zeaxanthin and lycopene were used for identification of peaks and also for quantifying them. The HPLC was calibrated daily by injecting a full loop of carotene standards. The concentrations of each carotene ranged from 1 to 5 ug per ml. The retention times in minutes were as follows: for lutein 2.0; zeaxanthin 2.2; B-cryptoxanthin 5.08, lycopene 8.3 – γ-carotene 12.8; α-carotene 13.5; and B-carotene 14.6. Peak identification of the sample was based on retention times and comparison with standards. Further confirmation was achieved by spiking the sample peaks with authentic standards of known concentration and co-migration of sample peaks. The increase in peak heights indicated confirmation of particular carotenoid. In addition to co-chromatography, carotene fractions were collected on HPLC and scanned for their spectra. Retention times were further confirmed by re-chromatography, where collected fraction of carotenoids, was once again injected on HPLC and compared for the retention time. The quantitation of carotenes in the sample was accomplished by comparing the sample peak area with that of a known concentration of standard. From the standard curve, the results were expressed as mg of carotenoid/100 g sample.

Recovery

Recovery experiments were carried out in triplicate by the addition of a known concentration of carotenoid standard solutions (various carotenoids in the range of 1-500 ug) to the sample extract during saponification step. Extracts of various food samples were used for this recovery check.

Vitamin A Activity

Vitamin A activity of vegetables were calculated according to the description of NAS-NRC 1980. Where retinol equivalents as equal to 1 ug retinol or 6 ug B-carotene or 12 ug of other provitamin A carotenoids.

Thus vitamin A activity of the vegetable

= 1/6 B-carotene content in ug + 1/12 of other provitamin A carotenoids content in ug.

= ug retinol.

ABBREVIATIONS

ITDA	: Integrated Tribal Development Agency
ICAR	: Indian Council of Agricultural Research
ICMR	: Indian Council of Medical Research
WHO	: World Health Organisation
TCR & TI	: Tribal cultural and Training Institute
NIN	: National Institute of Nutrition
PHC	: Primary Health Centre
RDA	: Recommended Dietary Allowances
RE	: Retinol equivalents
TC	: Total carotenoids
BC	: Beta Carotene
GLVs	: Green Leafy Vegetables
WI	: Wealth of India
IMP	: Indian Medicinal Plants
OL	: Orient Longman
AP	: Andhra Pradesh
VAD	: Vitamin A deficiency
FAO	: Food and Agricultural Organisation
BISR	: Birla Institute of Scientific Research
PTG	: Primitive Tribal Group

BIBLIOGRAPHY

A Report of Birla Institute of Scientific Research (Economic Research Division) 1984. Social forestry in India, Problem and Prospects.

A Report of Tribal Cultural Research and Training Institute Nov. 1993. Attitudes of tribals of A.P. towards joint forest management. Tribal Welfare Department, Government of Andhra Pradesh, Hyderabad.

Abdel-Kader Z.M. 1991. Determination of Carotenoids in foods with High Performance Liquid Chromatography. Die Nahrung 35 : 689-93.

Almeida L.B. and Penteado M.V.C. 1987. Carotenoids and provitamin A value of white fleshed brazilian sweet potatoes (Ipomoea batatas Lam) J. Food Comp Anal 1:341-52.

AOAC 1984 Official Methods of Analysis. Association of Official Analytical Chemistry. 14th Edition Arlington I/A USA.

Arima H.K., Rodriguez-Amaya D.B. (1988). Carotenoid composition and vitamin A value of commercial brazilian squashes and pumpkins. J Micrnutr Anal 4: 177-191.

Arima H.K., Rodriguez-Amaya D.B. (1990). Carotenoid composition and vitamin A value of squash and a pumpkin from north eastern brasil. Arch latinoam Nutr 40 : 284-292.

Asimas Chatterjee, Satyesh Chandra Pakrashi 1994. The treatise on Indian medicinal plants Vol. I-III. Publications and Information Directorate : Curios of Science and Indian Research, New Delhi.

BASF (1997) Human Nutrition, Antioxidant Nutrients (Ed. by Tonia Reinhard) New Jersey.

Baurnfeid J.C. (1972) Carotenoid Vitamin A precursors and analogs in food and feeds. J. Ag. Food Chem. 20 : 456-73.

Begum A and Perira S.M. (1977). The B-Carotene content of edible green leaves. J. Trop. Geogr. Med. 29:47.

Bennet S S R, San Biswas, Veena Chandra, Singh P J, Sumar Chandra,

Ramesh Dayal 1990, Food from forests. Indian Council of Forest Research and Education, New Forest, Dehradun.

Bhaskara Chary 1996. Studies on carotenoids in some plant foods as a source of vitamin A. Ph.D. Thesis submitted to Osmania University, Hyderabad, Andhra Pradesh, India.

Bose T.K., Das P, Maiti G G 1998. Trees of the World. Vol. I. Regional Plant Resource Centre, Bhubaneswara, Orissa, India.

Britton G. and Young A.J. (1993). In Carotenoids in Photosynthesis (ed. A.J. Young and G. Britton) pp. 409, Chapman and Hall, London.

Bureau J.B. and Bushway R.J. (1986). HPLC determination of Carotenoids in fruits and vegetables in the United States, J. Food Sci 51: 128-130.

Bushway R.J. (1986). Determination of alpha and beta Carotene in some raw fruits and vegetables by HPLC, J. Agri Food Chem., 34 : 409.

Bushway R.J. and Wilson A.M. (1982). Determination of alpha and beta Carotene in fruits and vegetables by High Performance Liquid Chromatography, Can Inst Food Sci. Technol. J, 15: 165-169.

Census of India 1991. Final population total paper-I of 1992, Vol. II.

Charles McCann 1985. Trees of India. Periodical Expert Book Agency, New Delhi.

Chen B.H. and Chen Y.Y (1993). Stability of Chlorophylls and Carotenes in Sweet potato leaves during microwave cooking. J. Agric. Food. Chem., 41 : 1315-1320.

Cherian A 1981. "Attitudes and practices of infant feeding in Zaria". Nigeria-Eco-food Nutr. 2:75-80.

Coloner Haber Drury Reprint 1985. The useful plants of India. International Book Distributors, Dehradun.

Delia. B, Rodriguez-Amaya (1997). Carotenoid and food preparation: The retention of provitamin A, Carotenoids in prepared, processed and stored foods, John Snow Inc./omni project.

Dietz J.M., S.S. Kantha, and J.W. Erdman, Jr (1988). Reversed Phase HPLC analysis of alpha and Beta Carotene from Selected raw and cooked vegetables. Plant Foods for Human Nutrition. 33:333-341.

Godoy H.T., Rodriguez-Amaya D.B. (1987) Changes in individual carotenoids on processing and storage of Mango (Mangifera indica) slices and puree. Int. J. Food Sci. Technol 22:451-460.

Godoy H.T., Rodriguez-Amaya D.B. (1991). Comportamento dos Carotenoides de pure de mamao (Carica papaya) Sob processamento estocagem. Cienc Techol Aliment 11: 210-220.

Godoy H.T., Rodriguez-Amaya D.B. (1994). Occurrence of cis-isomers of provitamins A in brazilian fruits. J. Agric Food Chem. 42:1306-1313.

Godoy H.T., Rodriguez-Amaya D.B. (1995a). Buriti (Mauritia Vinifera mart), uma fonte riquissima de pro-vitamina A. Arq Biol Tec 38: 109-120.

Godoy H.T., Rodriguez-Amaya D.B. (1995b). Carotenoid composition and vitamin A value of brazilian loquat (Eriobotrya japonica Lindl) Arch Latinoam Nutr 45: 336-39.

Gopalan C, Rama Sastry B.V. and Balasubramanian S.C., revised and updated by Narsinga Rao B.S., Deosthale Y.G. and Pant K.C. (1992). Nutritive value of Indian foods, National Institute of Nutrition, Indian Council of Medical Research, Hyderabad, Andhra Pradesh, India.

Gopaldas T, Gupta A and Saxena K 1983. "The phenomenon of Sanskritization in a forest dwelling tribe of Gujarat, India:

Nutrient Intake and Practices in the special groups" Ecol. Food Nutr. 13: 1-18.

Gregory J.F. III (1996). Vitamins In O.R. Fennema (ed). Food Chemistry 3rd ed. Marcel Dekker, New York, pp. 532-616.

Heinonen M.L., Ollilainen. V, Linkola E.K., et al (1989). Carotenoids in finish foods: Vegetables, fruits and berries, J. Agric. Food Chem. 37: 655-9.

Indian Council of Medical Research (ICMR) 1992 Nutrient requirements and recommended dietary allowances for Indians.

Jain S K 1996. Medicinal Plants, Director National Book Trust Publishers, India.

Kachik. F., Beecher G.R. and William R Lusby (1989). Separation, identification and quantification of the major Carotenoids in extracts of apricots, peaches, cantaloupe and pink grape fruit by liquid Chromatography. J. Agric Food Chem 37: 1465-1473.

Khachik. F., Beecher G.R., Whitaker N.F. (1986). Separation, identification and quantification of the major Carotenoid and Chorophyll constituents in extracts of several green vegetables by liquid Chromatography J. Agric Food Chem. 34: 603-616.

Kiritikar K R, Basu B D 1988 Indian Medicinal Plants Vol. I-IV. International Book Distributors, Dehradun.

Klein B.P. and Kurilich A.C. (2000). Processing effects on dietary antioxidants from plant foods. Hort. Science 35(4), 580-583.

Krinsky I N; M.M. Mathews-Roth and Taylor R.F. (1989), Carotenoids: Chemistry and Biology. Plenum press, New York.

Madhava peddi. R, Bhaskar chari. K, Sankar Rao D.S. Deosthale Y.S. an Vinodini reddy (1994). Effect of processing on Carotene content of vegetables. Applied Nutrition, 19 (122) 43-47.

Mangels A.R; J.M. Holden; G.R. Beecher; M.R. Forman and E. Lanza (1993) Carotenoid content of fruits and vegetables: An evaluation of analytical data. J. Amer. Diet. Assoc. 93: 284-286.

Mercadante A.Z. and Rodriguez-Amaya D.B (1990). Carotenoid composition and vitamin A value of some native Brazilian green leafy vegetables. Int J Food Sci Technol 25: 213-219.

Mercadante A.Z. and Rodriguez-Amaya D.B. (1991). Carotenoids composition of leafy vegetables in relations to some Agricultural variable,. J. Agric. Food Chem 39 : 1094-7.

Murphy, E.W., Criner P.E, Gray B.C. (1975). Comparisons of methods of calculating retentions of nutrients in cooked foods. J. Agric Food Chem 23: 1153-1157.

Nadkarni K M 1976 Indian Materia Medica Vol. I, II, Bombay Popular Prakashan, Bombay.

Nagra S.A., Shan. S (1988). Vitamin A (Beta carotene) losses in Pakistani cooking. J. Sci. Food Agric 46 : 249-251.

Narasinga Rao B.S. (1991). Use of B-Carotene rich foods for combating vitamin A deficiency. News Bulletin. Bulletin of the Nutrition Foundation of India 12(3) 1-6.

NAS-NRC 1980 Fat soluble vitamins : vitamin A. In recommended dietary allowances. 9th Ed. National Academy of Sciences, Washington D C 55.

National Institute of Nutrition 1980 Nutrition quarterly. Indian Council of Medical Research, Hyderabad.

National Institute of Nutrition 1997 Nutrition quarterly. Indian Council of Medical Research, Hyderabad.

Nelis W J C F, Deleenheer A P 1983. Isocratic nonaqueous reversed phase liquid chromatography of carotenoids. Analytical Chemistry 55: 270.

Onuoha G B I 1982 "The changing scene of food habits and beliefs among the Mbaise people of Nigeria", Ecol Food Nutr. 11: 245-250.

Padmavathi K, Udipi S.A. and Rao. M. (1992). Effect of different cooking methods on Beta Carotene content of vegetables J. Food Sci Technol., 29, 3: 137-140.

Padula M, Rodriguez-Amaya D.B (1987). Changes in individual Carotenoids and Vitamins C on processing and storage of Guava juice. Acta Alimentaria 16 : 209-216.

Pal D C, Jain S K 1998 Tribal medicine, Naya Prokash Publishers, Calcutta, India.

Pepping F, Vencken CMJ, West CE (1988). Retinol and Carotene content of foods consumed in East-Africa determined by High Performance liquid Chromatography. J. Sci Food Agric 45: 359-71.

Prasad V P and Daniel Mason, Joy E Marburger, Ajith Kumar C R 1996 Illustrated flora of Keoladeo National Park, Bharatpur, Rajasthan (A general guide to the wetland flora of the Gangetic plains). Bombay natural history society, Mumbai, India.

Pullaih T, Chennaiah E 1997 Flora of A.P. Vol. I. Scientific Publishers, Jodhpur, India.

Quackenbush F.W, Smallidge R.L (1987). Nonaqueous reverse phase liquid chromatographic system for separation and quantitation of provitamins Amer J. Assoc Anal Chem 69 : 767-772.

Rahman, M.M., Wahed, M.A, and Akbar Ali, M (1990). B-Carotene losses during different methods of cooking Green leafy vegetables in Bangladesh. Journal of Food Composition and Analysis 3 : 47-53.

Raju R A 1997, Forest Wealth of India. Daya Publishing House, Delhi.

Rajyalakshmi P 1991 "Tribal food habits" I. Edition, Gyan Publishing House, New Delhi.

Ramos D.M.R and Rodriguez-Amaya D.B. (1987). Determination of the vitamin A value of common Brazilian leafy vegetables. J. Micronutr anal., 3, 147-155.

Randall E and D Sanjur 1981 "Food preferences, their conceptualization and relationship to consumption" Ecol. Food Nutr. 11:151-161.

Rani Gopal K 1996. General profile of the tribal area of Visakhapatnam.

Rasheeduz Zafar, 1994. Medicinal plants of India, CBS Publishers. Shahdara, Delhi.

Reddy R D, Prasad M K, Venkaiah K 1991. Forest flora of Andhra Pradesh (Vernacular Names) Research and Development Circle, Andhra Pradesh Forest Department, Hyderabad.

Rock C.L. and M.E. Swendseid (1992). Plasma B-Carotene response in humans after meals supplemented with dietary pectin. Amer. J. Clin. Nutr. 55: 96-99.

Rock C.L., J.L. Lovalvo, C. Emenhiser, M.T. Ruffin, S.W. Flatt and S.J. Schwartz (1995). Bioavailability of B-Carotene is lower in raw than in Processed carrots and spinach in Women. J. Nutr. 128: 913-916.

Rodriguez-Amaya. D.B. (1993). Nature and distribution of Carotenoids in foods. In charalambous G(ed), shelf life studies of foods and beverages chemical, biological, physical and nutritional aspects, Elsevier Science Publishers, Amsterdam, pp. 547-589.

Seshagiri Rao.R, Sree Ramulu H 1986. Flora of Srikakulam district. Botanical Society Publication, Meerut, India.

Seshagiri Rao R, Sudhakar S and Venkanna P 1999. Flora of East Godavari district. The Indian National Trust for Art and Cultural Heritage (INTACH) A.P. State Chapter, Hyderabad.

Snedecor G W, Cochran W G eds 1965. Statistical methods 5th edition. The Iowa state university Press, Ames, Lowa USA 46 and 276-279.

Speek A J, Temalilwa C R and Schrijener J 1986. Determination of β-carotene content and vitamin A activity of vegetables by HPLC and spectrophotometer. Food Chem. 19:65.

Speek A.J., Supinum speek saichua and Wil HP schreus (1988). Total Carotenoid and B-Carotene content of Thai vegetables and the effect of processing. Food Chem, 27: 245.

Swamy P M, Thammanna 1985. Ferns and Fern allies of Tirumala. Tirumala Tirupathi Devasthanam Publication, Tirumala, Tirupathi.

Tadulingam C, Narayana V 1955-A handbook of some South Indian weeds.

Tee E.S, Lim C.L. (1991). Carotenoid Composition and content of Malaysian vegetables and fruits by the AOAC and HPLC methods. Food Chem 41 : 309-39.

Thamanna, Narayana Rao K 1990. Medicinal Plants of Tirumala. Tirumala Tirupathi Devasthanam Publishers, Tirupathi.

The Wealth of India 1948-1989. A dictionary of Indian new materials and industrial product Vol. I to X, Council of Scientific and Industrial Research, New Delhi.

Trujillo-Quijano J.A., Rodriguez-Amaya D.B., Esteres W, Plonis G.H., (1990). Carotenoids composition and vitamin A values of oils from four brazilian palm fruits. Fat Sci Technol, 6 : 222-6.

Varier P S 1995. Indian Medicinal Plants Vol. I-IV. Orient Longman Publishers.

Vedavathy S, Mrudula V, Sudhakar A 1997. Tribal Medicine of Chittor district. Herbal folklore Research Centre, Tirupathi, A.P. India.

Vinodini reddy, K. Vijayaraghavan, K. Bhaskarachary, M. Rani (1995). Carotene rich foods: The Indian experience, National Institute of Nutrition, Indian Council of Medical Research, Jamai Osmania, P.O. Hyderabad-500007, Andhra Pradesh, India.

WHO (1982) Control of Vitamin A deficiency and Xerophthalmia. World Health Organization, Technical Report Series No. 672: Report of a joint WHO/UNICEF/Helen Keller International/IVACG Meeting.

Wu. Y, A.K. Perry and B.P. Klein. (1992). Vitamin C and Beta Carotene in fresh and frozen green beans and broccoli in a simulated systems. J.Food Qual 15: 87-96.

Zakaria M, Simpson K, Brown P R, Krstulvic A 1979 Use of reversed phase High performance liquid chromatographic analysis for the determination of provitamin A carotenes in tomatoes. Journal of Chromatography 176: 109-17.

Index